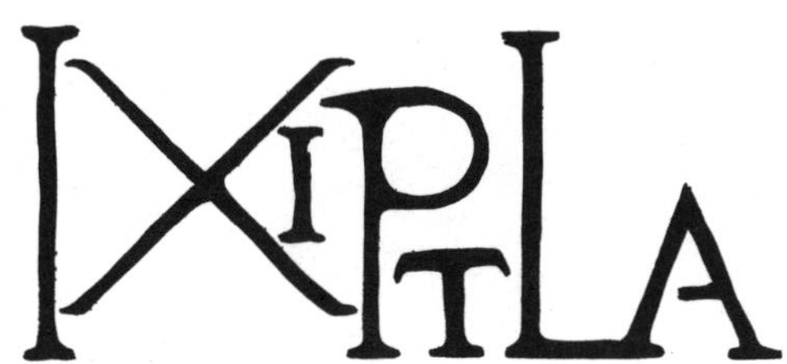

Editor: Mariana Castillo Deball

Production editor: Ana Ara

Translators: Jen Hofer, Amy Patton, John Pluecker

Proofreading: Courtney Johnson

Contributors: Kythzia Barrera, Maria Gaida, Moosje M. Goosen, Pablo Katchadjian, Paula López Caballero, Federico Navarrete Linares, Victoria Novelo Oppenheim, Sandra Rozental, Carlos Sandoval, Adam T. Sellen, Anna Szaflarski.

Design: Mariana Castillo Deball

Typographic design: Ayami Awazahara, Anna Szaflarski

Print: AZ Druck und Datentechnik GmbH, Berlin

Edition: 1000

This publication was produced with the support of the Berliner Künstlerprogramm/ DAAD

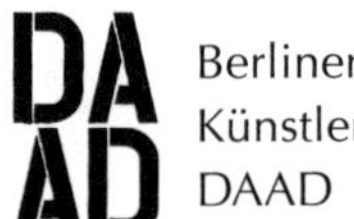

Berliner
Künstlerprogramm/
DAAD

and is published in the context of Mariana Castillo Deball's project *You have time to show yourself before other eyes*, 2014, commissioned and co-produced by the 8th Berlin Biennale for Contemporary Art.

BERLIN BIENNALE

With support by Ernst Schering Foundation

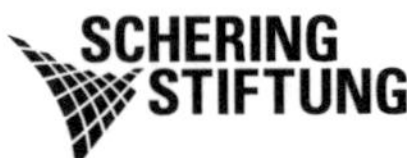

Thanks to Edwige Baron, Ariane Beyn, Maria Gaida, Juan Gaitán, Rodrigo Hernández, Amelia Hinojosa, Wilma Lukatsch, Manuel Raeder, Barbara Wien and all contributors.

Cover image: Wooden masks from Guatamala. Kept in the Studiensammlung (American Archeology) S:92, Ethnologisches Museum, Staatliche Museen zu Berlin. Photo © Mariana Castillo Deball, 2014.

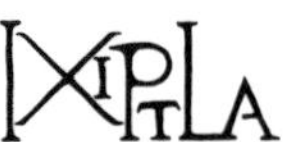

IXIPTLA, Spring 2014, Vol. I

www.ixiptla.org
info@ixiptla.org

Published twice yearly by

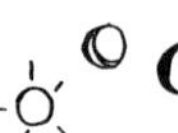

BOM
DIA
BOA
TARDE
BOA
NOITE

Rosa-Luxemburg-Strasse 17
10178 Berlin
Germany
www.bombiabooks.de

ISBN 978-3-943514-25-4

The Deutsche Nationalbibliothek lists this publication in the Deutsche Nationalbibliografie; detailed bibliographic data are available on the Internet at http://dnb.d-nb.de.

CONTENTS

IXIPTLA

The Nahua concept of *ixiptla* derives from the particle *xip,* meaning "skin," coverage or shell. A natural outer layer of tissue that covers the body of a person or animal, the skin can be separated from the body to produce garments, containers for holding liquids or parchment as a writing surface. Its material attributes allow it to become a container, or a coating. As an allegory, *xip* can be mold or cast, receptacle or costume.

Xipe Totec, "Our Lord the Flayed One," is an Aztec deity often portrayed wearing the skin that had been removed from a human sacrificial victim. His dress does not fit perfectly, so he shows his own hands and feet, while the hands and feet of the flayed skin appear hanging. Xipe may be recognized by observing the holes in the skin for mouth and eyes, through which the wearer of the skin can be seen.

Ixiptla is both a person capable of transforming himself into another, and an embodiment of the others he becomes, losing his skin and wearing the skin of someone else.

Originally a Nahua word, *ixiptla* has been understood as image, delegate, character, and representative. *Ixiptla* could be a container, but also could be the actualization of power infused into an object or person. In Nahua culture, it took the form of a statue, a vision, or a victim who turned into a god destined to be sacrificed. Without having to visually appear the same, multiple *ixiptlas* of the same god could exist simultaneously. The distinction between essence and material, and between original and copy vanishes.

For the first issue of the journal IXIPTLA, a group of anthropologists, archaeologists, artists, and writers have been invited to reflect on the role of the model, the copy, and reproduction in their areas of research and practice.

Since the nineteenth century, archaeologists have envisioned and implemented diverse techniques for capturing and replicating material evidence. The archaeologist collects fragments of material culture left by time, and while doing so, produces other objects in an attempt to better remember or observe those fragments. These techniques have included plaster molds, facsimiles, drawings, photographs, and scale models. When made, they emerge from a specific moment in time, producing a doppelgänger of the original milieu, which then takes its own course.

This edition of IXIPTLA is focused on the trajectory of such dislocated objects, which depart from direct contact with the original, and yet take a part of that original object along with them.

DIALOGUE WITH M BAKHTIN ABOUT THE CHRONOTOPE

FEDERICO NAVARRETE LINARES
UNAM

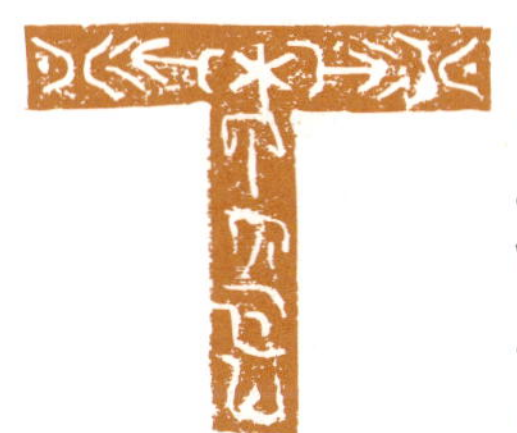

he purpose of this essay is to undertake a well intentioned but irreverent dialogue with the great Russian thinker Mikhail Bakhtin around his concept of the "chronotope."

Why a dialogue? Because one of the most fertile and enriching aspects of Bakhtin's thinking is precisely its *dialogical* nature, his refusal to turn his theoretical reflections into dogmatic impositions, his openness to hearing the reasoning of others. Why irreverent? Because what I seek to do is precisely to appropriate the concept of the chronotope and apply it to Bakhtin himself, in order to demonstrate the relative nature of his own conception of historical time. This act of irreverence will allow me, in turn, to reflect on the characteristics of what I will call the modern Western historical chronotope, and compare it with Mesoamerican chronotopes.

The Definition of Chronotope

At the beginning of his article titled "Forms of Time and of the Chronotope in the Novel," Bakhtin defined this seminal concept, the explanatory capacity of which I will be exploring in this essay:

> We will give the name chronotope (literally, "time space") to the intrinsic connectedness of temporal and spatial relationships that are artistically expressed in literature. This term [space-time] is employed in mathematics, and was introduced as part of Einstein's Theory of Relativity. The special meaning it has in relativity theory is not important for our purposes; we are borrowing it for literary criticism almost as a metaphor (almost, but not entirely). What counts for us is the fact that it expresses the inseparability of space and time (time as the fourth dimension of space). (Bakhtin 1981, 84-85)

Later on, he explains that the chronotope constitutes the backbone of any narrative:

> The chronotope is the place where the knots of narrative are tied and untied. It can be said without qualification that to them belongs the meaning that shapes narrative . . . Time becomes, in effect, palpable and visible; the chronotope makes narrative events concrete, makes them take on flesh, causes blood to flow in their veins. An event can

> be communicated, it becomes information, one can give precise data on the place and time of its occurrence. But the event does not become a figure. It is precisely the chronotope that provides the ground essential for the showing-forth, the representability of events. (Bakhtin 1981, 250)

That is, the way that a chronotope represents time and space allows for the organization of what is to come in a literary narrative, giving it meaning. Bakhtin proposes that the diversity of literary genres responds to a diversity of chronotopes, and in his article he takes on the task of defining some of these: the abstract chronotope of the classic adventure novel, the mythic chronotope of metamorphosis in Hesiod and Ovid, the primitive folkloric chronotope, etc.

The chronotope of each of these genres determines the types of events that are narrated, the forms and natures of the characters and the types of transformations they experience: thus, in the adventure chronotope, events are accidental, completely exterior to the heroes, who themselves appear to be immutable (this chronotope is identical, in fact, to contemporary animations like the Roadrunner); the chronotope of metamorphosis, on the other hand, causes the characters to experience constant successive changes, ones that assimilate the transformations experienced by nature. In short, the form a chronotope assumes determines the nature of a works characters and their psychology. As Bakhtin explains, in order to create a biography through which we might become acquainted, it was necessary to create a chronotope of the private life (focused on the home and the things that take place there) that would be clearly differentiated from the chronotopes of collective life.

On the other hand, Bakhtin asserted that the concept of the chronotope could extend beyond literature, because chronotopes of real life exist, like the chronotope of the encounter (manifested, for example, in diplomatic meetings), or that of the Greek agora or the Roman clan (Bakhtin 1981, 97–138). In short, the organization of time and space into coherent units charged with meaning was not achieved solely within literary texts, but rather was also a fundamental element of social life.

Real chronotopes determine, to a large extent, literary ones. This becomes particularly clear in the case of the folkloric chronotope. This unified and totalizing conception of time and space, according to Bakhtin, could only arise in classless agricultural societies, as it integrated agricultural cycles, seasonal cycles, astral cycles, and the cycles of human life into one harmonious whole. This was a time that was

> . . . profoundly spatial and concrete. It is not separated from the earth or from nature. It, as well as the entire life of the human being, is all on the surface. The agricultural life of men and the life of nature (of the earth) are measured by one and the same scale, by the same events; they have the same intervals, inseparable from each other, present as one (indivisible) act of labor and consciousness. Human life and nature are perceived in the same categories. (Bakhtin 1981, 208)

This primitive unity (suspiciously similar, as it happens, to a Christian lost paradise or to primitive Marxist communism) broke apart as private life grew more and more separate from collective life and chronotopes more suited to individuality developed, in a process that was linked to the rise of social classes (Bakhtin 1981, 206–210).

Bakhtin and the "True" Chronotope of History

Beyond the plurality of literary and real chronotopes, Bakhtin makes continuous reference to a plenitude of time that chronotopes express with greater or lesser exactitude. Thus, for example, he negatively judges the folkloric chronotope for being cyclical:

> All the peculiarities that we have pointed out so far may be said to be positive features in folkloric time. But a final feature of this time (on which we will now pause), its cyclicity, is a negative feature, one that limits the force and ideological productivity of this time. The mark of cyclicity, and consequently of cyclical repetitiveness, is imprinted on all events occurring in this type of time. Time's forward impulse is limited by the cycle. For this reason even growth does not achieve an authentic "becoming." (Bakhtin 1981, 209–210)

The classic conception that references a Golden Age lost in the past seems to him equally erroneous:

> To put it in somewhat simplified terms, we might say that a thing that could and in fact must only be realized exclusively in the future is here portrayed as something out of the past, a thing that is in no sense part of the past's reality, but a thing that is in its essence a purpose, an obligation.
> This peculiar "trans-positioning," this "inversion" of time typical of mythological and artistic modes of thought in various eras of human development, is characterized by a special concept of time, and in particular of future time. The present and even more the past are enriched at the expense of the future. (Bakhtin 1981, 147–148)

In this article, Bakhtin sketches the history of the progress of chronotopes toward a more fitting adaptation to the plenitude of time—that is, the development of a linear and progressive vision of the future, which the author considered to be the real vision and which is the one that prevails in modern Western culture.

In contrast, my purpose in this dialogue is precisely to question the supposed plenitude and reality of this linear, progressive, and irreversible time, and to demonstrate that it is much more fertile to analyze it as just another chronotope—that is, as another cultural construction that seeks to give *a* meaning to human occurrence. I want, in brief, to apply the explanatory richness of the concept of the chronotope to the Western conception of time and history itself. This exercise entails, of course, an undermining of the appraisals Bakhtin makes regarding the greater or lesser aptness of chronotopes to the plenitude of time, and a demonstration that the Western historical chronotope might end up being as far from or as close to that plenitude as any other.

This act seems to me to be the greatest homage I can make to the richness of Bakhtin's thought. In fact, the openness of his ideas is so great that those ideas themselves allow us to move beyond the cultural determinations of his chronotope—one that, like a universal Kantian category, the author himself considered to be unquestionable.

Bakhtin shows us the way when he signals that the relationships among chronotopes are necessarily *dialogic*—that is, that no one chronotope can hope to explain another, to subject another to its own logic. Rather, each has to begin a relationship of comprehension with the others, effecting an exchange from the irreducible alterity of their positions. (Bakhtin 1981, 252) Thus, a critique of what I will call the Western historical chronotope will allow me to establish the bases for a dialogue between this culturally determined conception of time and Mesoamerican historical chronotopes.

The Western Historical Chronotope, or "There Is No Way Other Than Ours"

Though I run the implicit risk inherent in any simplification, it seems to me that the modern Western historical chronotope can be represented as a path. The path, as Bakhtin himself signals, perfectly integrates time and space into one continuous line. The path necessarily entails a passage, and that passage is generally as linear as the path itself: we start from one end of the path (the beginning) in order to arrive at the other (the goal).

The conception of the historical chronotope as a path is evident in slogans as elemental as the one Luis Echeverría developed for his 1970 presidential campaign in Mexico—*"Arriba y adelante"* ("Onward and upward")—or in astronaut Neil Armstrong's comment when he walked on the Moon in 1969: "That's one small step for a man, one giant leap for mankind." In both cases, change is conceived as spatial progress, and this progress takes on temporal dimensions as well. The same conception is evident, of course, anytime we speak of progress, or of moving backward in history.

This linear conception implies, therefore, the division of history into stages that should be traversed in order and that should be left behind the moment a new stage initiates. From 1969 forward, in effect, there has been no shortage of pedants who claim we have entered the spatial age.

The metaphor of the path reveals another fundamental characteristic of the modern Western historical chronotope: its pretentions of universality. Time, in effect, is conceived as a singular line: it began with the creation of the cosmos (whether by divine agency or as a physical phenomenon) and leads inexorably to its destruction and/or its redemption.

The human evolutionary path, too, is universal according to this chronotope: the historical stages of social organization are conceived as a necessary and singular succession. Out of this conception arise Western obsessions with categorizing and explaining the developments of different societies as anomalous cases, and even as perversions, as these do not follow the supposedly unique pattern of evolution represented by European history. This was the case with societies that experienced an "involution" from state-based forms of organization to forms that were not state-based, or with those that maintained "ancient" social structures (like lineages) at the center of more "advanced" social structures (like the State).

This chronotopic conception is based, of course, on the conviction that a singular truth exists, and belongs to the West—either to the Christian religion or to modern science.

At the same time, the pretension of exclusivity of the modern Western chronotope explains another Western obsession: the equivalence it continually establishes between spatial distance and temporal distance. In a wide range of literary works, such as Carpentier's *The Lost Steps* (1972), a journey to a remote country with a different culture is considered equivalent to a journey to the past; the customs of faraway peoples become primitive customs.

This equivalency between distance and the past is inseparable from another chronotopic conception: that of the necessary spread of Western culture across terrestrial space, conceived as the expansion of faith, truth, technology, or reason into an unknown, dark, or primitive world. Bakhtin himself spoke positively of the way that the folkloric chronotope and Rabelais's work created equivalences between qualitative growth and quantitative expansion in space. This is the same idea that inspired the work that spread Soviet ideas of linear evolution and progress, *How Man Became A Giant*. Another manifestation of this chronotope is the way Western history ascribes an epic and necessary character to its "discoveries" and to conquests undertaken by Europeans, from the Americas to outer space. In fact, the very idea of "discovery"—dividing the cosmos into a known area and an unknown one based on the knowledge and prejudices of a particular culture—is rooted in the modern Western chronotope.

At the same time, according to this chronotope, the path of evolution and progress leads necessarily to a better future. The chronotope of the path requires, therefore, that we fix our gaze forward ("Facing the sun and wearing a clean shirt").[1] Thus history is presented to us as a succession of triumphs: that of the true religion over pagan ones, of reason over tradition, of knowledge over ignorance, or of technology over the intrinsic limitations of earthly life. As Reinhart Koselleck has noted, the European Enlightenment incorporated Christian scatological ideas into human history, presenting it as necessarily tending toward redemption. (Koselleck 1993).

Any reversal or delay in this preordained course (and these words already imply a very clear value judgment) is nothing more than a slight aberration in a predetermined and unstoppable trajectory. Thus history becomes a comedy in the Aristotelian sense of the term: a plot where the conclusion is reconciliation. All the destructions, all the aggressions toward other cultures are justified by their incorporation into this triumphal forward march.

One example among thousands of the force of this conviction is the text in which Gonzalo Aguirre Beltrán, the theorist and founder of modern Mexican indigenism, justifies the integration of indigenous people (that is, theft of their lands, the destruction of their culture, and their forcible incorporation into Mexican society) with the argument that when they become workers they can then access the possibility of being participants in a socialist utopia (Aguirre Beltrán 1970).

1 Facing the sun is the anthem of the Spanish Falange Facist party. Composed in 1935, it was thought necessary that Spain have its own anthem to represent the Falange party. Up until that point, anthems from Nazi Germany and Italy were adapted with Spanish lyrics.

The linear and exclusivist nature of the Western historical chronotope necessarily implies, therefore, a flight toward the future. When Bakhtin maintains that the Golden Age did not exist in the past, but must be sought in our future, he echoes that peculiar mythology that projects the most unlikely certainties onto tomorrow, and destroys what actually exists for the sake of something believed to be assured in the future. A particularly eloquent example of this faith in the future is the chapter in *Marxist Economic Theory* in which the Trotskyist theorist Ernest Mandel describes how life will be under a communist regime. I will cite just one example:

> A socialist society will never dictate to its members any obligatory use of collective services—while refusing to make available the means of assuring those same services on an individual basis. Such a society will satisfy all man's rational needs by any means necessary, respecting the need for periodic isolation and solitude, which is the permanent and dialectical corollary to his social nature. Similarly, if the individual automobile is manifestly irrational as a means of urban transport, it is undoubtedly the most nimble means of transport for pleasure trips . . . and even when travel by plane, train or bus should be free of charge, men will continue to want a private car . . . A socialist society will respect these desires, and far from condemning them as petit-bourgeois hold-overs, it will make an effort to satisfy those needs whose rational character is evident to any person of good faith. (Mandel 1980, 181)

In the end, it is simply unsustainable to claim that this vision of the future is more realistic, more scientific, or more rational than one that situates the Golden Age in the past. At best, we might assert that the latter claim is more scientific insofar as it is verifiable, as the past is, at the very least, susceptible to becoming known.

With respect to the consequences of this mode of thinking and acting, my only recourse is to recall the well known passage by Walter Benjamin, a man steeped in the Jewish and Marxist prophetic tradition, regarding the "angel of history":

> A Klee painting named 'Angelus Novus' shows an angel looking as though he is about to move away from something he is fixedly contemplating. His eyes are staring, his mouth is open, his wings are spread. This is how one pictures the angel of history. His face is turned toward the past. Where we perceive a chain of events, he sees one single catastrophe which keeps piling wreckage and hurls it in front of his feet. The angel would like to stay, awaken the dead, and make whole what has been smashed. But a storm is blowing in from Paradise; it has got caught in his wings with such a violence that the angel can no longer close them. The storm irresistibly propels him into the future to which his back is turned, while the pile of debris before him grows skyward. This storm is what we call progress. (Benjamin 1973, 183).

The genius of this vision lies in its very simplicity. The angel of history is trapped in the Western historical chronotope; the hurricane propelling him has all the required characteristics of necessity, universality, absolute linearity. But it is enough that the angel should reverse his point of view, that he should look backward instead of looking forward, as the chronotope demands, so that comedy might be converted immediately to tragedy, so that the triumphal march might become catastrophe.

On the Necessity of Dialogue

Beyond signaling the unfortunate consequences the imposition of Western culture and its historical chronotope has had on other cultures around the globe, I am interested in analyzing the way Western thinkers' immutable conviction that they are situated at the center of the only possible history, that only they possess true historicity, has facilitated the imposition of their domination over the rest of the societies on the planet.

There is no doubt that it is a significant advantage to conceive of historical becoming as a struggle between good or reason—which one ascribes to oneself—and evil or unreasonableness, which one ascribes to any other person one encounters. In the titanic confrontation between good and evil, in which the former will emerge victorious—as the Manichean chronotope establishes—it is most advantageous to believe oneself to be the representative of the triumphal side; this certainty permits judgment of and domination over foreign cultures with as little circumspection as Hernán Cortés had in relation to the Mesoamerican peoples.

A linear and unique chronotope is the basis for the very ancient Western conviction that the West's triumph, its imposition of relations of domination over other cultures, has always been the necessary result of its superiority, of its possession of the truth, of its greater evolution. A recent manifestation of this chronotopic syndrome is the book *The Conquest of America* by Tzvetan Todorov (1992), which claims to explain the conquest of Mexico as stemming from a very dubious notion of the superior capacity of Cortés and the Spanish to interpret and manage symbols (the result, of course, of their mastery of writing).

This comfortable certainty has allowed the Western historical chronotope to absorb other chronotopes and subordinate them to its uniqueness. In its own eyes, of course, this constitutes a triumph of history over fable and myth, of reason over ignorance, of writing over orality, of the new over the old.

Nonetheless, understood as a dialogic relationship, this capacity for absorption and subjugation loses its comfortable necessity and naturalness. It is not that the West incorporates other cultures and their different conceptions of the future into its own true version, but rather that it imposes a hegemony as part of a strategy of domination. Nor is this a dialectical process, in which thesis and antitheses merge in a synthesis that supersedes them; it is, rather, a fully dialogical relationship, in which incommensurate cultures exchange information and ideas, with inevitable misunderstandings, all within a clearly unequal power relationship.

Starting from this premise, the following notes will attempt to reconstruct some of the characteristics of Mesoamerican historical chronotopes—Nahuatl and Maya chronotopes in particular—based on their complex interaction with the Western historical chronotope.

Cycles and Conceptual Opening

A central characteristic of Mesoamerican chronotopes is their conception of time as a round of cycles. The importance of cycles in the Mesoamerican worldview is accepted by a diverse range of authors who have located this organizing principle at all levels of indigenous life: it organizes the calendar, conceived as a round of gods who carry time; it sustains the idea of the carriers of the years, who associate spatial paths with time; it determines the rhythm of festivals and ritual obligations, as well as the organization of the *tequio*[2] and the rotation of public posts; it is equally manifest in the sequence of cosmogonic suns.

This principle implies a historical praxis that is distinct from Western modes. While Western reason seeks unity, Mesoamerican reason is additive and seeks plurality. To return to metaphor: while a path suggests that the new necessarily leaves the old behind, the circle of cycles can grow to incorporate the new, without consequently displacing what already exists.

An eloquent example of this mode of reasoning is the way the Quiché Maya from Momostenango, in Guatemala, integrated the followers of Catholic Action, together with the traditional priests, or padres-madres, of the Indo-Catholic religion, into the cult of their patron saint Santiago. Some years ago, the pressure of the catechists on the community led authorities to name two of them as the saint's second and fourth stewards, in order to allow them to participate in the ritual round of his cult. The Mayan priests, as ethnologist Barbara Tedlock explains, adopted

> . . . a dialectical solution, not only interlacing converts and traditionalists in the confraternity's four leadership posts, but pointing out a useful complementarity of ritual abstinences in the Catholic Action avoidance of alcohol and the traditional avoidance of sexual relations. In effect, the dualism between converts and traditionalists shifted from an external opposition between institutions to an internal complementarity within a single institution. (Tedlock 1992, 43)

As Tedlock herself notes, the Western solution to a similar conflict would have entailed the nullification of one of the two traditions, either in the name of tradition or of progress. The conception of cycles, in contrast, is able to absorb the new without destroying the old, since as one Quiché padre-madre notes "you cannot erase time."

This radical difference between Mesoamerican and Western chronotopes helps to explain another cultural misunderstanding, one that is much older and more tragic.

For the Spanish in the sixteenth century, an indigenous acceptance of the Christian god implied, necessarily, a rejection of their ancient gods. Baptism and conversion, within a linear chronotope of Christian salvation, meant leaving the past behind, forever. These rituals signified a new birth, a tabula rasa (two obsessive concepts for Western chronotopes).

2 *Tequio*, derived from *tequitl* tribute in Nahuatl, has become the term to designate the free labor that members of a community are obliged to provide for public works.

In contrast, for indigenous people, the adoption of Spanish gods implied simply the opening of the circle and the incorporation of a new numen into the round. Muñoz Camargo explains it this way:

> Ask the captain why he wants to take away our gods, the gods we have who have served us and our ancestors so many times; tell him that without taking them away or moving them from their place he can put his God among ours, that we will also serve him and adore him and build him a house and a temple in itself, and he will be our God also, as we have done with other gods we have brought from other places . . . This way of speaking and of saying that he wants to give them another God occurs even knowing that when these people take notice of a God with good qualities, that they will receive him and accept him as such; because many people arriving from elsewhere brought many idols they held as gods: and toward this purpose they said that Cortés brought them another God." (Muñoz Camargo 1984, 245–246)

The result was one of those double confusions that James Lockhart has described so excellently in many colonial realms: the Spanish celebrated indigenous conversion, certain that it was an abolition of their old religion, and then felt disappointed and outraged when they discovered that the *Indios* had deceived them and that they were persisting in their superstitions (a term incomprehensible outside the Western linear chronotope). The *Indios*, for their part, felt disillusioned by the stubborn and intolerant monopoly the Spanish sought to exercise over religious truth, and by the repression to which they were subject when in fact they were adopting Christian gods and making them their own.

Temporal Rounds and Mesoamerican Restorative Hopes

In the Mesoamerican historical chronotope, cycles are organized in rounds or circles. In his *Segunda Relación* (*Second Relation*), the Náhuatl historian Chimalpain describes the indigenous calendar in the following way:

> When they counted the years, after they had all occurred they renewed them, they made them begin again; just like a temalácatl[3], they turned in circles, causing their records of the count of the years to spin, from fifty-two to fifty-two years, renewing with each wheel the count of the years.

This metaphor of the spindle, or wheel, seems to reveal a cyclical vision of time; this is apparently confirmed in the Náhuatl saying collected by Fray Bernardino de Sahagún:

3 *Temalacatl*, literally stone spindle in Nahuatl, a round stone that was used in sacrifice rituals and that signified the circularity of time.

> *Occepa iuhcan iez, occepa iuh tlamaniz iniquin in canin*
>
> *Intlein mochioaia cenca ie uecauh, inaiocmo mochihua: auh occepa mochioaz, occepa iuh tlamaniz, iniuhtlamanca ievecauh: iniehoantin, in axcan nemi, occeppa nemiquizque, iezque. (Sahagún 1979: vol. 2, fo. 296v-297r)*
>
> Once again it will be; once again it will be customary, sometime, somewhere
>
> What was done in very old times, is no longer done, but once again it will be done, once again it will thus be customary as it was customary in ancient times. Those who live now will live, will exist once again. (Sahagun 1950-70, v. 6, p. 235).

In his Spanish gloss, Sahagún eloquently expresses his indignation in the face of this idea:

> What is will be restored again, and what was will be again.
>
> This proposition is Plato's, and the Devil taught it here, because it is erroneous, it is extremely false, it is against faith, which is to say: the things that were will return to be as they were in times past, and the things that are now will be again; so that, according to this error, those who live now will return to live, and as the world is now it will be again in the same way, which is extremely false and extremely heretical. (Sahagún 1988, 451)

By attributing a Platonic origin to this idea, Sagahún assimilates it to the conception of the eternal return as an infinite doubling back of the same. Nonetheless, despite Plato, the Brahmans, and Mircea Eliade, it seems to me that this abstract conception has little to do with the Mesoamerican historical chronotope, or with the majority of the historical chronotopes that actually exist.

If we read the Náhuatl text, and not the diatribe of the hunter of heresies, the idea of the indigenous historical chronotope is revealed to us in all its richness. In the first place, the Náhuatl explanation indicates that what was done in the past is no longer done now, and what the saying offers is the certainty that it will be done again in the future. The past and the future appear as distinct from the present.

The future return of the customs of the past indicates a circle, in effect, but it is not a matter of a philosophical speculation, but rather a political program. If we consider that this saying was not collected until the second half of the sixteenth century, from a generation that grew up under the colonial Christian regime, the expectation of a return of ancient customs seems to be a longing for the restoration of a pre-Hispanic reality. At the same time, the final phrase promises that those living in the present (that is, those who no longer live as those who lived before did) will once again live in the world, presumably in that future in which they will have once again imposed the old customs.

In short, it does not seem preposterous to propose that this saying expresses a hope of restoration—perhaps supernatural restoration—of independent indigenous life and an end to colonial domination. If correct, this interpretation would reinforce Bierhorst's hypothesis (1985) with regard to the *Cantares Mexicanos*, a contemporary manuscript crafted by Sahagún's same indigenous informants, as an expression of a movement from colonialism to restoration. A movement that might be analogous to the revitalizing movements of the *taki ongos* in Perú (Stern 1982), also in the sixteenth century, and of the indigenous people on the North American prairies (McLoughlin 1990) and the Amazonian people (Brown 1991) in recent centuries.

In this dialogue between such different chronotopes, we cannot be sure to what extent Sahagún understood the historical project implicit in this saying, or in the *Cantares* in general, or to what extent his indignation was a response to more general convictions. In any case, for the linear chronotope, the imposition of Christian faith, like revelation, needed to be definitive, and it marked an irreversible transformation in America, as it had in the Old World: a change of era. From that perspective the very idea of any type of return seemed positively heretical.

The historical chronotope expressed in this sixteenth century Náhuatl saying brings us back to the better known historical ideas of the Maya. It is fundamentally analogous to this statement gathered in the *Chilam Balam of Chumayel:*

> It is the 18th day of August in this year of 1766. There was a wind storm [hurricane]. I am writing a record of it so that we might know how many years later there will be another. (*Chilam Balam of Chumayel* 1988, 149)

Against a simplistic cyclical interpretation, it is sufficient to note that the Mayan priest declares that there will be another windstorm, not the same one. The same idea is expressed, with equal eloquence, by a contemporary Maya Cruzob when he speaks of the war that will come:

> Hah! It will. That's what's coming to pass, so it will remain so.
> Not like it was, perhaps. Its form is different.
> Different, but still that's it —
> Only its form is different as it is instituted again.
> . . .
> Well, here go things getting bad again.
> First you get fucked. Well, isn't that how it happened long ago?
> First they got fucked, because of hunger. Well, because my late father told me, hunger made the war happen, he said. (Sullivan 1988, 177–178)

My hypothesis is that the historical chronotope these statements manifest is essentially the same as the one that expresses the cycle of the thirteen *katunes*[4] so deeply rooted in pre-Hispanic life. Regardless of which calendar system is used (the Christian solar year or the long count), both conceptions of historical cycles are based in the same ambiguous relationship of similarities and differences.

4 Yucatec Maya term for a calendar period of approximately twenty years, which was the basis for the long-range calendar counts utilized for historical texts.

On the wheel of the *katunes*, in effect, historical repetition does not imply identical sameness, as the extremely long succession of misfortunes that befell the Itza in katún 8 Ahau, mentioned in the *Chilam Balam of Chumayel* (with the Christian dates in brackets):

> [672–692] Chichén Itzá was abandoned after thirteen folds of the *katún*. And they settled in Chakán-Putún, in their homes there, in the time of this *katún*.
> [928–948] Chakán-Putún was abandoned by the Itza people. And they came to put their homes there again. Their homes at Chakán-Putún were settled there thirteen folds of the *Katún*. During this same katún the Itza left to live beneath the trees, beneath the ash, beneath their misery.
> [1185-1204] The Itza people were dispersed from their homes for the second time, for the sin of the word of Hunaceel, for his altercations with the people of Izamal. They had been settled there thirteen folds of the *katún* when they were dispersed by Hunaceel; this is what the Itza people understand.
> [1441-1461] Mayapán, the walled city, was demolished, because those who were behind the wall destroyed the fortress, in order to empty the city of Mayapán of the power that had gathered there.

It is clear that these events are similar, but never equal, as they occur in different places and with different characters. Nonetheless, their regularity is confirmed by the enumeration of four successive cases.

For that reason, it is not surprising that the fall of the Itza in Tayasal in 1697 should have coincided with another return of the terrible *katún 8 Ahau*. It seems to me that the analysis Jones (1989) provides of the history of the region throughout the seventeenth century demonstrates that the historical consciousness of this repetition among the Maya, perfectly objective within their premises, played an important role in these events.

Another eloquent manifestation of this chronotope and its effects on the historical actions of the Maya is the return of *katún 9 Ahau*. The *Chilam Balam of Tizimín* describes the passing of this *katún* in the sixteenth century in the following way:

> 9 Ahau
> Was the second *katun*.
> Heaven Born Merida
> Was the seat of the *katun* being
> counted; And there was the beginning
> And rise of Christianity, Which was spread to the wicked world
> In the adjacent lands.
>
> And there was the beginning
> And the construction of the god house
> That is in the middle of the city Of Merida.
> Piling on work
> Was the burden of the katun.
> And there was the beginning Of the noose.
> And started was the fever of the nose and limbs

> Of the white lima bean Grove lands,
> Bringing with it their poison And their ropes over the world—
> Affecting children
> And younger brothers
> With the harsh lash,
> With the harsh tribute.
> And there was great theft of tribute:
> There was the great theft of Christendom.
> There was the establishment of the seven sacraments:
> The word of God is great. Take it
> And welcome it, Coming to the city
> Of our older brothers.
> (Edmonson 1982, 59–60)

In this interpretation of the events that took place between 1559 and 1579, the arrival of Christianity is viewed positively, but the imposition of Spanish domination (conquest, construction of churches, tributes, encomienda, epidemics, inquisition) is judged negatively.

For this reason, it's not surprising that throughout the colonial period the return of 9 Ahau should begin to be conceived as a new coming of Christianity, dissociated this time from dreaded colonial domination. A similar occurrence, another arrival of the cross, would acquire a completely different shade of meaning, since it would now be beneficial for the Maya:

> Then they shall come forth from the forests and from [125] among the rocks and live like men; then towns shall be established [again]. There shall be no fox to bite them. This shall be in *Katún 9 Ahau* . . . Then there shall be an end to the paying for the wars which our fathers raised [against the Spaniards]. You shall not call the katun which is to come a hostile one, when Jesus Christ, the guardian of our souls, shall come. Just as [we are saved] here on earth, so shall he bear our souls to his holy heaven also. You are sons of the true God. Amen. (Roys 1967, 124–125).

In order to evaluate the possible significance of this vision, it is enough to signal that the *katún 9 Ahau* recurred in the year 1848 (since the cycle shifted with the refashioning of the wheel of katunes at the end of the eighteenth century (Edmonson 1982) and that the Cruz Parlante and San Juan de la Cruz were revealed to the Maya in 1850, effectively fulfilling the prophecy of the *katún,* since the latter figure presented himself as Christ reincarnated (Reifler-Bricker 1977).

Because she has proposed this interpretation, Reifler-Bricker has been accused of being an idealist, since some claim that proposing this type of interpretation—one that attempts to take into account indigenous peoples' own historical consciousness—implies a devaluation of the objective social causes that actually govern history (and that obey the rules of the Western historical chronotope). Nonetheless, studies of this type, which are more and more numerous and rich, have demonstrated that an open attitude that does not disqualify historical chronotopes from other cultures allows us to begin to understand those cultures' ways of acting historically, and above all to make meaning from it. In order to achieve this openness of perspective, we should not attempt to reduce a consciousness that is foreign to our own, nor seek to dissolve its chronotope into a Western one, but on the contrary, we should recognize the alterity of that consciousness and initiate a dialogue with it.

Eras And Their Transformations

Beyond the cycles and the wheel, the Mesoamerican chronotope conceives the future as divided into eras organized in a more linear fashion. The nature of these eras, and the transformations they imply, seem to me to be complex and elusive; hence I will present just a few hypotheses. Another problem still to be resolved is the question of the degree of influence the Western historical chronotope has on these conceptions.

A better known manifestation of this division into eras is the sequence of creations and destructions that precedes the current cosmogonic era. Within this sequence, we find a combination of a certain cyclical impulse—as each era is created and destroyed in a constant play of cosmic forces—with an undeniable linearity: previous eras are considered as imperfect preludes of the current era; previous instances of humanity are nothing more than failed versions of the present humanity; their foods are imperfect attempts at the corn we know now. This conception is equally evident in both the *Popol Vuh* (1985) and in the *Leyenda de los Soles* (*Códice Chimalpopoca* 1992; *Legend of the Suns, Chimalpopoca Codex*).

Some writers have made attempts—not entirely convincing ones—to identify these cosmogonic eras with Mesoamerican historical stages (Graulich 1982). My hypothesis is that rather than a division in great cosmogonic eras, it is more accurate to consider that the current era, the era of human beings, is also divided into clearly distinct eras that are defined not by great cosmic cataclysms, but by human events. These eras go beyond those discussed above, as they mark irreversible transformations in men and in societies. In this way, they introduce a strong element of linearity into the Mesoamerican temporal conception.

There are two examples I can present in order to demonstrate the existence of this division of Mesoamerican historical chronotopes into discontinuous and successive eras.

Mexica, or Aztec, history seems to be clearly divided into distinct eras, each with a different corresponding chronotope. The first is that of migration, which was initiated with the departure from Aztlán in *one year 1 Tecpatl* (a date charged with deep symbolism) and ended with the founding of Mexico in *one year 2 Calli*. As it begins, this era marks the end of a previous era: that of life in Aztlán. Almost nothing is known about this previous historical period, not because no history exists, but because Mexica history is defined as a break with that past: hence the initiation of a new count on the calendar.

The migration was an era with very particular characteristics: it was defined by the constant search for a homeland, for a spatial center that might substitute for the one that was left behind. In another work (Navarrete, 2000) I have analyzed the characteristics of what we might call the migratory chronotope: time and space are represented as a continuum, defined by the movement of the people in search of a site they might definitively settle. The narrative conventions of the codices underscore the unity of this journey, its irreversible and univocal nature, over and above the multiple vicissitudes that define it.

The founding of Mexico marks the end of the migratory era and the establishment of a new historical chronotope. It seems to me that images like the first illustration of the *Códice Mendoza* (*Mendoza Codex*, 1979) clearly represent the establishment of México-Tenochtitlan as the center of the world around which Mexica historical time will spin from that point forward.

This center defines a new chronotope: history is no longer the movement of a people in search of their homeland, but rather the expansion of this same people from an already established center. The Mexica god Huitzilopochtli himself explains the way this expansion will come about thus:

> . . . so that my will shall govern in villages everywhere I will wait, I will confront, I will meet with people from the four cardinal points (*Crónica Mexicáyotl*, 29).

Therefore the codices that address this period adopt narrative conventions that are radically different, including in their representation of the conquests (not of the journey) and a periodization based on the coronation and death of the *tlatoques*[5] (and not on stays in or departures from places). Along with changes in the chronotope, the protagonists also change: during migration, the people as a whole were guided by the god Huitzilopochtli; after the founding, everything turned on the individual figures of the *tlatoques* and their exploits.

It seems to me that the radical differences in the chronotopes of the two eras reflect the radical transformations in the historical nature of the Mexica, from a miserable and wandering people to a conquering and high-flying empire. The indigenous people themselves were conscious of the irreversible nature of this transformation, as demonstrated in the episode of the failed return to Aztlán, recorded by Diego Durán (1967).

At the same time, the Mesoamerican eras combined the linearity of these irreversible transformations with a certain cyclical impulse. The Mexica knew that their imperial splendor was destined to collapse, as the reign of the Toltec, the Culhua, the Acolhua, and the Tepaneca had fallen before them. This consciousness was not so different from the awareness that caused them to fear the end of their cosmogonic era, that it might disappear just as previous eras had disappeared.

For this reason, it seems to me natural that the arrival of the Spanish and the conquest would have been interpreted as another change of era, a change similar to those that had occurred previously. This conception might explain the constant allusion to the Spanish as beings that were returning, as well as Moctezuma's failed attempt to take refuge at Cincalco, as Huémac had done. Other analogies between indigenous narratives of the conquest of the Mexica and the narratives of the fall of the archetypical city of Tollan

5 *Tlatoani* (plural *tlatoque*). Nahuatl term for rulers or kings. It means literally "he who speaks," and refers to the role of the ruler as representative of his people and of the gods.

(another change of historical era) have been located by Olivier (1999).

The hypothesis that the Spanish conquest marked a change of era in indigenous historical consciousness is yet to be fully demonstrated. Likewise, it is yet to be determined to what extent an originally indigenous conception was reinforced by the analogous Spanish idea that conceived of the conquest as the arrival of Christianity to America and as the beginning of a new Christian era on that continent. The apparent combination of these two ideas appears in the following fragment from Cristóbal del Castillo:

> . . . all the things written in this book are the end, the destruction, the conclusion of the being [custom] of the Mexica, ever since the holy water was expanded, and the bonfire, until they were conquered by Captain Hernando Cortés, Marquis of the Valley, when he introduced, when he caused to enter México Tenochtitlan for the first time, such that the divine light entered, the divine solar radiance of Our Lord, God the only god, Jesus Christ, his true faith, his knowledge, the divine words of his faith. (Del Castillo 1991, 163)

The Mexica era, marked by its being or custom (*yeliztli*), began with the expansion of sacrificial war (holy water, bonfire) and ended with the arrival of Cortés and the beneficent rays of the new religion. In other parts of Del Castillo's work, we learn that the Mexica era (appraised in the most negative way) came to destroy a previous era in which peasant peoples lived peacefully, adoring false gods and not the devil, as the Mexica did. In this way, the author turned the tables on the Catholic accusation that all *Indios* were devil worshippers.

A similar conception of the Spanish conquest and the arrival of Christianity can be found in this Mayan prophecy from the *Chilam Balam of Chumayel*:

> In the year Trece Ahau, in the final stages of that katún, the Itza people will be destroyed and will wander through Tancah, Father. As a sign of the only God of the heavens the Sacred Tree will come, made manifest to all so that the world might be illuminated, Father . . . The earth will awaken to the North and to the West. Itzam will awaken . . . Receive these your guests, who are bearded and come from the lands to the east, transmitters of the sign of God, Father. Good and wise is the word of God, which comes down to you. The day of your life is come. Do not become lost from that day here in this world, Father. "You are the only God who created us:" thus will be the kind word of God, Father, Lord of our souls. He who shall receive Him with all his faith, shall follow Him to heaven.
>
> But this is the beginning of the people of the Second Time. When they send their signal up to the heavens, when they raise it up with the Tree of Life, everything will change at once. And the successor of the first tree of the earth will appear, and will be manifest for all people. The sign of the only God above, that is the one you shall adore, Itza people. Adore the new sign of the heavens, adore Him with your whole will, adore the true God, this one, Father. Accept the word of the Only God into yourselves, Father. From heaven comes the one whose word overflows for you, to enliven your spirit, Itza people. For those who believe, it will dawn during the next Katún, Father. And now my

> word enters the night. I, Chilam Balam, I have explained the word of God across the world, so that all who live in this great region of this earth might hear, Father. This is the word of God, Lord of heaven and of earth. (*Chilam Balam de Chumayel* 1988, 184–185)

This passage seems to confirm that for the Maya, the arrival of the Spanish and of Christianity also marked a change of era. Edmonson asserts that in colonial times, the wheel of the katunes was reshaped, so that *katún 11 Ahau,* the *katún* of conquest, would be shifted to become the beginning of that era. (Edmonson 1982, 17)

The Chumayel text might explain the constant concern among the Maya, throughout the colonial epoch, with appropriating the Christian religion and turning it into the basis for a new social order free from Spanish domination; this concern became especially evident during the rebellion of Cancuc and the War of Castes. It would seem, in effect, that the Maya perceived the arrival of a new religion as the nullification of their old beliefs.

It is equally interesting that even this irreversible break within the religious order, and the raising of a new tree of life, might be incorporated into the Mayan historical chronotope, and that the Maya might construct an efficacious political program of adaptation and appropriation of this new reality.

Chronotopes and the "Plenitude" of Time

These reflections lead to a double conclusion. In the first place, they confirm the value and the explanatory power of the concept of the chronotope as it was defined by Bakhtin. Second, they suggest that the "plenitude" of time that Bakhtin located as a referent for chronotopes is much more elusive and complex than he himself thought.

In effect, it seems to me that the linearity, irreversibility, and uniqueness of the modern Western historical chronotope is a poor reflection of that "plenitude." The fact that modern historical consciousness should conceive of time as an uninterrupted and linear continuum starting with the Big Bang should not imply that there might not be a plethora of much more complex cycles—from terrestrial and stellar movements to biological rhythms—inserted into that linearity. In fact, the theory of relativity contains a much more complex conception of time than that of this linear historical chronotope. At the same time, it is impossible to deny the negative effects of a vision that originates in the imposition of a singular truth and reason and the destruction of what already exists in the service of a better future that does not yet exist. In contrast, the Mesoamerican chronotope, with its extremely complex game of rounds, cycles, and irreversible transformations, seems much closer to a true "plenitude."

However, we must start from the premise that a plenitude of time is by definition unattainable. Any human chronotope necessarily arises out of cultural determinations, out of indemonstrable premises (based in a cultural conception of reality), and thus constructs a system that is rational and functional but does not encompass reality in itself. In this sense, we might aptly apply Weber's reflections on the forms of rationality and their inescapable limits.

This affirmation, in turn, implies a practical and moral conclusion. If we cannot be certain of the superiority of our chronotope, and of our culture, then our attitude toward other cultures should no longer be to explain them in order to integrate them into our conception of reality and historical coming into being, but rather to attempt to dialogue with them in order to comprehend them, while always respecting their fundamental alterity.

Translated by Jen Hofer

BIBLIOGRAPHY

Aguirre Beltrán, Gonzalo. "Encuentro sobre indigenismo en México", *América Indígena,* Revista del Instituto Indigenista Americano, 1970.

Bakhtin, Mikhail. "Forms of Time and of the Chronotope in the Novel: Notes towards a Historical Poetics." in *The Dialogical Imagination: Four Essays by M. M. Bakhtin.* Austin: University of Texas Press, 1981, 84–258.

Benjamin, Walter. "Tesis de filosofía de la historia." *Discursos interrumpidos I.* Madrid: Taurus Ediciones, 1973, 175–192. Bierhorst, John, ed.

Bierhorst, John. *Cantares Mexicanos. Songs of the Aztecs,* Palo Alto: Stanford University Press, 1985.

Brown, Michael F. "Beyond Resistance: A Comparative Study of Utopian Renewal in Amazonia." *Ethnohistory* 38:4 (1991) 388-413.

Carpentier, Alejo. *Los pasos perdidos.* Barcelona: Barral Editores, 1972.

Chilam Balam de Chumayel. *Libro de Chilam Balam de Chumayel.* Mexico City: Secretaría de Educación Pública, 1988.

Códice Chimalpopoca: Anales de Cuauhtitlan y Leyenda de los Soles. Mexico City, UNAM-IIH. 1992 [1945].

Del Castillo, Cristóbal. *Historia de la venida de los mexicanos y otros pueblos e Historia de la conquista.* Trans. Federico Navarrete. Mexico City: INAH/GV Editores/Sociedad de Amigos del Templo Mayor, 1991.

Durán, Fray Diego. *Historia de las Indias de Nueva España.* Mexico City: Editorial Porrúa, 1967.

Edmonson, Munro S., ed. *The Ancient Future of the Itza: The Book of Chilam Balam of Tizimin.* Austin: University of Texas Press, 1982.

Graulich, Michel. *Mythes et rituels du Mexique ancien préhispanique.* Brussels: Académie Royales de Belgique, 1982.

Jones, Grant D. *Maya Resistance to Spanish Rule: Time and History on a Colonial Frontier.* Albuquerque: University of New Mexico Press, 1989.

Koselleck, Reinhart, "Historia, historias y estructuras formales del tiempo." *Futuro pasado. Para una semántica de los tiempos históricos.* Barcelona: Ediciones Paidos, 1993, 127–140.

García Quintana, Josefina and Alfredo López Austin, eds. *Historia General de las Cosas de la Nueva España*. Madrid: Alianza Editorial, 1988

Ernest Mandel. *Tratado de economía marxista.* Mexico City: Ediciones Era, 1980.

McLoughlin, William. "Ghost Dance Movements: Some Thoughts on Definition Based on Cherokee History." *Ethnohistory* 37:1 (1990) 25-44.

Muñoz Camargo, Diego. "Relación geográfica de Tlaxcala." *Relaciones Geográficas del Siglo XVI: México.* Ed. René Acuña. Mexico City: UNAM-IIA 4 (1986) 229-269.

Navarrete, Federico. "The path from Aztlan to Mexico: On Visual Narration in Mesoamerican Codices." *Res. Aesthetics and Anthropology* 37 (2000) 31–48.

Olivier, Guilhem. "Entre transgresión y renacimiento, el papel de la ebriedad en los mitos del México antiguo." *El héroe entre el mito y la historia,* ed. Guilhem Olivier and Federico Navarrete. Mexico City: Instituto de Investigaciones Históricas-CEMCA, 1999, 101–121.

Popol Vuh: The Mayan Book of the Dawn of Life. Translated by Dennis Tedlock. New York: Simon and Schuster, 1985.

Reifler-Bricker, Victoria. "The Caste War of Yucatán: The History of a Myth and the Myth of History." in *Anthropology and History in Yucatán.* Edited by Grant D. Jones. Austin: The University of Texas Press, 1977, 251–258.

____. *El Cristo indígena, el Rey nativo.* Mexico City: Fondo de Cultura Económica,1993.

Roys, Ralph L. *The Book of Chilam Balam of Chumayel.* Norman, OK: University of Oklahoma Press, 1967.

Sahagún, Bernardino de. *Códice Florentino.* Mexico City: Archivo General de la Nación, 1979

——. *The Florentine Codex: General History of the Things of New Spain.* Translated by Arthur J.O. Anderson and Charles Dibble. Santa Fe, NM and Salta Lake City, UT: The School of American Research and the University of Utah Press,1950.

Stern, Steve J. *Los pueblos indígenas del Perú y el desafío de la conquista española.* Madrid: Alianza Editorial, 1982.

Sullivan, Paul. *Unfinished Conversations: Mayas and Foreigners Between Two Wars.* Berkeley, CA: University of California Press, 1989.

Tedlock, Barbara. *Time and the Highland Maya.* Albuquerque: University of New Mexico Press, 1992.

Tezozómoc, Fernando Alvarado. *Crónica Mexicáyotl.* Mexico City: UNAM-IIH, 1992 [1949].

Todorov, Tzvetan. *La conquista de América. El problema del Otro.* Mexico City: Siglo XXI Editores, 1992.

Villar, Ernesto de la Torre, ed. *Códice Mendocino.* Mexico City: San Ángel Ediciones, 1979.

Fold-out map in Edith Mackie and Sheldon Dicks   Mexican Journey: An Intimate Guide to Mexico, Dodge Publishing, 1935

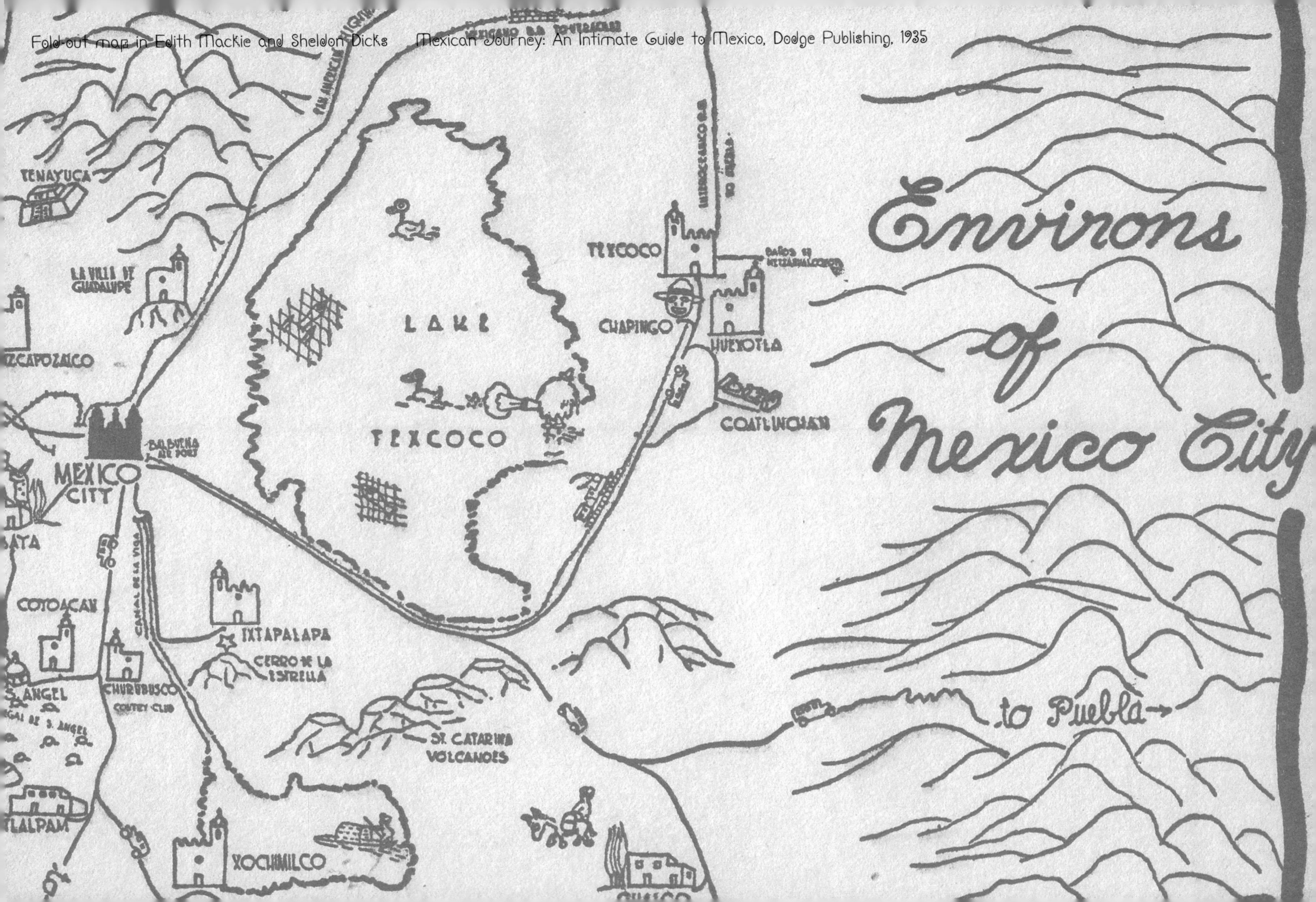

COATLINCHAN IN FRAGMENTS WHERE DO THEY BELONG ?[1]

SANDRA ROZENTAL
UNIVERSIDAD AUTONOMA METROPOLITANA

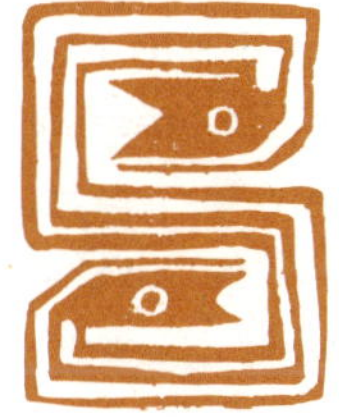an Miguel Coatlinchan is a town in the Texcoco municipality, a region of the Estado de Mexico that makes up the blurry boundary that separates, or rather gradually seeps from, Mexico City's asphalt landscape to its eastern semi-urban, semi-rural periphery. A relatively quiet agricultural town during most of its post-conquest history, Coatlinchan's fate changed dramatically in the second half of the nineteenth century, when a colossal pre-Hispanic sculpture was found buried in one of the town's surrounding ravines. Although scholars of ancient Mexico agreed that the statue represented an anthropomorphic rain deity, they debated for decades regarding its gender and identity (Batres 1890, 1903, 1905; Chavero 1904; Noguera 1964). The "Idol of Coatlinchan," as the object came to be known, was featured in travel guides and became a quintessential stop on the Interoceanic Railroad of Mexico, along with the Baths of Nezahualcoyotl (near Texcoco) and Huexotla, for antiquarian collectors, amateur archaeologists, and tourists interested in the ruins of ancient Mexico (Batres 1903).

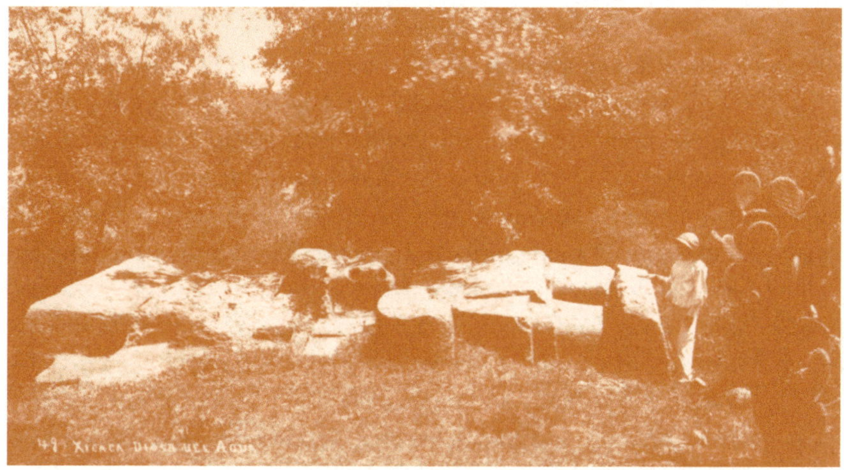

Monolith of Coatlinchan
Ibero-amerikanisches Institute, Berlin

1 The research for this article was conducted from 2007–2012 in New York, Berlin, Mexico City, and Coatlinchan, and was funded by the Wenner-Gren Foundation and by the Andrew W. Mellon/ American Council for Learned Societies. I am very grateful to Mariana Castillo Deball for the opportunity to publish the work in this journal and to Richard Kernaghan, Adam Sellen, and Matthew Robb for their helpful comments and suggestions. All translations and images are mine unless otherwise noted.

In 1964, after almost a century of marking the town as an archaeological destination, the 167-ton monolith was removed from its former abode and transported to Mexico City, where it was upended as the monument and marker signaling the entrance of the newly inaugurated National Anthropology Museum. Although Coatlinchan is most famous for this object and its subsequent removal and transformation into both a national and public urban monument, other artifacts from the town's territory have been excavated, removed, and exchanged since at least the mid-1800s.

The region surrounding the former Texcoco lake and its towns, built over pre-Hispanic settlements, were known treasure troves for museum professionals and private collectors who enjoyed the area's proximity to Mexico City for unearthing, buying, or looting ancient material culture. Such collectors visited Coatlinchan as a place to find and acquire ancient artifacts beginning in the nineteenth century, scattering the tangible traces of the town's pre-Hispanic past all over the world. Although a walk in the town's arable plots after the rainy season still reveals shiny pottery shards (lavishly decorated with black and red paint and known locally as *tepalcates*[2]), small clay figurines (*ídolos*), and broken obsidian blades, many more such objects have been excavated, extracted, purchased, and sold for over a hundred years. To this day, these itinerant objects circulate, travel, and lurk in collections, galleries, museum storage spaces, and private homes in Mexico and abroad.

Coatlinchan's ancient material culture might be thought of as a broken vessel, a dispersed collection of broken pieces, of fragments that could potentially be reconfigured by tracing historical pathways and current whereabouts. Since the 1970s and 80s, fragments, and fragmentation more broadly, have been at the core of postmodern critiques of what had up until then been imagined as the unified master narrative of modernity (Lyotard 1984; Harvey 1989; Jameson 1998). Gilles Deleuze has also written about fragments, albeit in the form of islands characterized by a double movement—élan that pushes the severed pieces away from one another and from the mainland that formerly incorporated them—and drift, a gravitational force that draws them toward one another. Élan and drift, in turn, both push and draw us away and toward fragments. For Deleuze, "Dreaming of islands—whether with joy or in fear, it doesn't matter—is dreaming of pulling away, of being already separate, far from any continent, of being lost and alone—or it is dreaming of starting from scratch, recreating, beginning anew" (2004,10). In addition to my own dreaming of islands, drawn by this double force of élan and drift, what interests me about fragments—these very tangible islands of clay that have drifted away from the spatially and temporally bounded continent of Coatlinchan's ancient past—is their inherent indexical potential. Incomplete and broken as they are, severed from place and context as isolated bounded entities, these fragments, stored as inert specimens in museums and kept as valuable treasures in personal collections, are always pointing toward something more. Fragments are as such always fragments of something else, connected and related to other fragments and to an ostensible origin through their very severance and fragmentation. Although they reveal the fissures and breaks, they also always bear the scars of their past connections, or of their former lives as incorporated parts of something else.

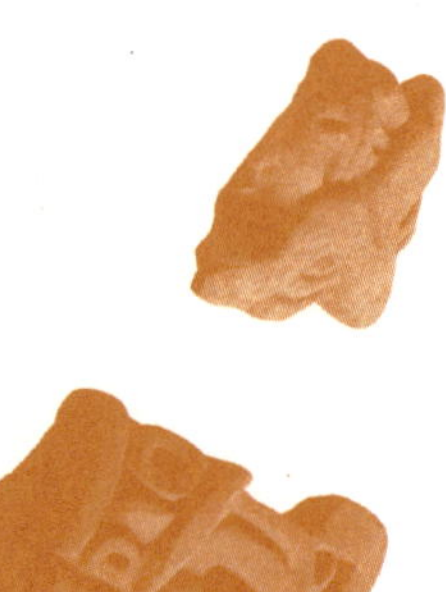

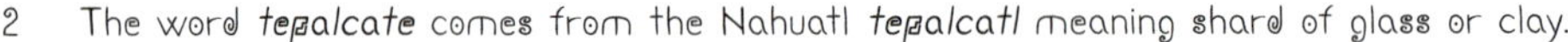

2 The word *tepalcate* comes from the Nahuatl *tepalcatl* meaning shard of glass or clay.

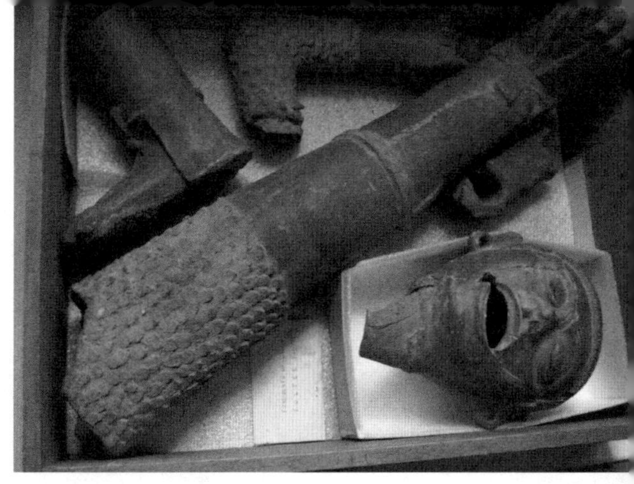

The Saville Collection at AMNH, 2007

In this article, I trace the history of Coatlinchan's severed past, mapping the trajectories of its tangible fragments—the élans and drifts— that crafted their pathways and led to their current sites. Rather than a life history of a single shard that traces its transformation into an ancient artifact and form of evidence (Holtorf 2002), I am interested in analyzing the temporal and spatial relationships that fragments have with each other and with their sites of origin. I therefore describe the social lives of fragments from Coatlinchan as they went from objects found buried in Coatlinchan's soil to museum pieces and scientific specimens in faraway lands. I then contrast the ways in which these fragments have become incorporated into collections, catalogued and framed as art and artifacts, with the ways in which they are displayed, kept, and cherished by Coatlinchan's contemporary residents, who are also invested in picking up the pieces and returning to a long-lost origin by gathering its parts. Unearthing the histories of Coatlinchan's ancient material culture, and locating its traces in collections, in museum storage drawers, and in the homes of Coatlinchan's contemporary residents, I ask, where do these fragments belong?

The first pieces of Coatlinchan's past that I located were catalogued and stored in the American Museum of Natural History (AMNH) on New York's Upper West Side. The collection was acquired by Marshall H. Saville when he was the Mexico and Central America Hall's curator between 1894 and 1907, during Frederic Putnam's tenure as head of the Anthropology department. From 1895–1896, Saville was commissioned on the Mexico Expedition to amass a representative collection of Mexican antiquities, under the patronage of the Joseph Florimond Loubat (Saville 1911; Mc Vicker 1989). In his correspondence with the museum's authorities, Saville mentions his negotiations with the government of Porfirio Díaz for a special contract similar to the one a German specialist on ancient Mexico, Eduard Seler, had negotiated with the government of Honduras, where the AMNH was allowed to conduct excavations for ten years and would split the findings equally with the local government, bearing the entirety of the expedition's costs and being guaranteed no export fees. Casts would be made of the entire collection so that each party would have its original half in addition to the other's half in replicas (AMNH-*Marshall H. Saville Archive*/Box 7/Folder 1). This amounts to a collection made up of fragments, one half original, the other half made up of plaster casts. This collection of both artifacts and casts also produced a new set of incorporated fragments: a collection of late-nineteenth-and early-twentieth-century matchboxes from Mexico that were used by Saville to store and transport the artifacts he gathered during the Mexico Expedition.[3]

3 I am very grateful to Elise Alexander, curatorial assistant at the AMNH for her help during my research in the storage areas and archive at the AMNH in 2006.

Most of Saville's letters are about his frustration with the Mexican government, namely the Congress, whose opposition to the bill resulted in a considerably delayed stay in Mexico. During these negotiations, Díaz apparently related to him an anecdote showing the importance of archaeology in Mexico: during his campaign against the French in Oaxaca, when they ran short of bullets, the Indians brought in cargos of old copper axes that they had dug out of the ruins, and that he and his troops used to make bullets (AMNH-*Accession Records* 1896–32). Díaz's anecdote, folded into the AMNH collection through Saville's writings, shows another élan, a patriotic force, pushing the fragments of Mexico's ancient past, repurposed as bullets, against an army of foreign invaders.

Saville took advantage of his delay in Mexico to travel to nearby towns in search of artifacts for the AMNH's collection. His correspondence does not say much about his collecting missions in Coatlinchan itself, but his accounts of other pieces collected during his time in the region surrounding Mexico City show us a glimpse of his methods and interests in artifacts. For example, he traveled to Tepoztlán, Morelos in late April 1895, and there investigated a temple where he located potential objects for the collection:

> In the vicinity, I saw a number of green stone beads, perhaps jade, and the most prominent mountain is named Chalchihuitepetl, or the mountain of chalchihuite, the Indian name for Jade. I was told of an old quarry there and shall explore the place as soon as possible. There are in this primitive Indian village two old teponoaxtlis or drums, handed down for centuries. They are still used by the Indians during their feasts and I secured a photograph of them. I hope eventually to get one of them (Letter to John Winser, Secretary of the Museum, April 23, 1896).

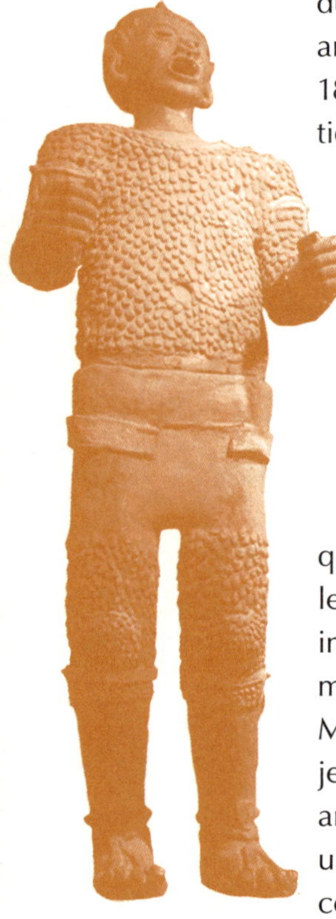

Xipe Totec Mexico and Central America Hall, AMNH

Saville considered these objects valuable because of their material and aesthetic quality, but also because of their relationship to other museums with pre-Hispanic collections: "There are several in the European museums and here in Mexico. The people in Mexico do not know of their presence here otherwise they would probably be in the museum. They are beautifully carved and very valuable. I know of no specimen from Mexico of a carved teponaxtli in the U.S." For Saville, the value of these and other objects collected during the Mexico Expedition was based on a competition with European and Mexican museums, as well as with other museums in the U.S., to have the most unique and complete collection. The fact that the Tepoztlán drums were in use by local communities and had been passed down for centuries is mentioned only in passing. In his letters, Saville also explains the classification scheme that he favored. He mentions, for example, that

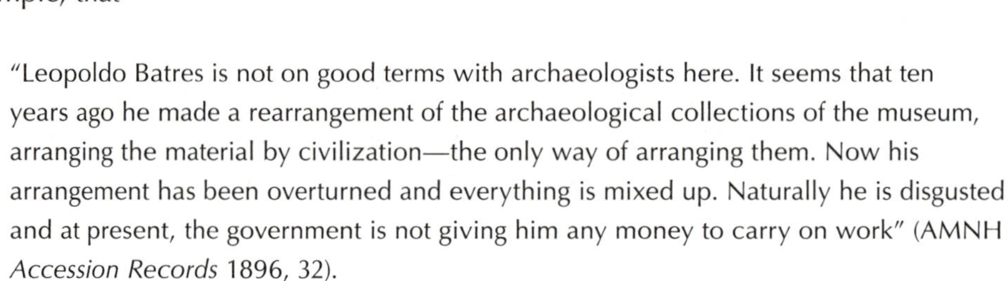

> "Leopoldo Batres is not on good terms with archaeologists here. It seems that ten years ago he made a rearrangement of the archaeological collections of the museum, arranging the material by civilization—the only way of arranging them. Now his arrangement has been overturned and everything is mixed up. Naturally he is disgusted and at present, the government is not giving him any money to carry on work" (AMNH *Accession Records* 1896, 32).

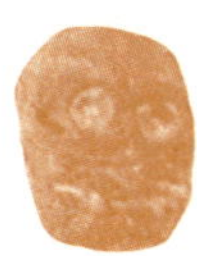

Saville's comments in favor of Batres's classification scheme show that he was himself also engaged in creating an object-based epistemology on a culture-area basis, a model put forth by Franz Boas and Frederic Putnam at the AMNH and at the Chicago Columbian Exhibition (Jacknis 1988). Thus, the collections Saville gathered during his time in the region, including in Coatlinchan, were carefully selected to build a specific narrative of the pre-Hispanic past through objects and displays.

Saville collected artifacts from Coatlinchan, including one of the Mexico and Central America Hall's highlights: a striking life-size terracotta figure comprised of detachable parts. In the catalogue, Saville's description of the standing figure as a "singing priest with feather garment" was crossed out, probably at a later date, pointing to a possible reinterpretation of the figure's identity. In the hall itself, the label states that the figure is made of terracotta and that it is from the Toltec period. It is described as a Xipe Totec, meaning "the flayed one," a deity related to fertility. The label further details: "It represents a practice repellent to us: a person is wearing the skin of a sacrificial victim. Rough areas on the surface apparently depict dried skin tied together at the back and the figure has an open mouth characteristic of Xipe Totec images." A life-size stone skull, probably from a Tzompantli, is also designated as being from Coatlinchan and is displayed nearby. This skull is almost identical to several such skulls encrusted in the

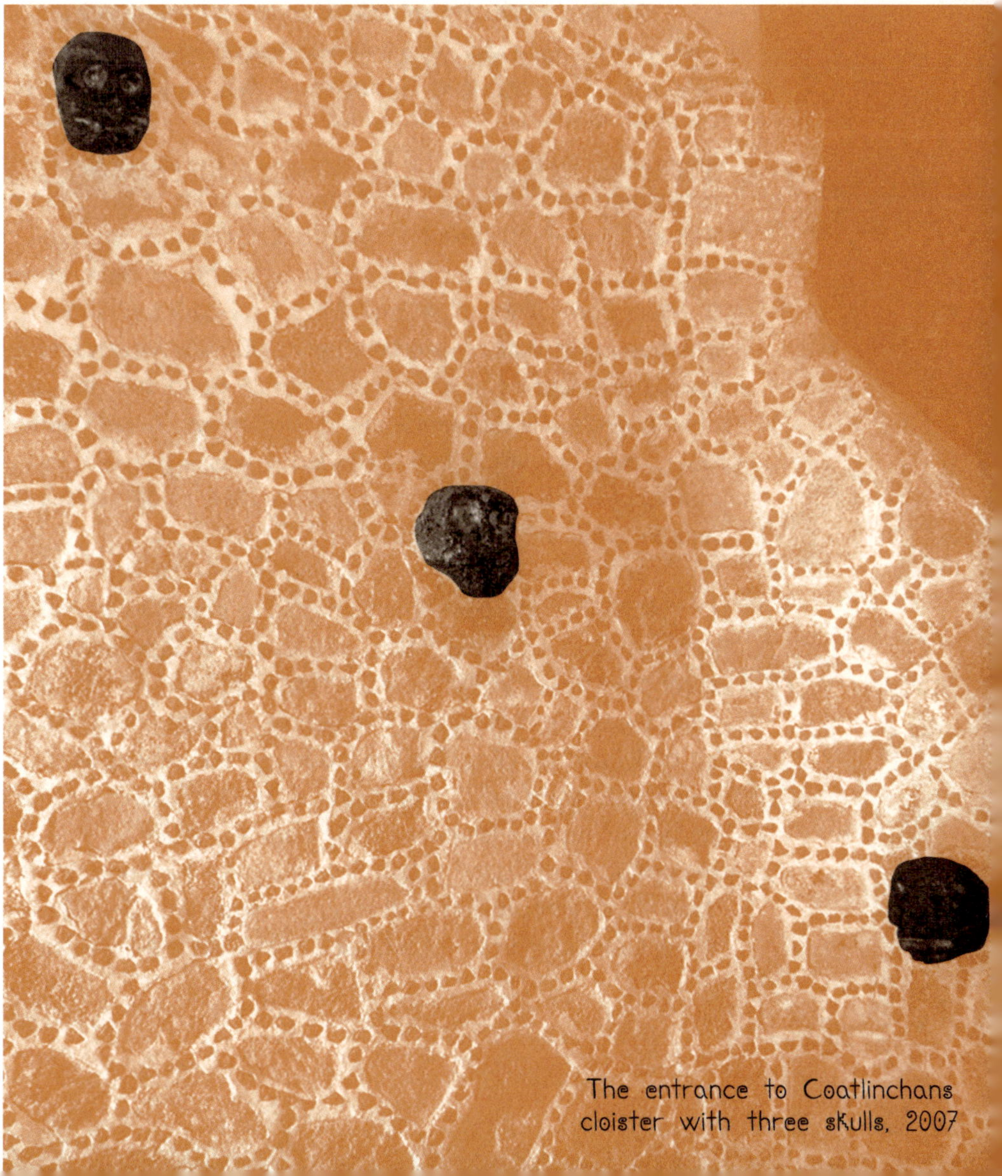

The entrance to Coatlinchans cloister with three skulls, 2007

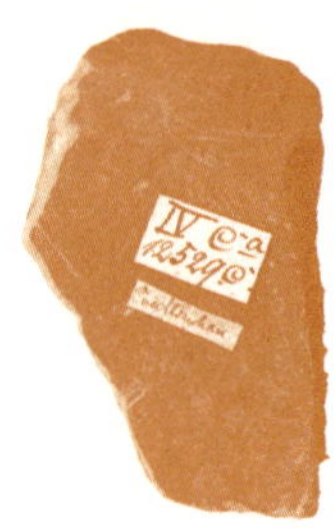

entrance to Coatlinchan's sixteenth-century cloister, plastered into the walls in the 1970s after they were found in the area by town residents.

The original catalogue listed several other objects as part of the same accession number. The Xipe in the gallery was numbered 30–499, but was grouped with 500–502 with an annotation that read "same place as 499." Objects 734, 760, 723, 800, and 801 are also from Coatlinchan (often misspelled as Cuautlanchan and corrected in pencil). These objects were stored in clusters: 500–502 in Cabinet 20, drawer 4, and 734–801 in Cabinet 19, drawer 7. Handwritten labels were attached to each piece, although many also sport the handwritten evidence of a second incorporation, of their becoming part of the AMNH collection—marked with tangible traces of Saville's *flâneries* through accession numbers, dates, and place names written in blue and black ink.

The majority of these inscriptions are hidden from view in discrete places—behind a head, under a foot—places that would be out of sight if these artifacts were ever placed on public view. In some cases, the objects bear two different numbers, marking moments of institutional renewal and new forms of collections and data management within the AMNH. A few pieces have markings on their faces or across a painted design, showing that they were probably acquired as scientific specimens rather than for exhibition.

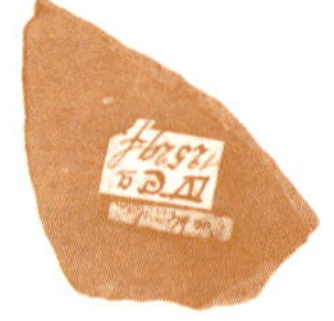

Saville donated these objects to the museum in April 1896, and in the catalogue gave only a vague indication of their provenance: "found in a cave at Coatlinchan, near Texcoco." The catalogue entries show that none of these objects were actually excavated by Saville since, despite his training as a field archeologist, he gives no further information on their precise location or on the site of their origination, data he provided for collections that he did excavate. The Saville collection from 1898, also in this catalogue, has very different descriptions. Objects are entered with much more detail given to their location. For example, 6393 is "a pottery plate, diameter 7 in. Tomb 3. Mound 9, Main Floor, North part" and 6453 is "a dark jar, contained (when found) ashes and obsidian knife. Was covered with plate 30/6454 which had ashes above it. 29 feet from commencement of trench in mound 9." Collected only two years after the Coatlinchan objects, the difference in description and detail cannot be due to a fundamental disciplinary change in how knowledge was organized and prioritized. Clearly, Saville conducted archaeological fieldwork in 1898 as part of his collecting mission, whereas he only went shopping in 1896.

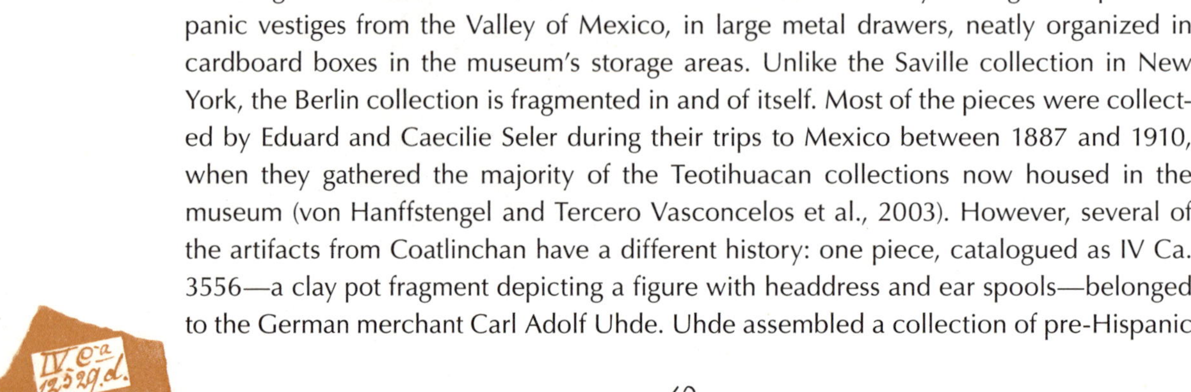

Another, much larger collection of artifacts from Coatlinchan is stored in Berlin's Ethnologisches Museum. The artifacts are stored indiscriminately among other pre-Hispanic vestiges from the Valley of Mexico, in large metal drawers, neatly organized in cardboard boxes in the museum's storage areas. Unlike the Saville collection in New York, the Berlin collection is fragmented in and of itself. Most of the pieces were collected by Eduard and Caecilie Seler during their trips to Mexico between 1887 and 1910, when they gathered the majority of the Teotihuacan collections now housed in the museum (von Hanffstengel and Tercero Vasconcelos et al., 2003). However, several of the artifacts from Coatlinchan have a different history: one piece, catalogued as IV Ca. 3556—a clay pot fragment depicting a figure with headdress and ear spools—belonged to the German merchant Carl Adolf Uhde. Uhde assembled a collection of pre-Hispanic

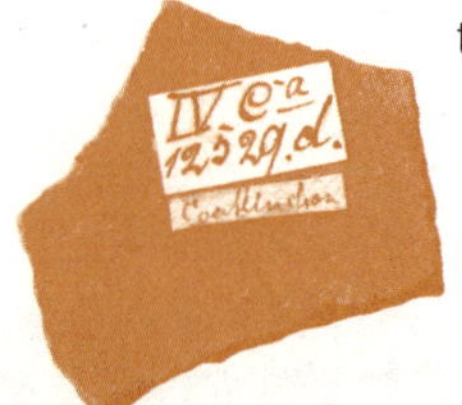

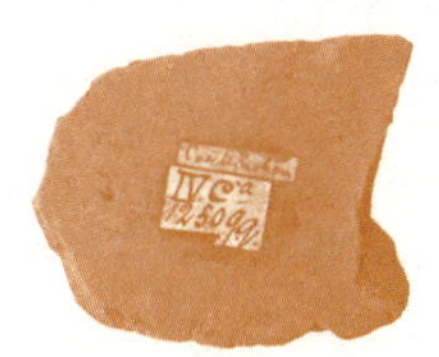

objects during the first half of the nineteenth century that was subsequently brought to Berlin in 1862. Another set of pieces was collected by Wilhelm Bauer and sold to the museum at the beginning of the twentieth century along with thousands of ancient Mexican objects. Bauer was an independent collector and dealer who lived in Mexico City and who would travel to surrounding villages in search of artifacts, which he would purchase, catalogue, and photograph to then sell to various European Museums, including the Berlin Ethnographic Museum, the Stuttgart Museum, the Budapest Ethnographic Museum, and the Museum für Völkerkunde in Leipzig. Seler sometimes commissioned Bauer to locate objects for his own collecting endeavors until he realized that many of the artifacts he sold him were fakes (Adam Sellen, personal communication).

According to János Gyarmarti, Bauer wrote about his collecting techniques in his letters to museum curators: "He embarked on a few days or occasionally, few weeks long tours from his home in Mexico City, in the course of which he acquired both ethnographic and archaeological objects from the villagers. There is but one single reference that he had personally conducted an excavation; he usually bought the items dug up by the locals and if possible, he observed how the villagers opened the graves and recorded what he saw—the position of the deceased, the grave goods and where they were deposited in the burial." Bauer also apparently collected artifacts far from the location of their provenance: an object from Morelos in Mexico City and one from Veracruz in Cordoba (Gyarmarti 2004). Thus, we might never know whether Bauer went to Coatlinchan, where he might have also watched and recorded as "the villagers" unearthed goods, or whether he simply bought them far away from their source community.

Nevertheless, the largest collection of Coatlinchan artifacts in Berlin is the result of Eduard and Caecilie Seler's collecting missions. Eduard Seler served as the director for the American Division of the Königlichen Museum für Völkerkunde, as it was then called, and was, therefore, in charge of the museum's acquisitions of ancient artifacts from the Americas from 1904–1922. Eduard and Caecilie Seler collected objects for the Berlin Museum: clay figurines, vessels, and other fragments. They visited Coatlinchan together at least once in 1910, and photographed the monolith that is now in front of the National Anthropology Museum lying in situ with the caption "Tepetitlan: la Diosa del agua"; the image is now in the Seler Archive at the Ibero-American Institute in Berlin. The most striking feature of the Seler Coatlinchan collection is that it is made up of a large number of broken pottery shards, listed as having been collected by Eduard Seler alone. Unlike Saville, who collected largely whole artifacts fit for display—fragmentary pieces of Coatlinchan's material culture, but whole objects nonetheless—Seler collected a great number of shards and fragments of pots and vessels, broken pieces that he catalogued, drew, and stored. Seler's interest was not in the whole object as a possible artwork or exhibition piece, but in the designs that these shards sported—etched, painted, and sculpted onto the baked clay, which he classified according to scientific taxonomies. Each shard was inscribed on the unpainted side, with a handwritten description of provenance and catalogue number written in black ink onto a white paper label, privileging the side bearing a design as the "front" of the object. The Selers did not inscribe the objects' surfaces, unlike Saville, whose handwritten dates and numbers have now become part of the AMNH artifacts' patina.

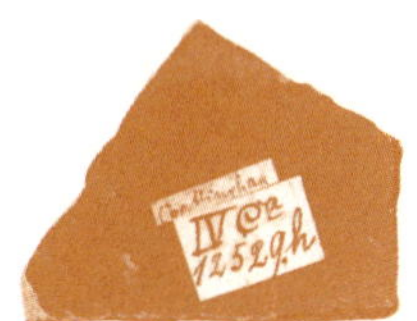

The Seler Collections of Shards in Berlin, 2014

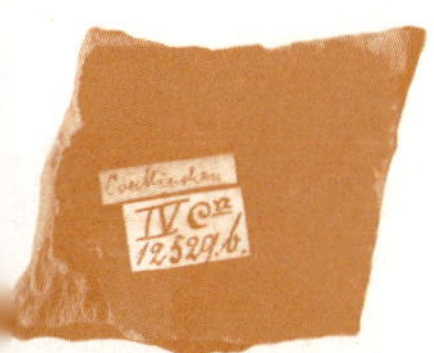

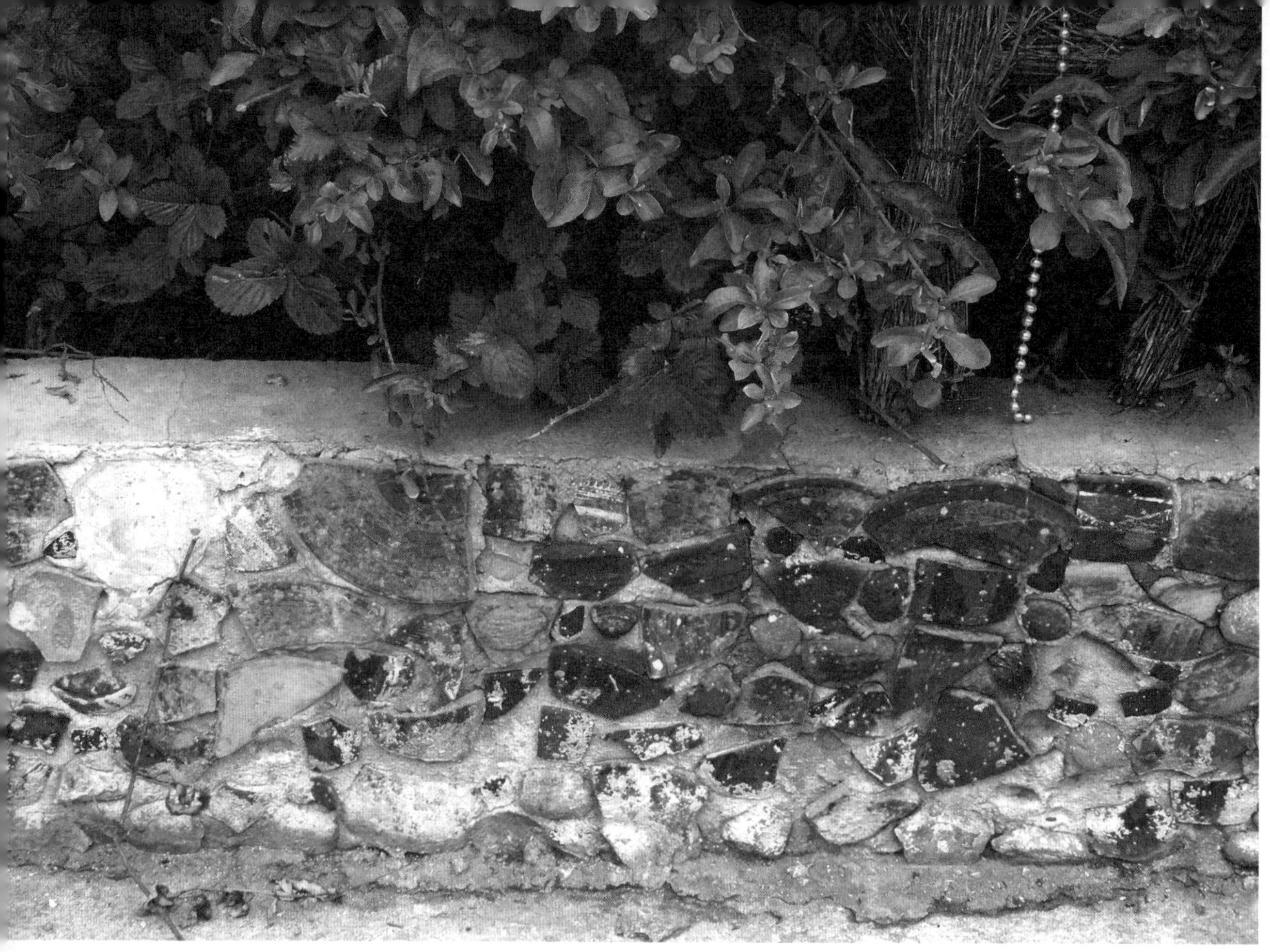

Spolia in Coatlinchan
2013

In Coatlinchan today, townspeople nostalgically reminisce about the presence of pre-Hispanic artifacts—*ídolos* and *tepalcates*— in their everyday lives. Marcelo, a man in his forties who works as a designer, recalls his childhood working with his father in the fields, picking up small figurines and obsidian blades left in the wake of the plow. Children would collect these objects and sell them to the *idoleros* (idol people) who, like the Selers, Saville, and Bauer, came to Coatlinchan on weekends looking for pre-Hispanic artifacts. Marcelo explained to me: "I would sell the *ídolos* in exchange for a few cents, enough to buy a soft drink or sweets—we didn't know what they were worth." Doña Flora, a woman in her late nineties, complained "there are hardly any *idolitos* or tepalcates left to collect." Whereas *Tlacuaches* or opossums, as town residents are known locally, lament the recent scarcity of these precious objects in their lands—artifacts many believe were left behind by ancient ancestors for contemporary residents to find, decode, and cherish—the town itself is full of fragments. Painted shards and little faces peek out from the adobe walls of old houses. A manhole on Independencia, one of the town's main streets, is decorated with old coins and ancient spindles—known as *malacates* or *pirinolas*— whose designs have faded under the wheels of passing cars and trucks.

Inside homes, it is not unusual to see similar spindles and broken shards encrusted in cement walls decorating patios and gardens. These fragments have been turned into contemporary spolia, ruins from a distant past reused and repurposed to embellish and imbue the present. In addition to these objects' presence in the town's built environment, residents have created their own curiosity cabinets and display cases. Often in living rooms or social spaces within their homes, these collections are carefully arranged according to Tlacuaches' own taxonomies.

The local schoolteacher, for example, fixed her collection of spindles and figurines onto cardboard frames that she takes to classroom demonstrations on the pre-Hispanic past. When I asked her how she organized the artifacts, she explained: "Well, there are things here from very different time periods. You can tell their age by looking at the ways they were manufactured; some are more complex, others more rudimentary." She also added, "You can classify them by what they depict too, so for example there are these little oval heads with features that look like aliens. I don't know if our ancestors saw aliens, but I call them UFOs (*ovnis*) and have them all together on a single frame." The town's local chronicler, Salvador, has a different set of criteria for displaying his own collection. He explains that he places only certain objects in what he calls his "mini-museum"—the ones he likes the most, the ones that impress him because of their designs, beauty, or rare features: "There are many objects that are similar in Coatlinchan, but some are very rare, special. They are the really beautiful ones, the ones that I have found and know to be unique."

Others do not display their collections at all, keeping objects around the house in cardboard boxes, paint cans, plastic bags, or tupperware. Concha, for example, has only a handful of artifacts on display in her living room, next to family photographs and souvenirs from friends' baptisms, first communions, and weddings. The rest she keeps in boxes stored in her closet. "I just like having them there. Sometimes I take them out, clean them with a toothbrush. I take them out sometimes to handle them, or just to look at them." Her daughter chimes in: "The whole family gets involved. As soon as we find something we all gather to look at it, to try and make sense of what it is, what meaning it might have had for people so long ago, then we put it away in one of these boxes, until we find another one, and so on." For Concha and her family, these objects represent an enigma, a puzzle to be solved about a mysterious and inaccessible past, not unlike what fascinated the archaeologists and antiquarians who collected them for museums and private collections around the world.

Other town residents keep these fragments far from sight, in plastic bags, canisters, and buckets, adding to their collection sporadically. Don Pablo, a man in his seventies, explained to me that he liked to keep them because they reminded him of his land, of the plots that he and his family have owned and tilled for three generations. He pulled a seated figure out of a bucket full of figurines and pottery shards and knew exactly in which part of town, in which of his family plots, he found it. He picked out another figure randomly, this time a small broken snake's head with protruding eyes, and again told me exactly where it came from. Like Pablo, for many townspeople, these fragments are not fragments of an unknown past at all, of a lost origin, but rather present-day indices of their lands, of their property and deep-seated relationship to the soil.

As part of my on-going collaboration with Coatlinchan's residents, I brought them photographs and as much information as I could gather on both the AMNH and Berlin collections. A few weeks later, Marcelo, who also runs a community website where he regularly posts events and news, posted a page called "The looting: April 2 1896." In this page, he included images of the AMNH collection and information about the artifacts collected by Marshall Saville at the end of the nineteenth century. Marcelo also included the postings of websites featuring ancient artifacts from Coatlinchan: a spindle collected by Zelia Nuttall and exhibited in a show at the Hearst Museum in Berkeley, California; and an anthropomorphic figurine and a snake's head collected in the 1950s in Coatlinchan, featured on websites selling antiques. On his webpage, Marcelo warns: "This should make people conscientious so that nothing like this ever happens again. Without a past there is no future. Think carefully next time you want to sell your past, your identity!" When I asked Marcelo about the webpage, he explained that he wanted to use it to show Tlacuaches the dangers of selling artifacts on the black market, and show new generations to care for and preserve their heritage, their past, their history. He said sharply: "We have to care for what little or what more we have left, but we can't keep having people chip away at what is ours."

Many town residents who like Marcelo saw my images of the Saville Collection began asking me for copies to display in their homes. As Doña Flora explained, she had a figure in her personal collection that looked just like the one in one of the photographs. But authenticating it or its value was not her main concern: "Imagine, she said, my little *ídolo* in New York! And laughing: I will probably never be able to see New York, but my *ídolo* might" Others also underlined their interest in the images because one or several of the objects at AMNH were similar to something they had found in their own land, in their community's territory. Rather than serving as certificates of authenticity or economic value, my images of these lost fragments functioned as vectors connecting, perhaps even transporting, Coatlinchan to New York City.

The reactions to the collections in Berlin were strikingly different, as were the collecting projects that Carl Adolf Uhde, Wilhelm Bauer, and Eduard and Caecilie Seler, had been engaged in in the first place. I watched time and again as my informants in Coat-

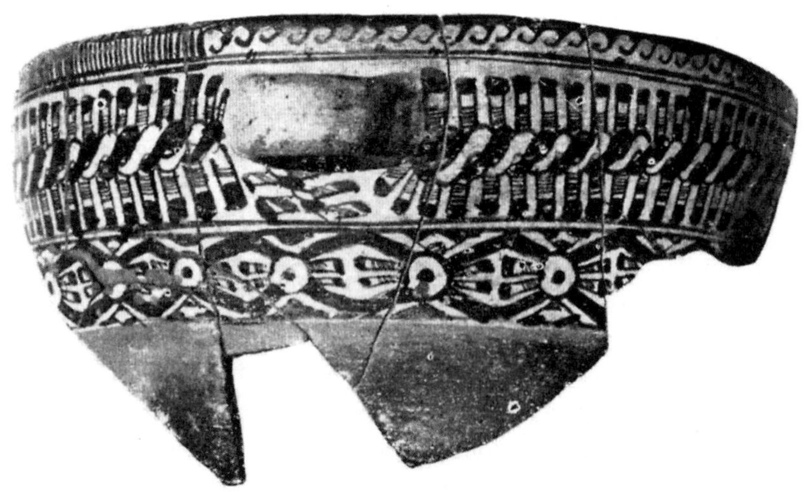

Fragment of a bowl photographed by Jímenez Moreno, Espejo and Peterson during their study of Coatlinchan ceramics (Peterson 1950:29)

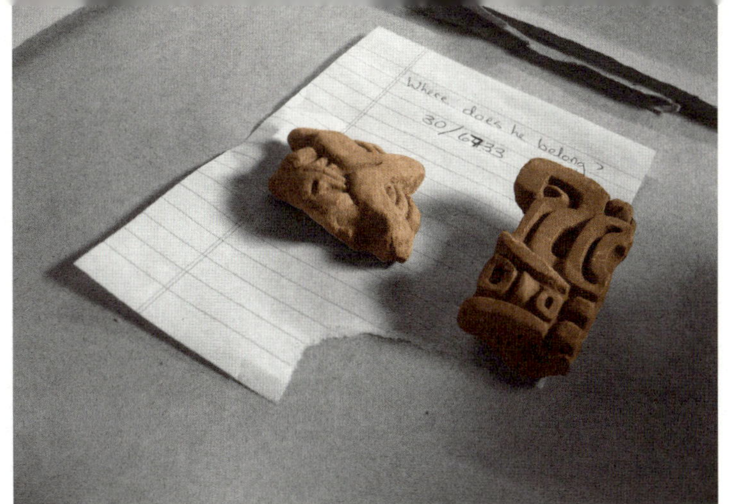

The Saville Collection at AMNH, 2007

linchan flipped through the images and catalogue entries sent to me by the Ethnographic Museum's curator.[4] Having invited me to her home, one elderly woman looking at the images of the collection exclaimed: "Our gigantic idol, I can understand. It is unique. The only one in the world, made here by our ancestors. I can understand people wanting to keep *ídolos* too. They are pretty, many have decorations and designs, many have faces and features, but these knick-knacks? What was so special about them?" She continued: "I remember the *ídoleros*, they came and chose the best, the most valuable pieces, the ones that were whole. We were ignorant, we had so many, we never attributed value to *idolitos*. But I don't remember anyone ever coming to buy tepalcates!" She showed me a pile of dirt in her back yard that her grandson was digging out to build a cistern. Among the rubble, stones and dirt, there were hundreds of shiny pottery shards, some polished, some painted. "We just toss this stuff out. They are just tepalcates, pieces of dry clay!" She could not understand why a museum would go to such pains to catalogue, store and preserve these broken fragments—damaged goods—that she and others in Coatlinchan discarded.

The fragments of Coatlinchan's past, whether whole objects with intact features or broken shards and fissured artifacts, will inevitably remain scattered and incomplete. Some objects are lost in museum collections with no marker of their provenance, while others are traded on the black market, making sporadic appearances on auction websites selling antiquities. Some collections that are known to have been excavated and removed from this location—the urns, bowls, and figurines described and photographed by Wigberto Jímenez Moreno, Antonieta Espejo, and Frederick Peterson following the 1948 excavations conducted by the Mexico City College (Peterson 1950)—have yet to be located in Mexican or foreign collections.

Many objects from Coatlinchan are likely to have ended up in Mexico City's National Anthropology Museum, but this patrimonial leviathan does not have a comprehensive catalogue of its collections organized through data that would allow the singling out of artifacts from Coatlinchan. In fact, much of the information regarding the collection's provenance was already missing in 1907 when Eduard Seler classified the museum's holdings (Solis 2003). Thus, as of yet, there is no way of knowing what artifacts from the museum's Central Valleys collections actually came from Coatlinchan. Many of these objects were probably found and donated to the Museo Nacional by the

4 I am very thankful to Maria Gaida, the curator and director of the Mesoamerican collections at the Ethnologisches Museum, Berlin, for her help locating the artifacts from Coatlinchan amid the Museum's Central Valleys holdings.

elite residents of the nearby haciendas, or perhaps sold by locals to idoleros who in turn sold their findings, which eventually made their way to the museum. Whereas artifacts from Coatlinchan are likely folded into its Central Valleys and Aztec collections, the Coatlinchan monolith stands proudly at the museum's entrance, its provenance clearly marked by a metal plaque and by the still relatively recent memories of its 1964 transfer.

Tangible traces from Coatlinchan's ancient past have been incorporated into private collections of archaeological or Mexican art in Mexico and beyond. They are also kept in private spaces by Coatlinchan's contemporary residents, who hoard them as fragments indexing their very own history and patrimony, far from the patrimonial gaze of the Mexican state and the scientific and artistic pretentions of museums and collectors. And finally, hundreds of artifacts lie to this day buried under Coatlinchan's territory, fragments of an ancient past that haunts town residents' contemporary social lives and whose élans and drifts remain to be seen. A single artifact that I found in the AMNH's collections, excavated in Coatlinchan by Marshall Saville and stored in the museum for over a hundred years, haunts my own thinking on Coatlinchan's fragments. It is a broken clay figure placed in a wooden drawer under a note written relatively recently by the museum's staff on a sheet of paper that is itself torn, missing a piece. An island on an island. The note says: "Where does he belong?" I ask again, where do Coatlinchan's fragments belong?

BIBLIOGRAPHY

AMNH (1892/32) *Accession Records* 1896–32. New York: Division of Anthropology Archives, American Museums of Natural History.

AMNH *Marshall H. Saville Archive*. Box 12, Folder 29 "Mexican Notes (topical)." New York: Division of Anthropology Archives, American Museums of Natural History.

AMNH *Marshall H. Saville Archive*. Box 7, Folder 1 "Concession in Mexico Granted 1896." New York: Division of Anthropology Archives, American Museums of Natural History.

Batres, Leopoldo. "Archéologie Mexicaine: Le Monument de la "Déesse de l'Eau." *La Nature*, Paris, 1890

——.*¿Tlaloc?* Mexico City: Secretaria de Justicia e Instrucción Pública, Inspección y Conservación de Monumentos Arqueológicos, 1903.

——.*El Senor Chavero y el Monolito de Coatlinchan*: Mexico City: Imprenta Fidencio S. Soria, 1904.

——.*Contestación a la duplica del señor licenciado Alfredo Chavero en la controversia del monolito de Coatlinchan*, Mexico City: Imprenta Fidencio S. Soria, 1905.

Chavero, Alfredo. *El Monolito de Coatlinchan*. Mexico City: Imprenta del Museo Nacional, 1904.

Deleuze, Gilles. *Desert Islands: and Other Texts, 1953--1974*. Los Angeles: Semiotext(e), 2004.

"¡El Saqueo!," accessed May 1, 2014, http://koatlinchan.jimdo.com/02-abril-1896/

Gyarmati, János. "Wilhelm bauer, a german collector and his mexican collections in the German Museum of Ethnography, Budapest and in other museums." *Baessler-Archiv* 52: 47–53, 2004.

Harvey, David. *The Condition of Postmodernity*. Oxford: Blackwell, 1989.

Holtorf, Cornelius. "Notes on the Life History of a Pot Sherd." *Journal of Material Culture* 7.1: 49–71, 2002.

Jacknis, Ira "Franz Boas and Exhibits: On the Limitations of the Museum Method of Anthropology." In *Objects and Others: Essays on Museums and Material Culture*, ed. G. W. Stocking. Madison: University of Wisconsin Press, 1988, pp 75-111.

Jameson, Fredric. *The Cultural Turn: Selected Writings on the Postmodern, 1983–1998*. New York and London: Verso, 1998.

Lyotard, Jean-François. *The Postmodern Condition: A Report on Knowledge*. Minneapolis: University of Minnesota Press, 1984.

McVicker, Donald. "Prejudice and Context: The Anthropological Archaeologist as Historian." In *Tracing Archaeology's Past: The Historiography of Archaeology*, ed. Andrew L. Christenson. Carbondale: Southern Illinois University Press, 1989, pp.113-126.

Noguera, Eduardo. "El Monolito de Coatlinchan." In *Anales de Antropología*, 131-143. Instituto de Investigaciones Históricas, Mexico City: UNAM, 1964.

Peterson, Fredrick A. "Notes on Coatlinchan Ceramics." In *Mesoamerican Notes*, Mexico: Mexico City College 1:29–33, 1950.

Saville, Marshall H. *The Work of the Loubat Expedition in Southern Mexico*. New York: Privately printed, 1911.

Solís, Felipe "Eduard Seler y las colecciones arqueológicas del Museo Nacional de México." In *Eduard y Caecilie Seler, sistematización de los estudios americanistas y sus repercusiones*, ed. Renata Von Hanffstengel and Cecilia Tercero Vasconcelos. Mexico City: UNAM, 2003, pp.211-224.

Von Hanffstengel, Renata, and Cecilia Tercero Vasconcelos. eds. Eduard y Caecilie Seler, sistematización de los estudios americanistas y sus repercusiones. Mexico City: UNAM, 2003.

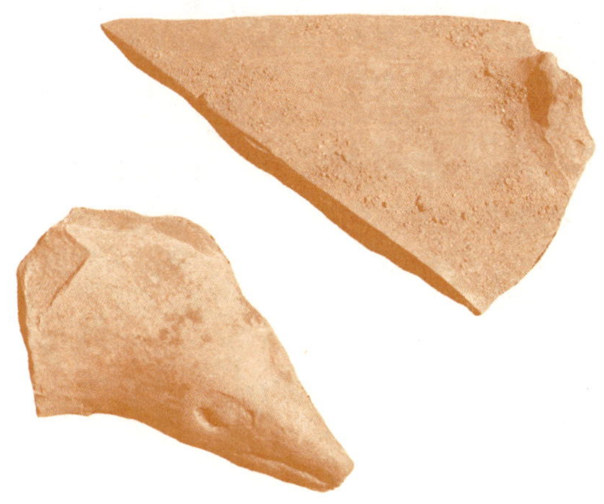

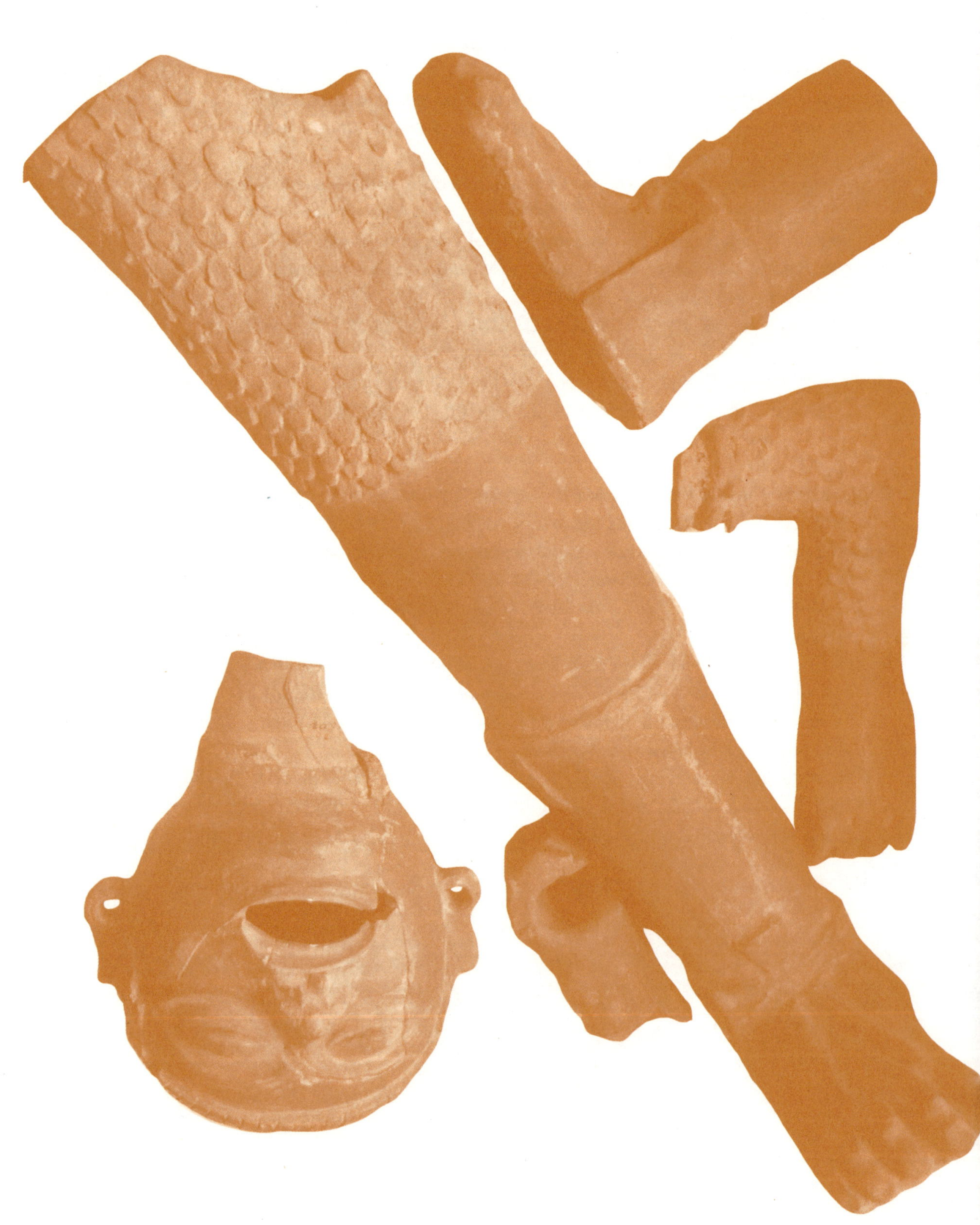

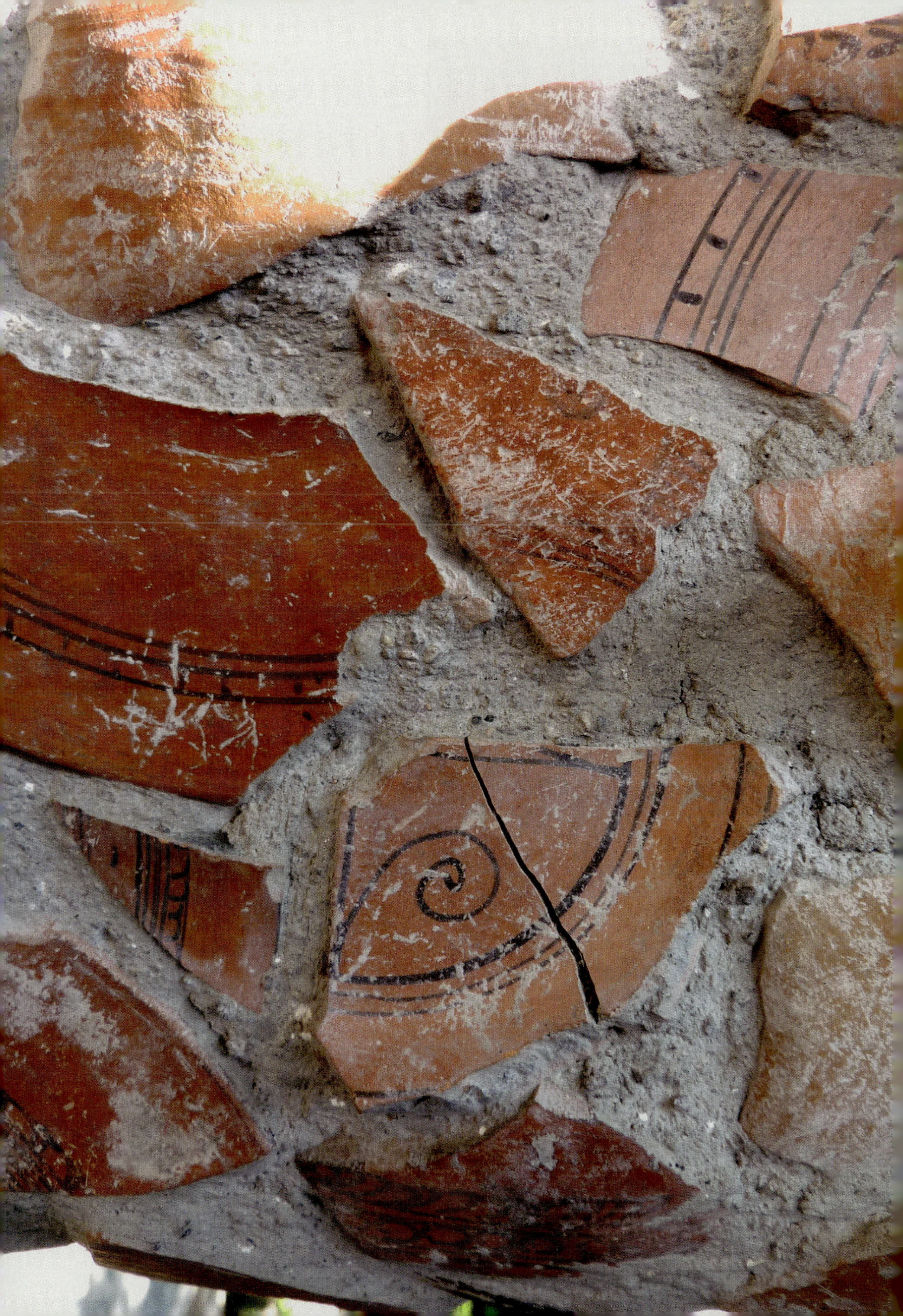

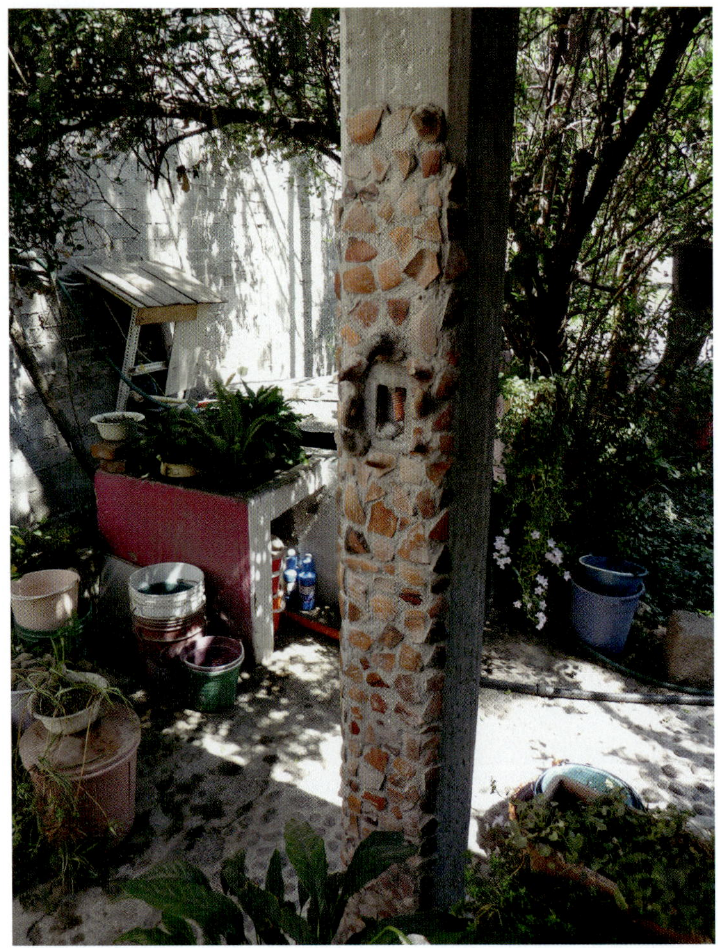

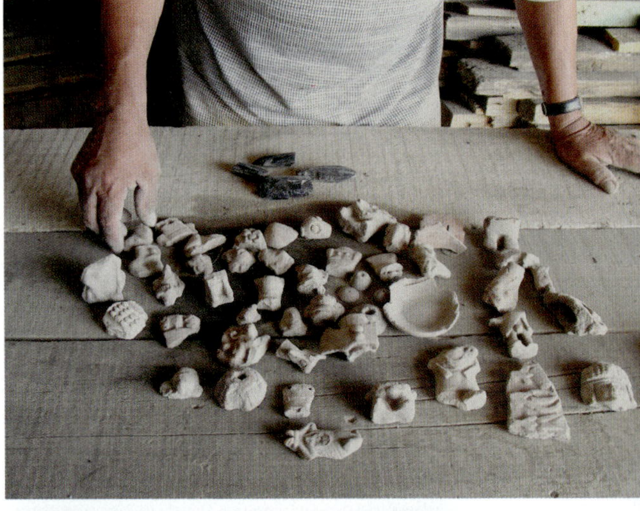

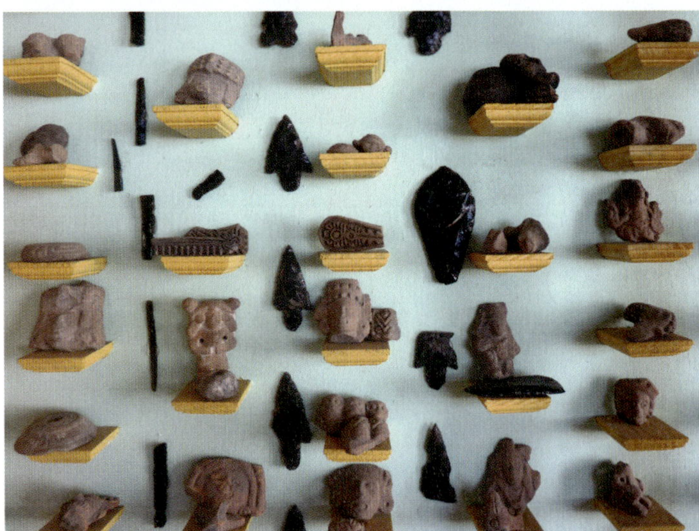

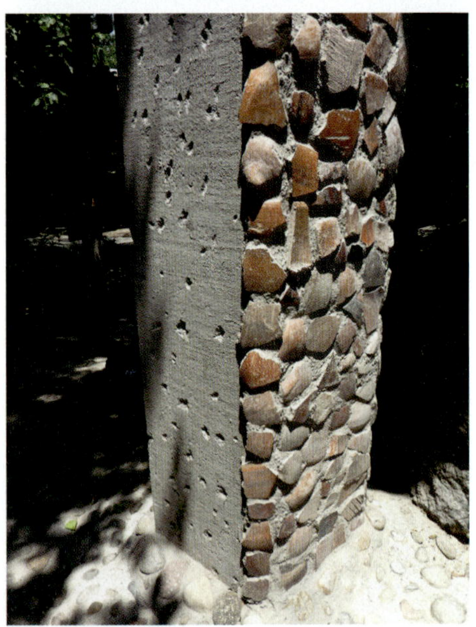

Fragments and
collections in
Coatlinchan
2009-2014

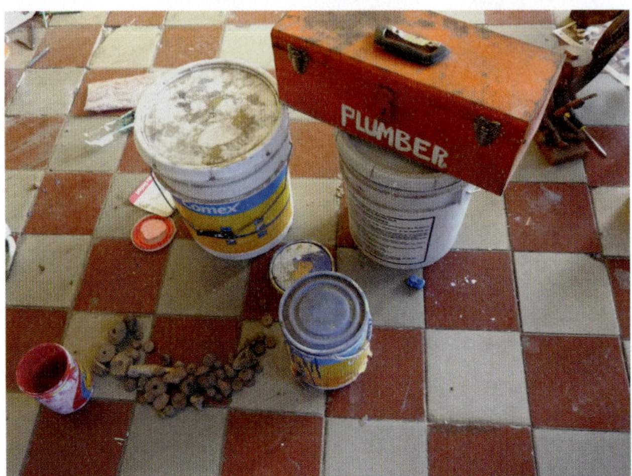

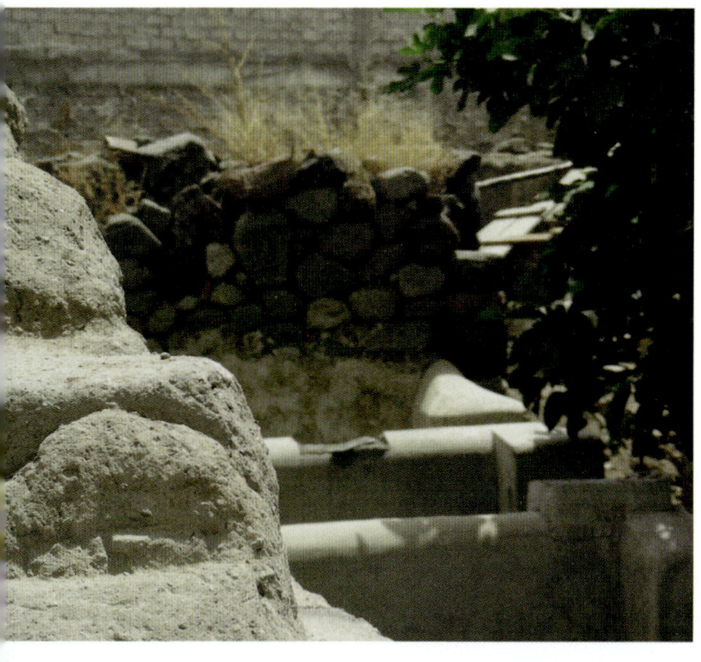

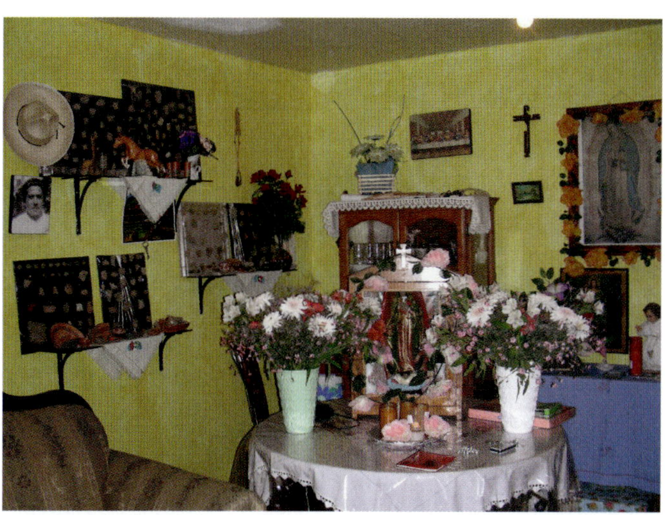

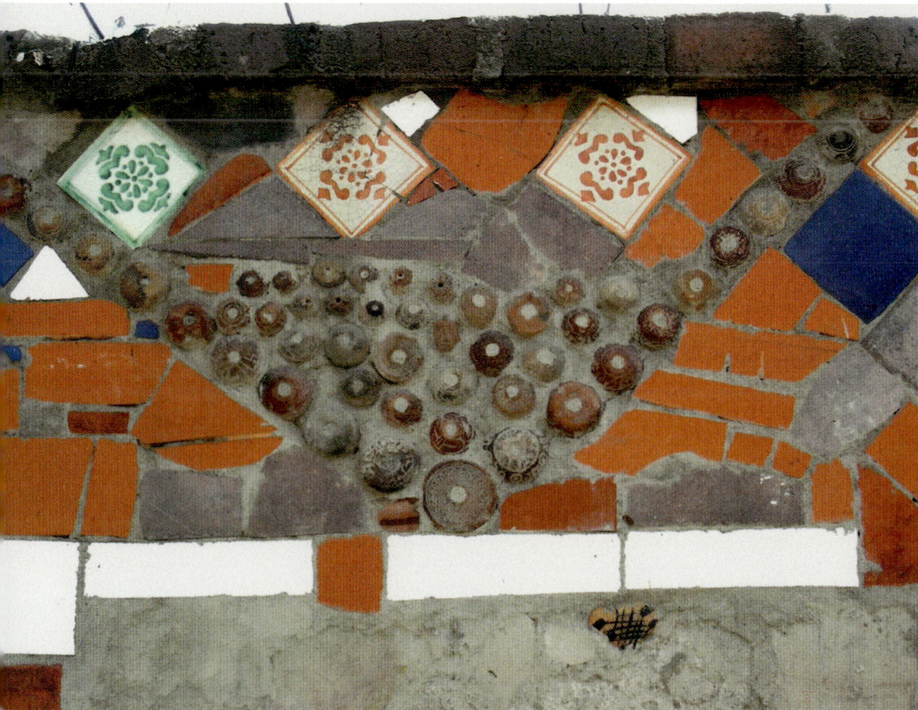

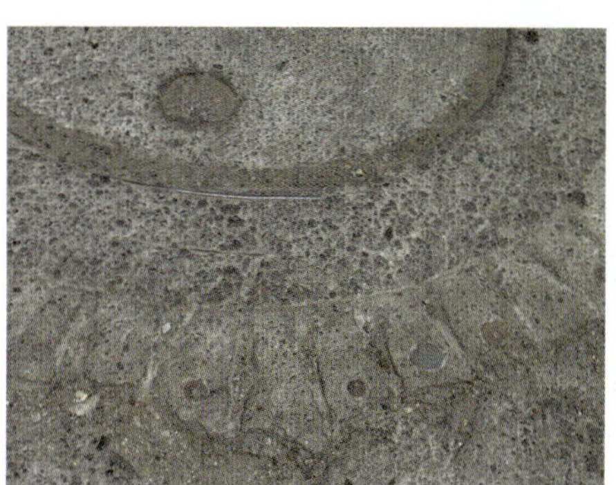

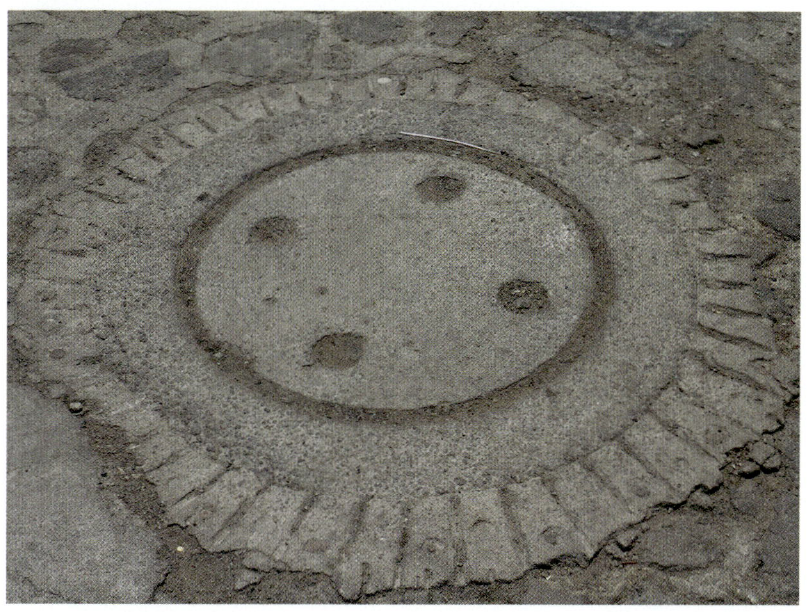

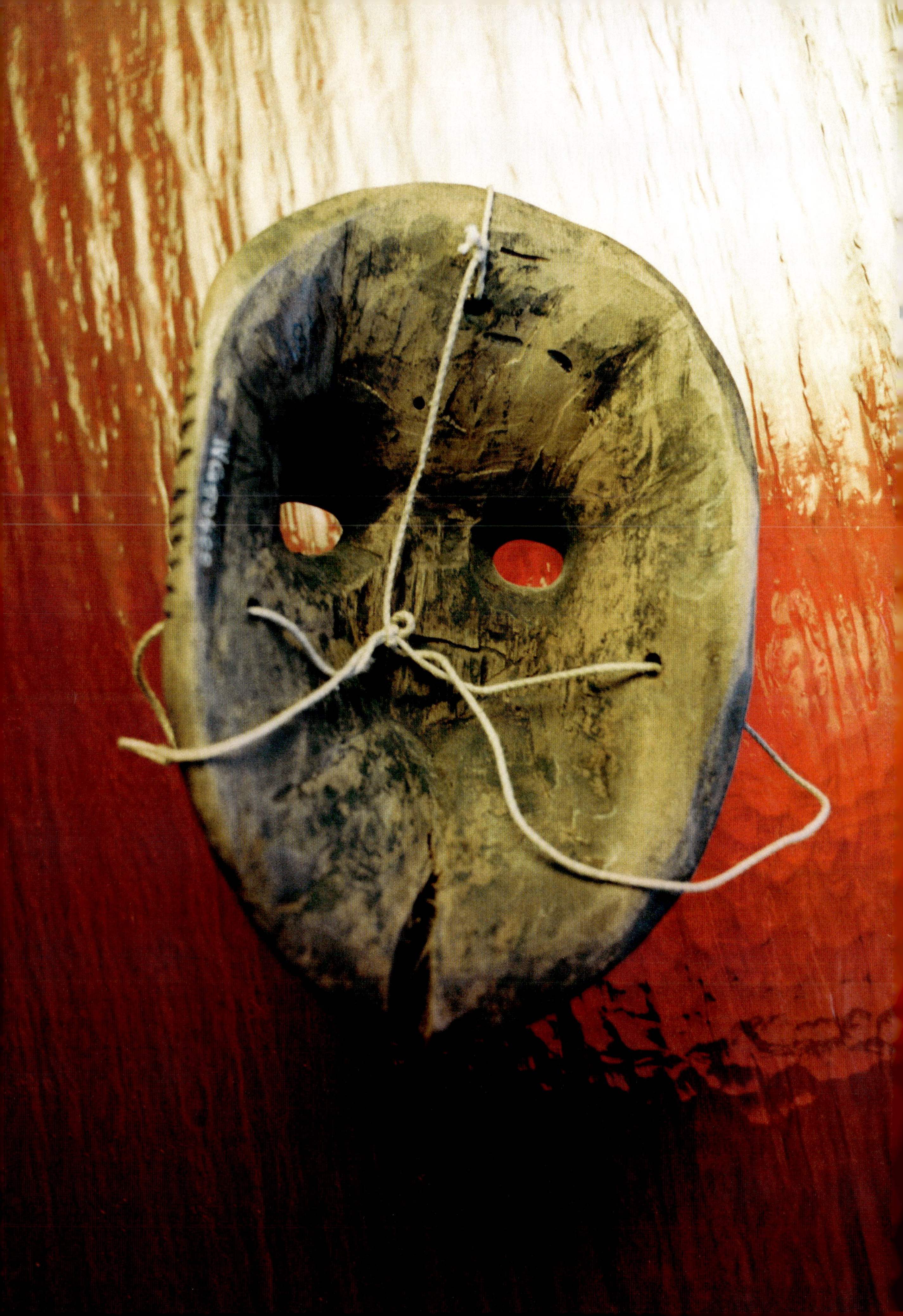

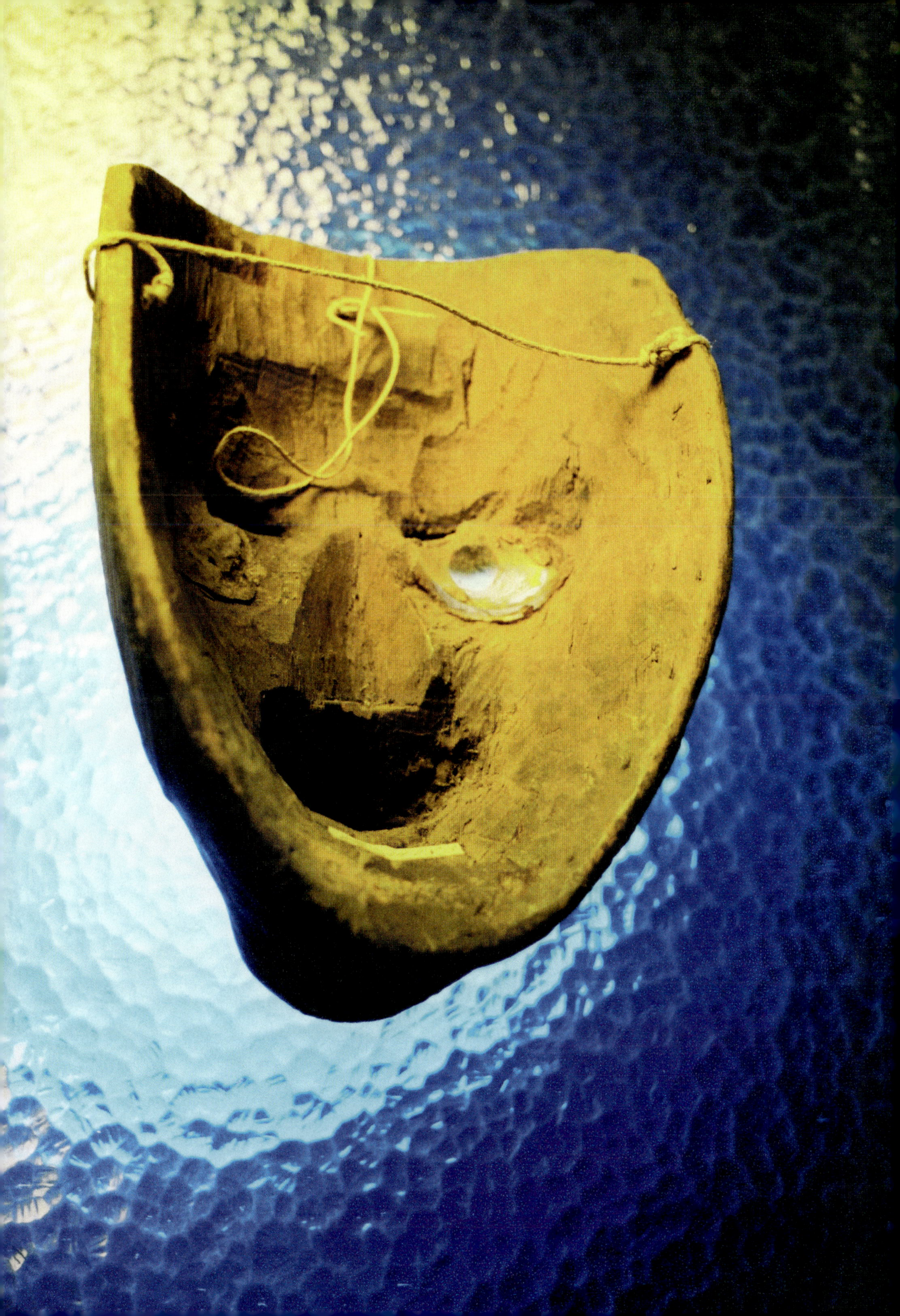

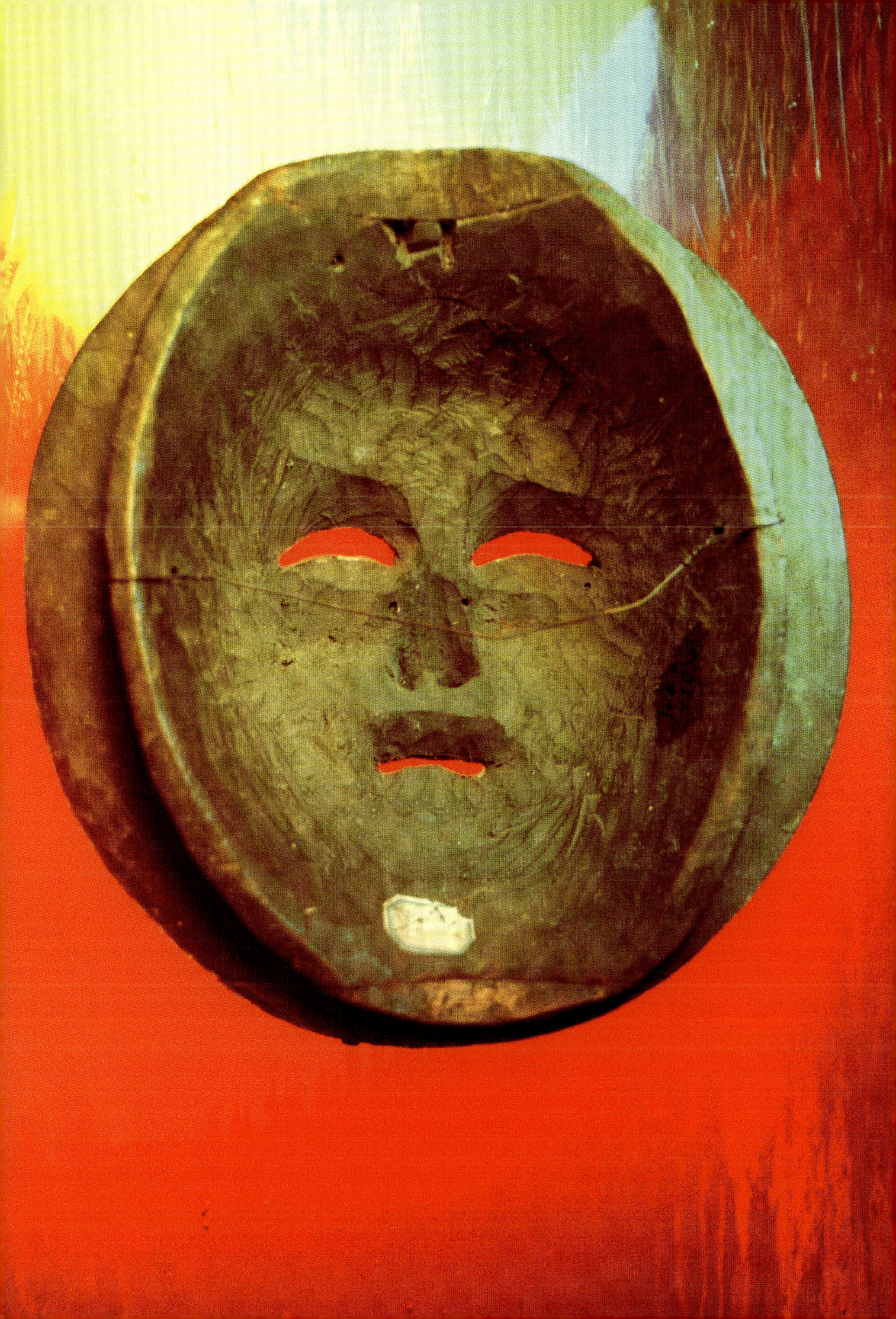

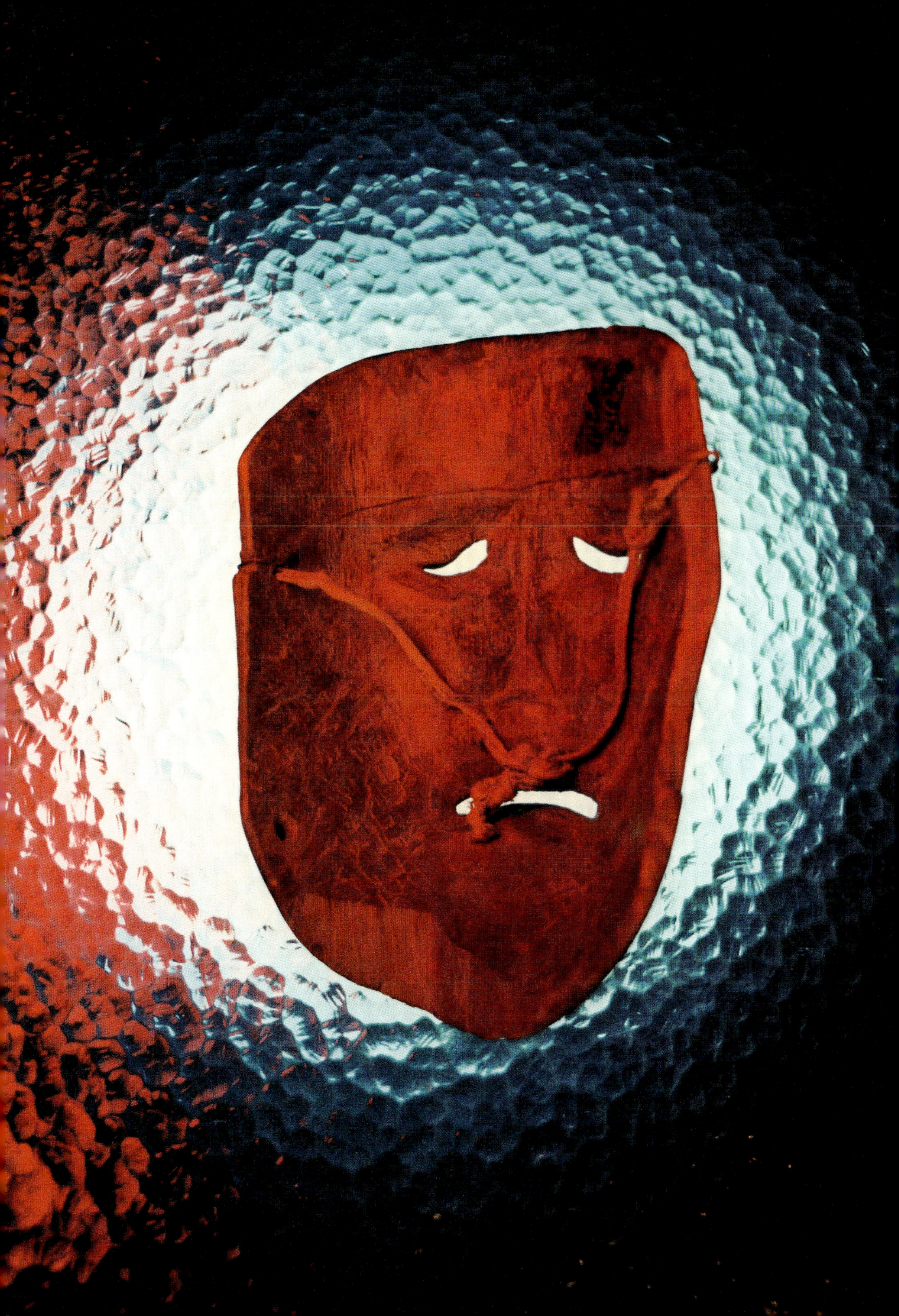

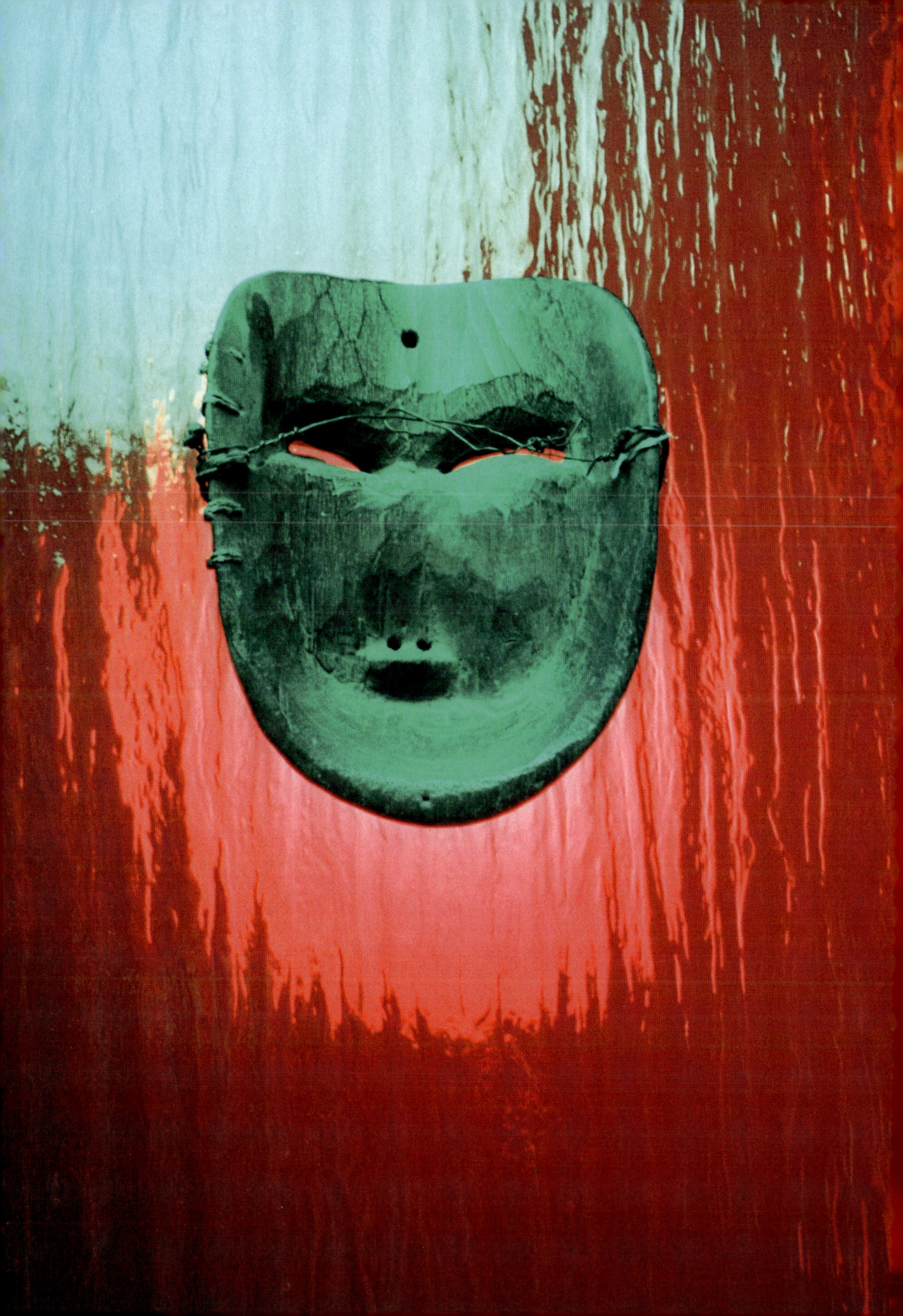

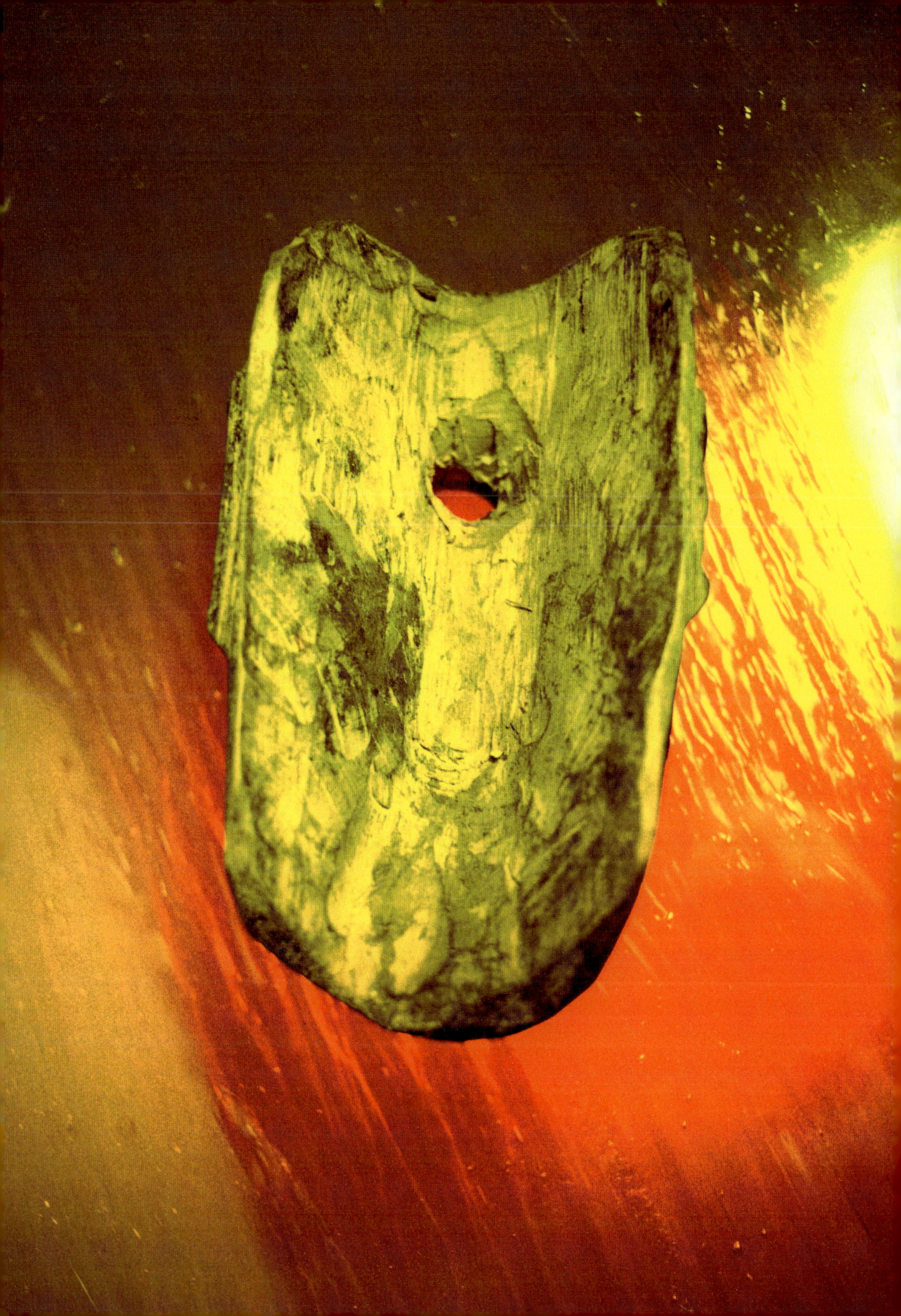

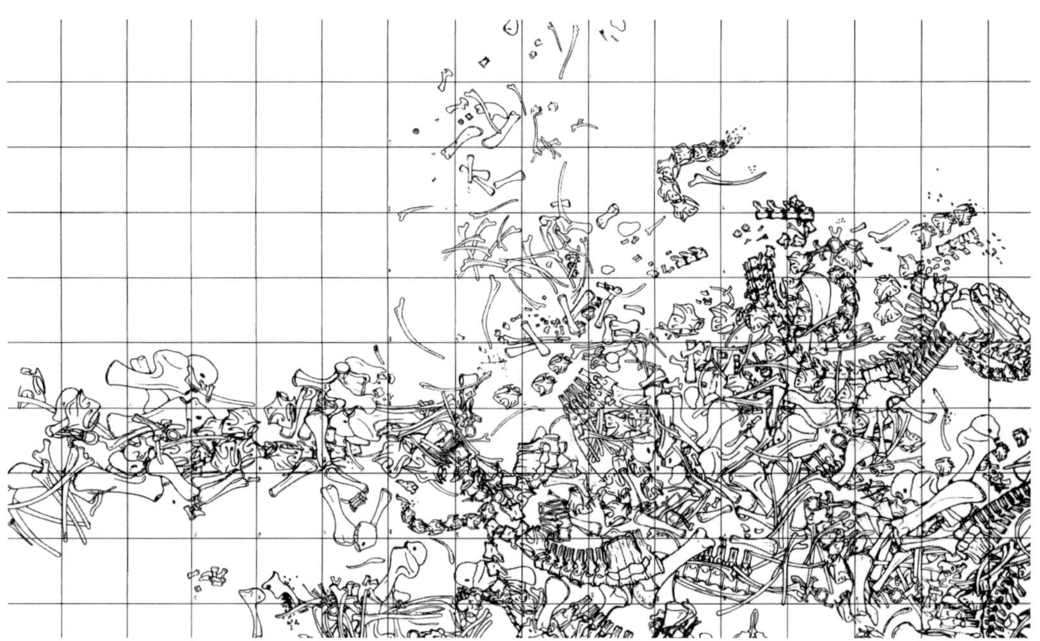

Map of dinosaur bones found in the Howe Quarry by Barnum Brown, ca. 1930

THE DINOSAUR THAT WAS STILL THERE

MOOSJE M. GOOSEN

"Dawn glows along the shore of a lagoon near the sea three millions of years ago in Montana. The landscape is of low relief; sycamores and ginkgo trees mingle with figs, palms and bananas. There are few twittering birds in the tree-tops and no herds of grazing animals to greet the early sun. A huge herbivorous dinosaur Trachodon, coming on shore for some favorite food, has been seized and partly eaten by a giant Tyrannosaurus. Whilst this monster is ravenously consuming the carcass another Tyrannosaurus draws near determined to dispute the prey. The stooping animal hesitates, partly rises and prepares to spring on its opponent. With colossal bodies poised on massive hind legs and steadied by long tails, ponderous heads armed with sharp dagger-like teeth three to five inches long, front limbs exceedingly small but set for a powerful clutch, they are the very embodiment of dynamic animal force."
Barnum Brown, "Tyrannosaurus, the Largest Flesh-Eating Animal That Ever Lived," *The American Museum Journal* (1915)

I have a dream and it involves a few dinosaurs. I want to lift their ancient bones from the stratum and put them back on their fossilized feet. I want these feet to abandon the vast plains where no language is spoken, and I want them to walk into a story. The story that awaits them is a distorted mirror built with words. A dinosaur looks at it and laughs at its reflection.

"El Dinosaurio" is possibly the shortest story in the world. It was written in 1959 by the Guatemalan writer Augusto Monterroso, and it reads as follows: "Cuando despertó, el dinosaurio todavía estaba allí" ("When he/she/it woke up, the dinosaur was still there").

This single sentence—a story's minimum—enables a world of possible fictions, each of which may produce multiple subplots of its own: (1) the dinosaur was transposed from a dream to reality; (2) dinosaurs come out at night when the world is asleep, and go into hiding at dawn when the humans are about to wake up; (3) A nonexistent dinosaur can only dream of its existence on earth, and then to its surprise wakes up into the surroundings it just dreamed about; (4) a prehistoric human being sleeps among the dinosaurs; (5) the child never goes to sleep without its dinosaur toy; (6) someone is delusional; and so forth. But how does a sentence succeed in becoming a story? Why is this sentence more than the sum of its words? It is from the continuity of the adverb *still* that the reader is asked to imagine a before and after, so that its seven words acquire a phantom structure, an imaginative front and back holding up these words' assumptions. Beginning, middle, end: once the three dimensions of the narrative order have been established, the reader—any reader—has the power to breathe life into the dinosaur.

Though Monterroso's story can grow as large as one's imagination, his actual text really only has a middle, hurrying straight, as the poet Horace would say, to where the action takes place (From *Ars Poetic, written sometime between 20 BCE and 13 BCE*: "nec gemino bellum Trojanum orditor ab ovo: semper ad eventum festinat et in medias res ("nor does [Homer] begin the Trojan war from the egg, but always he hurries to the action into the middle of things"). In other words, this dinosaur need not come from the egg in order to appear to us as alive—perhaps disturbingly so. This reminds us that dinosaurs exist only in our dreams and as fictional characters.

Who dreams of dinosaurs today? In the heyday of fossil hunting, some men did. In his memoir, fossil collector and amateur paleontologist Charles Sternberg recounts the first prehistoric objects that featured in his dreams:

> I walked up this ravine and was at once attracted by a large cone-shaped hill, separated from a knoll to the south by a lateral ravine. On either slope were many chunks of rock, which the frost had loosened from the ledges above. The space left vacant in these rocks by the decayed leaves had accumulated moisture, and this moisture, when it froze, had had enough expansive power to split the rock apart and display the impressions of the leaves. Other masses of rock had broken in such a way that the spaces once filled by the midribs and stems of the leaves admitted grass roots; and their rootles, seeking the tiny channels left by the ribs and veins of the leaves, had, with the power of growing plants, opened the doors of these prisoners, shut up in the heart of the rock for millions of years.
>
> Sternberg remembers the dream so clearly because, as he claims, he went to the place and found everything there just as it had been in his dream. At night Sternberg had excavated hidden treasures from his subconscious, which pointed to their doubles out there in the real world—though this occurred only once. Through his dream the past became accessible, within reach, yet always as a matter of the past: in petrified, fossilized, skeletal form. But Sternberg also recalls the nightmares of Edward Drinker Cope of the Academy of Natural Sciences in Philadelphia, whose excavated fossil bones came to life at night to take revenge on him as a dreamer, "tossing him into the air, kicking him, trampling upon him." (Sternberg 1909, 19,75)

◗

I have a dream and it involves a few dinosaurs. I see them while I lay asleep. One of the dinosaurs notices my presence: we look each other in the eye, traversing time. "History," I stumble, is when time is absorbed into a story and becomes invisible —a bit like in this dream. "Gururrru gurruru," the dinosaur responds. I look this up in a special dictionary and it turns out to mean "no meaning."

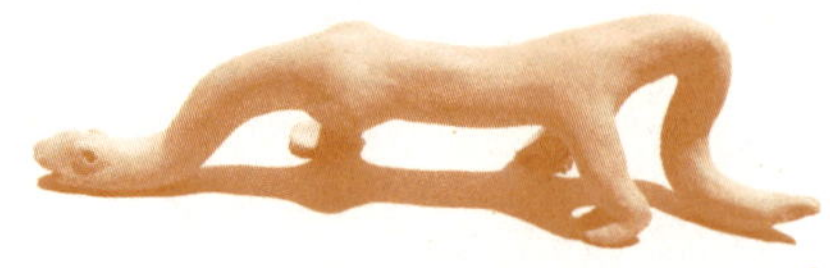

To make a story, one needs: time outside of the story, time inside the story, and good timing; a sentence (to begin with); and a rumor, a proposition, a problem, a mystery, a thief, a puzzle, a question, a sudden disappearance, an egg, a Trojan war, a dream with many symbols, a blind man, a labyrinth, or a grave from which the dead can rise. A story needs so much more, but at minimum it needs something that can be resolved with words, or brought into existence by a stream of language rolling from the tongue or onto the page.

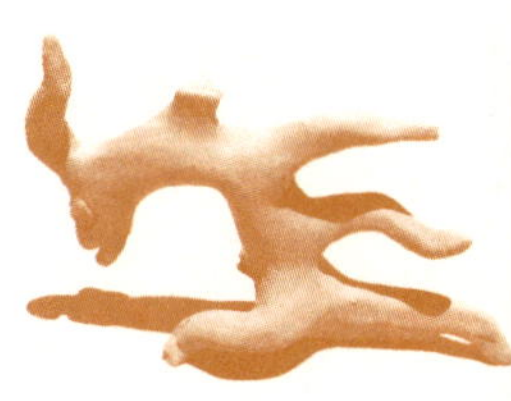

History is linear and irreversible. Dreams are timeless. Stories always keep time in order, even when they evoke a future, contain flashbacks, or are written backwards from the present into the past. But try any of that with a prehistoric creature from a world without clocks and you will produce a monster: Edward Cope's preliminary images of an elasmosaurus depicted its head and tail on the wrong end of its body, telling the most incoherent of dinosaur tales. (This should have been a story with a long-necked beginning and a short-tailed end).

IN THE BEGINNING WERE THE DINOSAURS

Waldemar Julsrud was a German hardware merchant and amateur archaeologist who lived in Mexico. In 1944 or 1945, when he was in his sixties, he discovered some ceramic figurines at the foot of a hill near Acámbaro, a town located in the southeastern corner of Guanajuato. Julsrud, excited about his findings, hired the local farmer Odilón Tinajero to do further excavations at the site, offering him a peso for each piece he would dig up and bring to him intact. With the help of the farmer and over the course of a decade, Waldemar Julsrud amassed more than 30,000 clay figurines, the majority of which had been fabricated simply as a result of Julsrud's dream to own an archeological collection of major historical significance. No one knows who produced these fake archeological finds, but before they were dug up from the soil and handed over to Waldemar Julsrud, they had first been retrieved from the imagination of their maker(s), and molded by unknown amateur hands.

Julsrud's collection most prominently features dinosaur creatures: two feet tall, three feet tall, four feet tall, three-clawed, two-toed, mostly friendly in appearance, sometimes in the company of human beings. These clay creatures, much beloved by their owner, gradually took over the merchant's twelve-room mansion—at first lining the floor, then occupying the furniture, until Julsrud had to sleep in the bathtub. Among his dinosaur friends, he could count: the trachodon, the gorgosaurus, the horned monoclonius, the ornitholestes, the titanosaurus, the triceratops, the stegosaurus palaeoscincus, the diplodocus, the podokesaurus, the struthiomimus, the plesiosaur, the iguanodon, the pteranodon, the dimetrodon, the brachiosaurus, the tyrannosaurus rex, and other unknown or as yet unidentified dinosaur species.

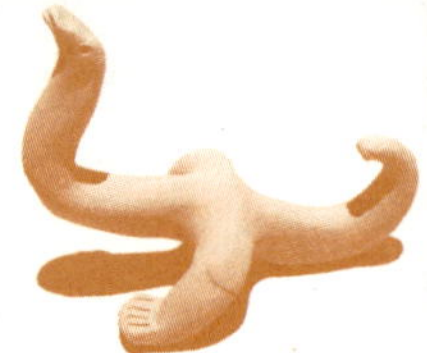

Sometimes the circumstances are such that the story begins to tell itself, and all that the characters need to do is to carry out their role. The Acámbaro collection traces the evolution of a desire: Waldemar Julsrud, an idiosyncratic, aging man with money and time on his hands; Odilón Tinajero, a farmer in need of extra cash; thousands of clay dinosaurs appearing at the point of mutual interest, steering the story out of control and into fantasy mode.

When Waldemar first discovered a clay dinosaur among Tinajero's finds, what would have astonished him most: That the dinosaur was still there, or that the human being was already there? For this narrative to make sense, Waldemar turned the obvious anachronism of the prehistoric animal into a plot, and hypothesized that people and dinosaurs had once coexisted in this area of Mexico.

◗

> "Every work of art can be regarded both as a historical event and as a hard-won solution to some problem. It is irrelevant now whether the event was original or conventional, accidental or willed, awkward or skillful. The important clue is that any solution points to the existence of some problem to which there have been other solutions, and that other solutions to this same problem will most likely be invented to follow the one now in view. As the solutions accumulate, the problem alters. The chain of solutions nevertheless discloses the problem." (George Kubler, *The Shape of Time: Remarks on the History of Things*)

The Acámbaro collection is layered with stories. It is the tale of thousands of dinosaurs, but also of desire and demand, of cause and effect. I think of a single movement that progresses into a dance; an accident that sets a chain of events in motion. One dinosaur giving birth to another to another to another to another and so forth.

The evolution of story, form, species.

In the summer of 2011, I stayed in Mexico for a project about storytelling, organized by the Uqbar Foundation. I planned to make a visit to Julsrud's collection in Acámbaro, and to see what happened from there—perhaps as a calculated accident that would lead up to a narrative that would tell itself. After all, I have little to add to this story. As a writer, I expected to write during my stay in Mexico, but Julsrud's dinosaurs took over and sabotaged my plans.

MID - AUGUST 2011 / IN MEDIAS RES

It's 11 a.m. and I am trying to figure out how to turn five kilos of brown-bagged crumbs of dry Oaxaca soil into a clay that I can bend, mold, and shape into a dinosaur creature. I am an amateur. I am a writer, my hands produce words, not form. There is always form, of course, if only because my thoughts take shape in my brain, but I have never played with thoughts so literally. I have seen many of the clay figures in small, low-resolution pictures online, and I have collected these images in a computer folder, which I have been using as my source of reference. My eyes turn from the "model" on the computer screen to the ball of yellow-brown clay in front of me. Translation: from image to form, from writing to making. Amateurism: something we all master in some fields and to some degree. This is what I think about as I scrutinize the pixelated images on the screen, trying to interpret a dinosaur's angles and curves, its depth, its approximate size.

I will visit the Museo Julsrud in Acámbaro later this month, but having looked at this collection of clay dinosaur images on my computer over and over again, I have come to realize: What better way to actually see these forgeries than to forge them myself, here at my kitchen table, copying these dinosaurs with my own amateur hands?

I have no feeling for material, and I don't know anything about clay. At the store I asked for *barro* and they gave me a bag of dry mud. "Just add water." Now, a bucket with the mud is on my table: a mess of unarticulated ideas. Once I have turned it into a workable substance, the first dinosaur begins to manifest itself. I created a creature, I think—possibly a hybrid of a herrerasaurus and a tuojiangosaurus. The forms that follow mostly underline the repeated failures of my attempts to achieve something spontaneously successful, once again. My dinosaurs look harmless, seemingly laughing at the joke I produced with my own hands.

◗

Most of the information about the Acámbaro collection is found on amateurishly designed and outdated websites and in the occasional book that, along with the collection of figurines, often also promotes the Bible, God, and creationism.

Fossil hunters and early paleontologists who tried to be good Christians at the same time argued that God had created dinosaurs *as an extinct species,* just like he had created everything else prehistoric in a fossilized or petrified state, to provide humans with the fantasy of a time from which they had once been missing. "Before the first day, God made the world that came before the world."

◗

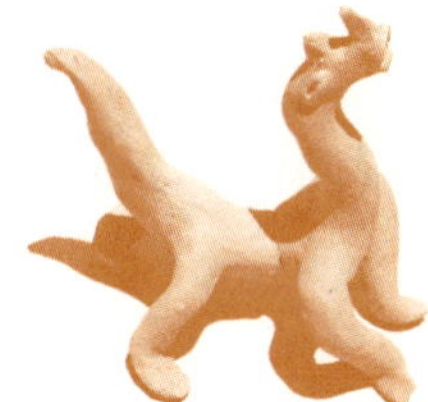

This practical (tactical) clay joke is an experiment in amateurism as much as it is an exercise for my writing—the latter of which always succeeds in territorializing my thoughts, molding them, as it were, into the autopilot direction of language, structure, and plot. That doesn't mean I am ever prepared for the writing that is about to come. Sometimes it's as if I can feel this molding take place inside my brain—to no avail. Too much traffic in my head clutters the flow of words. Indeed, words cannot express the frustration of the writer who can't find the proper words to express him- or herself. That of course is a tautology, or a roundabout: a great way of simply not getting there, unless you wish to swallow your own tail.

◗

After a month, I have made some thirty dinosaurs. I have never made something else in my life that looked happy. Most people laugh at my clay dinosaurs when they see them, too.

With the dinosaurs occupying my days, I try to summon them in my dreams as well, but each morning I wake up in sheer disappointment.

"When she fell asleep, the dinosaur was never there."

To this day, I have not managed to see a dinosaur in my dreams. Could it be that my subconscious is so irrefutably apathetic to my prehistoric fantasies simply because it has no idea about this reptilian gibberish of the conscious mind? In Italo Calvino's *Cosmicomics,* a "New One"—a species inhabiting the earth after the extinction of the dinosaurs—has a strange dream about a dinosaur, a species that, to the knowledge of the New Ones, has only survived in stories. The New One shares her dream with the "Ugly One," a stranger who has recently arrived at their camp. The Ugly One suspects that she is trying to tell him something with her dream. Perhaps it is in her dreams, and only in her dreams, that she recognizes the Ugly One for what he really is: the last remaining dinosaur on earth.

We cannot suppress the memory of the dinosaur, because we have no memory of the dinosaur—only figments of imagination, fueled by historical clues. Any encounter with a prehistoric being provides us with an ahistorical plot and is thus immediately subjected to the laws of fiction.

Therefore it doesn't matter whether I'm a sculptor or an amateur, or whether dinosaurs and humans did or did not once coexist in Mexico.

A SHORT AFTERWORD

We drive for about four hours, on nearly empty highways. I doze off, glad to be out of the city for the day. When we arrive in Acámbaro we ask for the museum. In the museum we ask for the dinosaurs—but the dinosaurs are everywhere around us. I look at each one of them, and each one them responds in utter silence. Or maybe not: "Gurrurrru gurruru."

BIBLIOGRAPHY

Charles H. Sternberg, The Life of a Fossil Hunter (New York: Henry Hold and Company, 1909), 19, 75

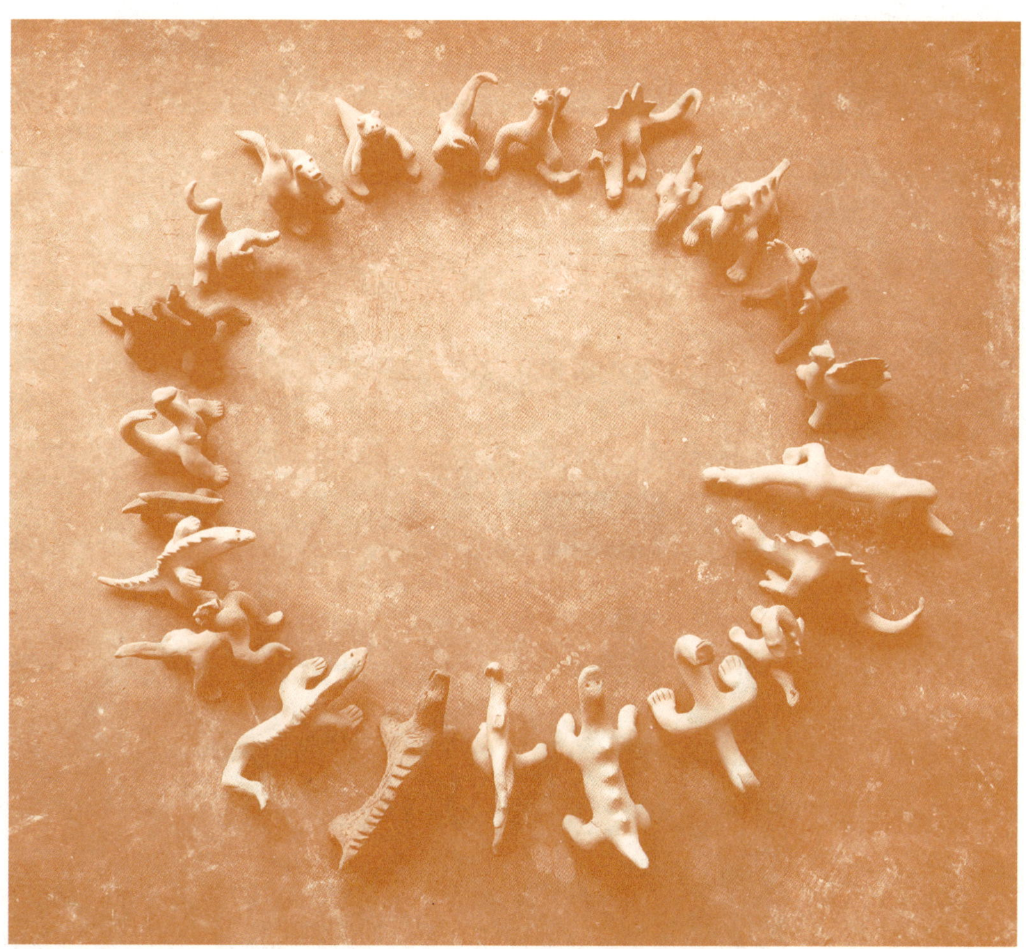

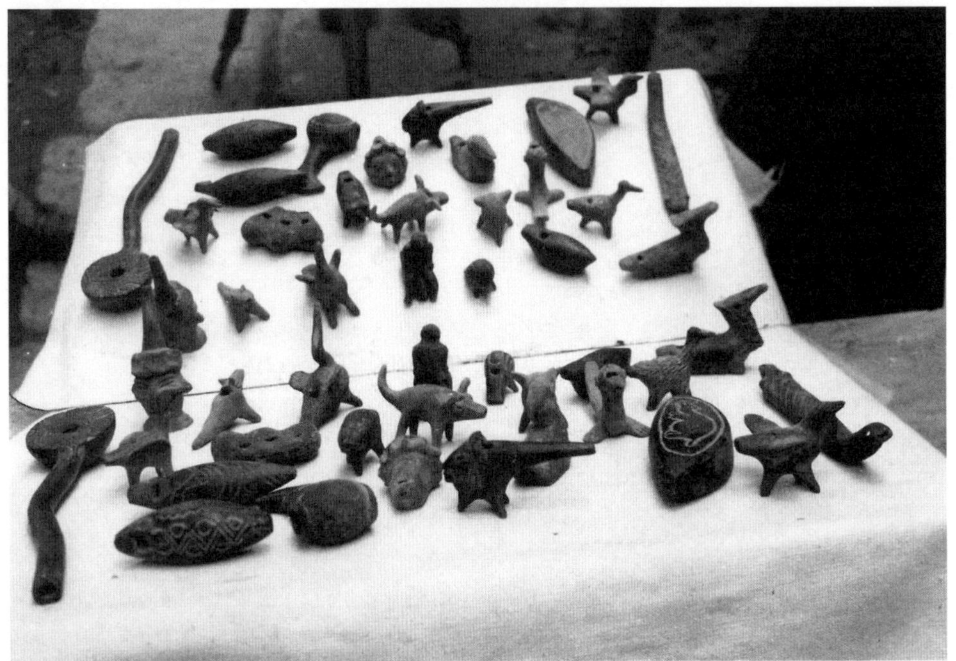

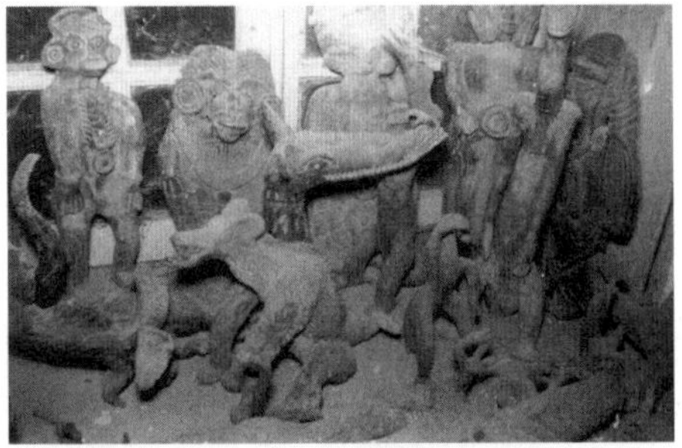

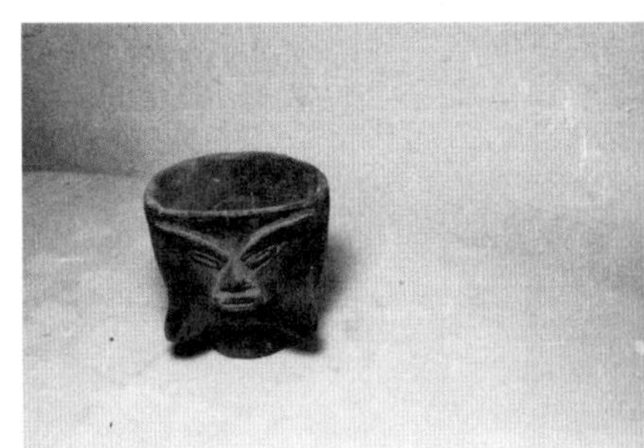

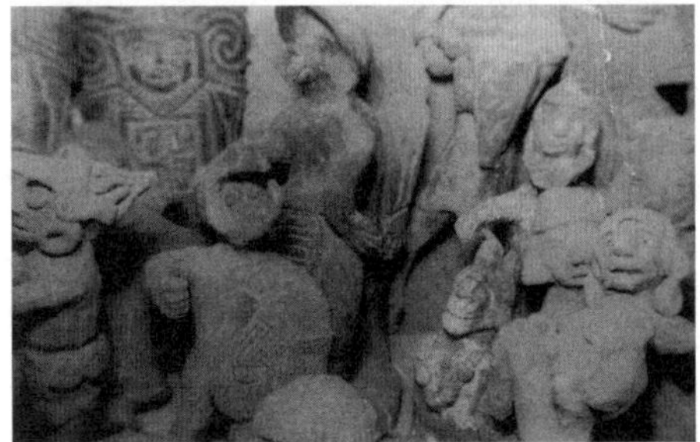

Pictures of the Acámbaro figures in 1953
© Abraham Veneciana Gutiérrez

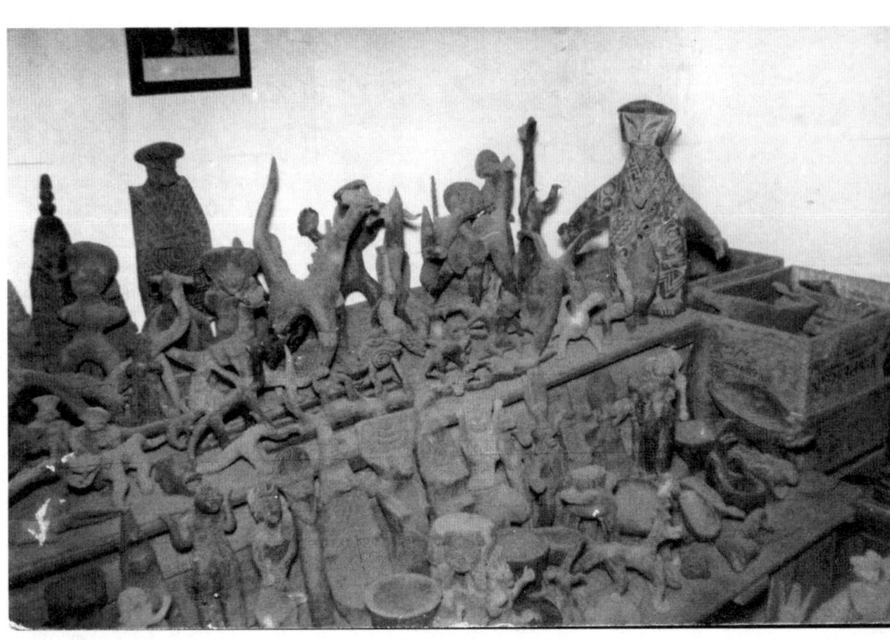

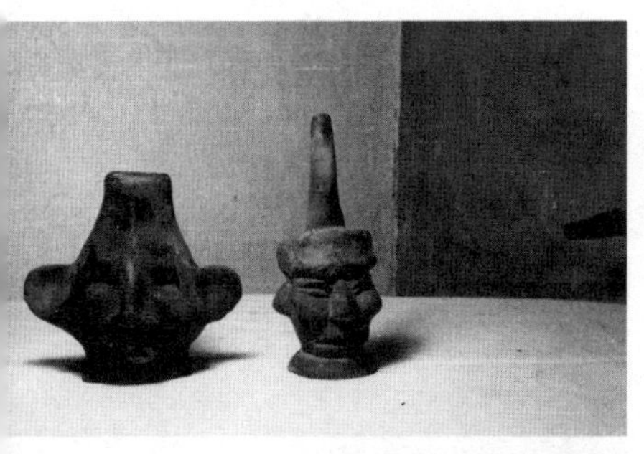
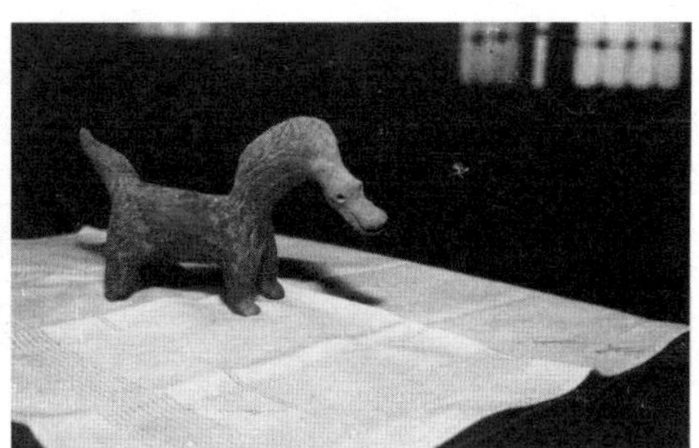
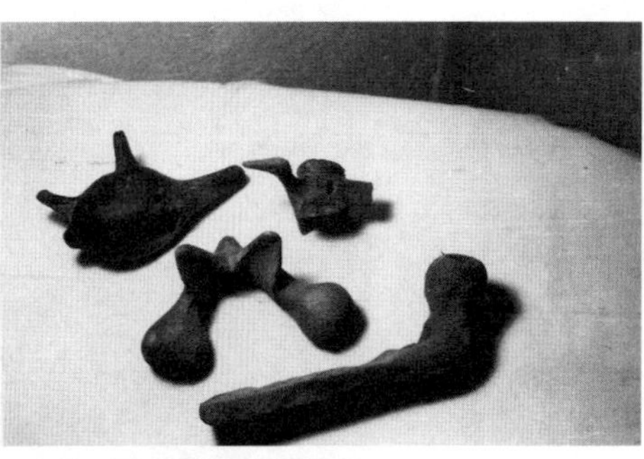
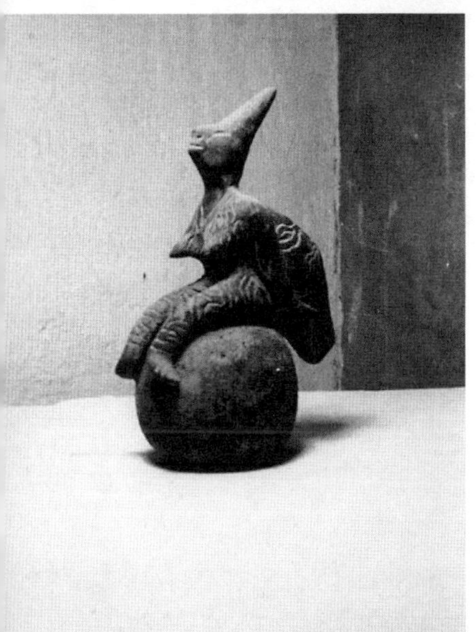
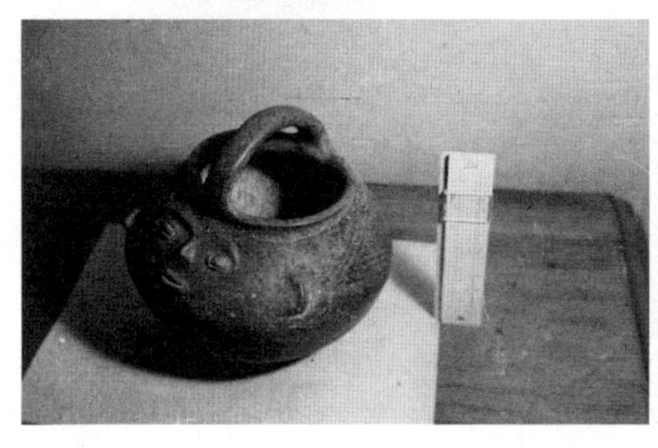
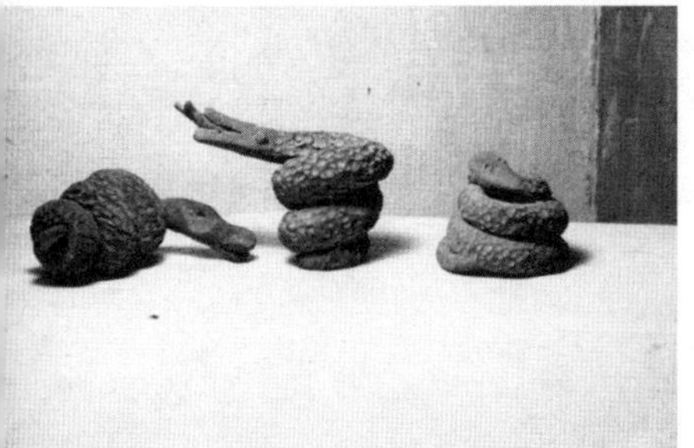
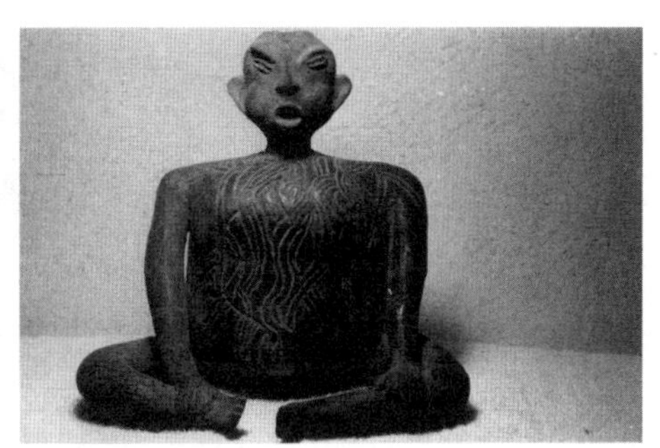
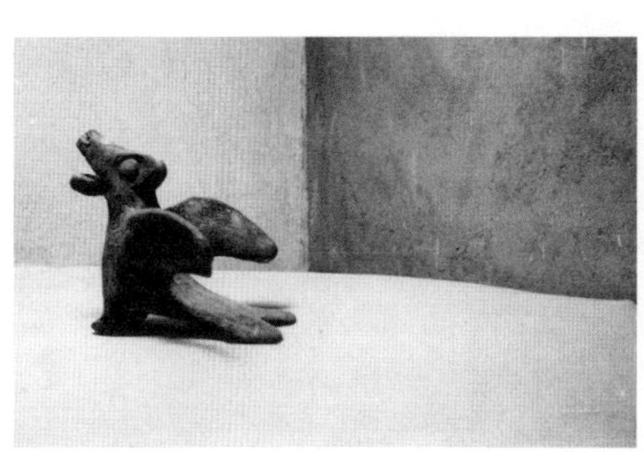
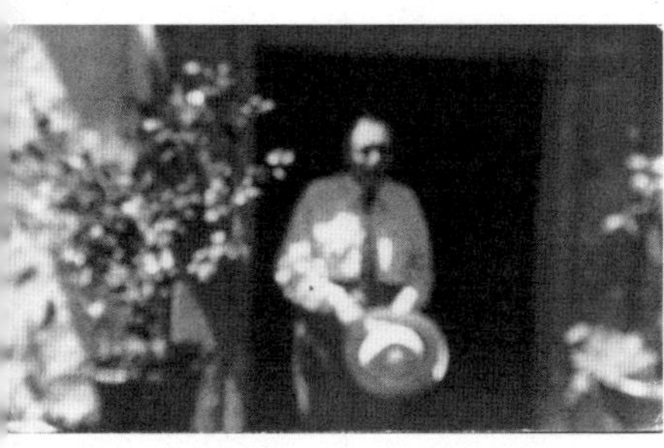

diversas especies de dinosaurios por la
altar el dinamismo y plasticidad que los
s de la colección. El domino de los
ra fue de decenas de millones de años y
mas allá de 300 mil años de antiguedad,
Neanderthal, el cual fue una raza de

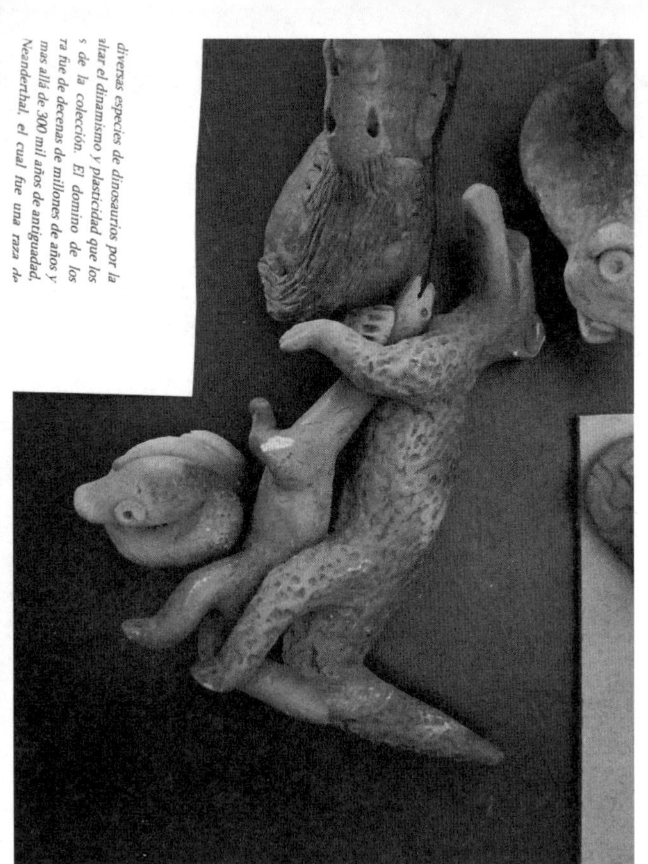

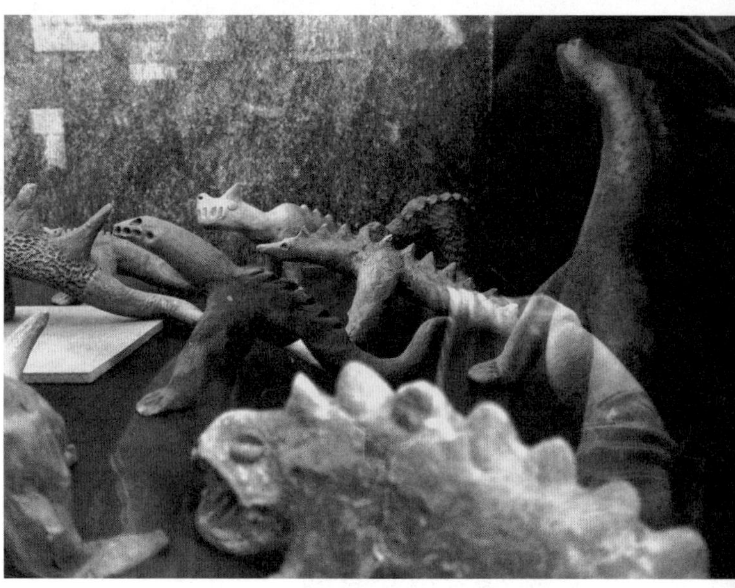

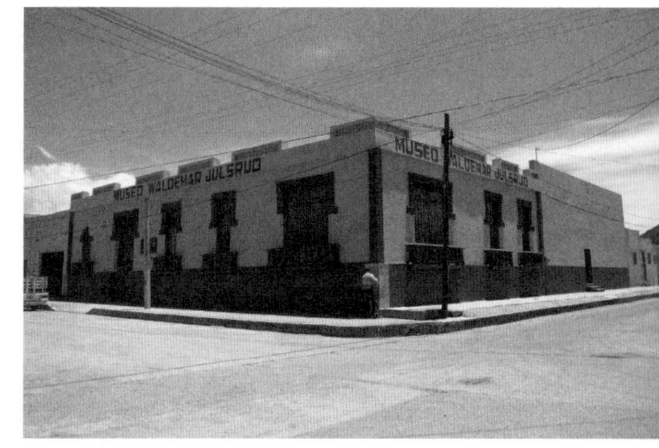

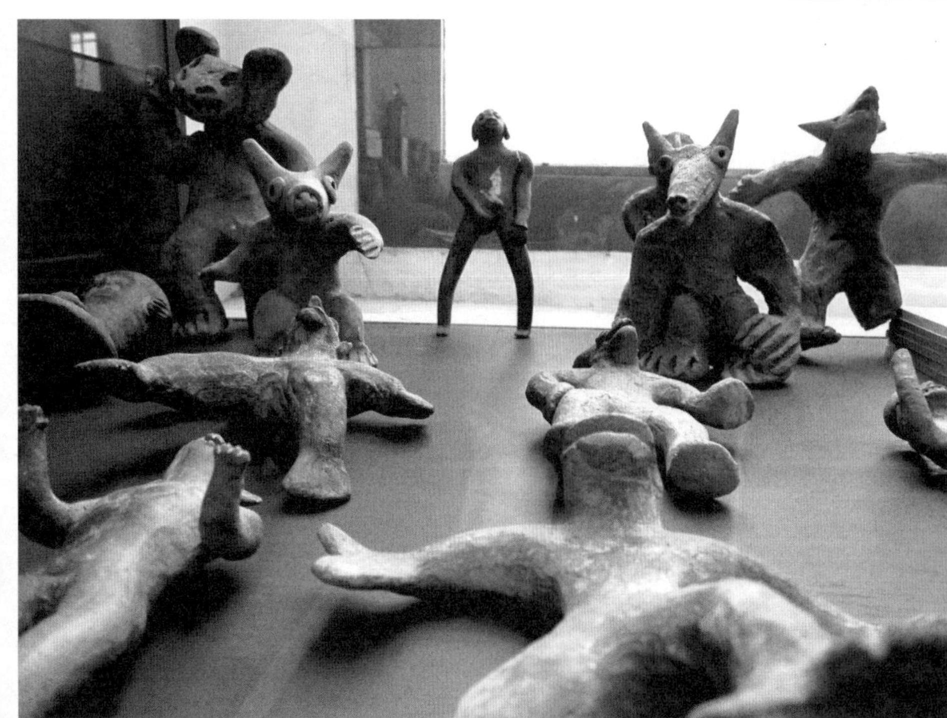

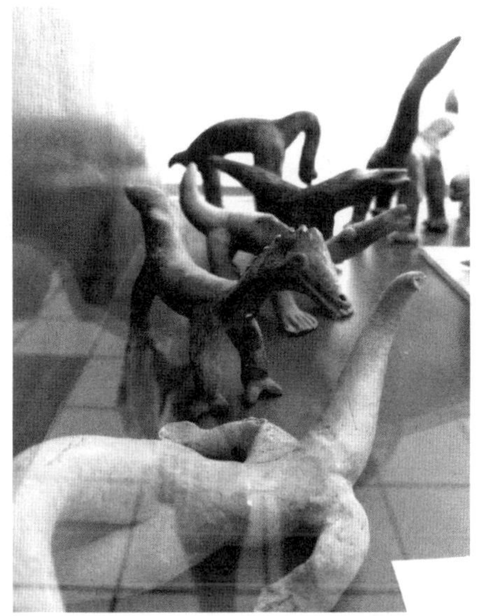

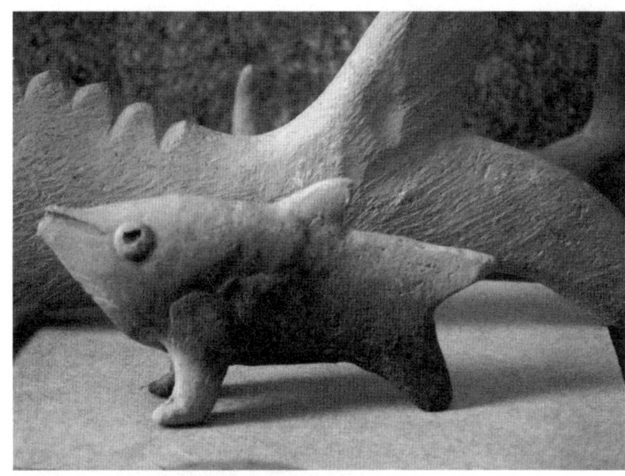

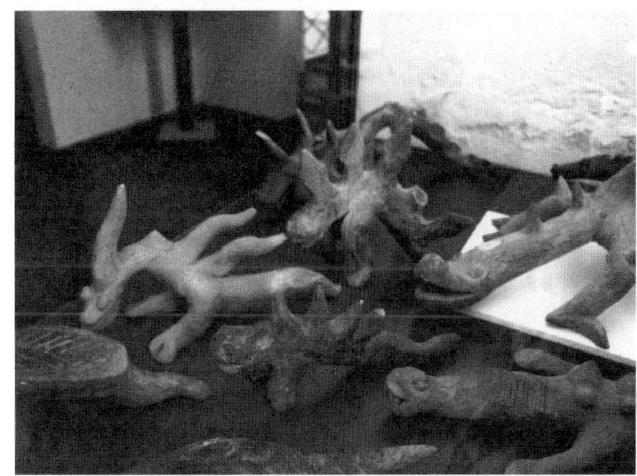

Acámbaro
Museum
Moosje M. Goosen
2011

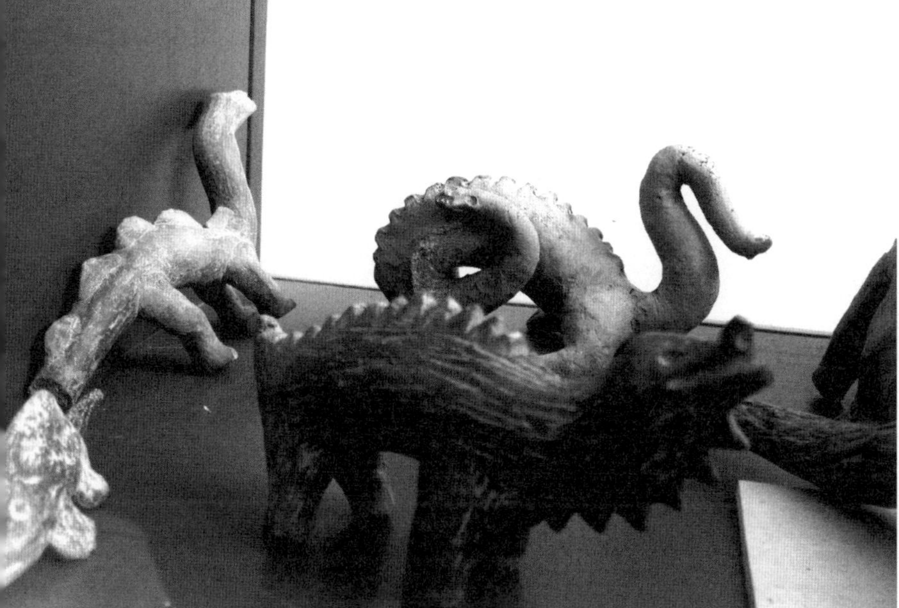

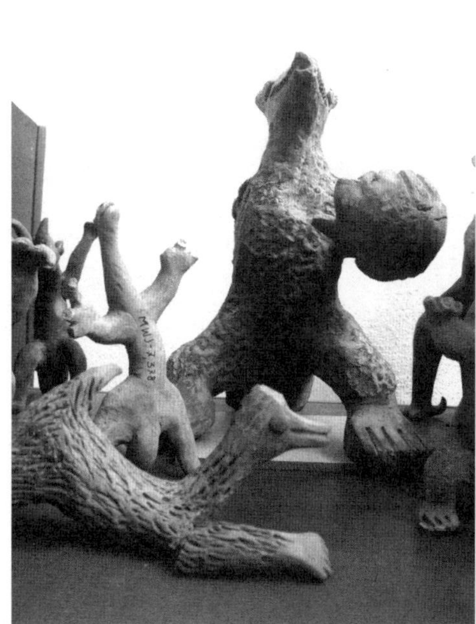

REAL OR FAKE ? GERMAN POST-WAR NATIONALISM AND THE FORGED MAYA STUCCO HEAD IN THE ETHNOLOGISCHES MUSEUM

MARIA GAIDA
ETHNOLOGISCHES MUSEUM, BERLIN

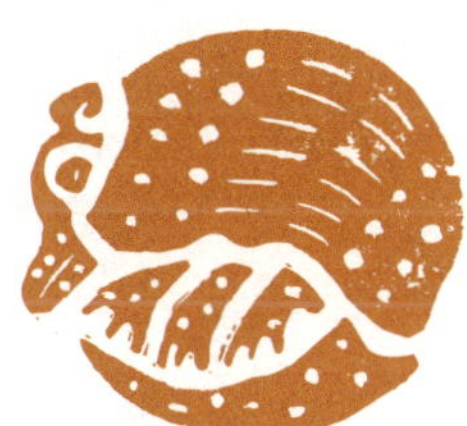

ne can say, with a fair degree of certainty, that counterfeit versions of special objects from the pre-Hispanic cultures in Mexico existed even before the Spanish conquest in 1521 as well as during the colonial period. But there can be no doubt that after independence, when the Spanish viceroyalty opened its borders, it also opened a very broad field of possibilities for local forgers.

It was not just the published works of European travelers such as Alexander von Humboldt, John Lloyd Stephens, and Frederick Catherwood that fanned Europe's interest in the hitherto unknown pre-Hispanic cultures, but also the ideas of the Enlightenment and notions of the "noble savage" and "primitive" cultures (Kelker and Bruhns 2010, 15). Moreover, it was in the nineteenth century that many European museums laid the groundwork for their collections. Suppliers generally consisted of travelers, missionaries, merchants, the crews of merchant ships, adventurers, and diplomats. It was, or so it appears, in this initial phase that many counterfeit objects entered the museums, as the sudden increase in demand proved greater than the available "supply" (the actual pool of pre-Hispanic antiquities).

This network of copyists, forgers, collectors, enthusiasts, dealers, and curators, which grew in complexity over time, eventually became a very controversial subject among experts (Holmes 1886; Batres 1909; Blom 1935; Ekholm 1964; Kelker and Bruhns 2010). One can assume that many of today's archaeological collections also include pieces that were offered to curators under the pretense that they were "authentic," were not recognized as forgeries, and were thus acquired as alleged originals. A forgery is an object that is passed as an original with the intent of deceiving the buyer.

Being forced to admit that a museum-preserved piece has turned out to be a fake is a painful realization for any collection curator, as one can read in Kelker and Bruhns's important and instructive publication *Faking Ancient Mesoamerica* (2010). Among the more interesting cases to occur at the Ethnologisches Museum Berlin was that of a forged Maya stucco head (IV Ca 44330).

In tracing the object's biography and correspondence surrounding the acquisition of this non-genuine stucco head, as well as the events leading up to its "unmasking," the following analysis attempts to shed light on the circumstances that contributed the

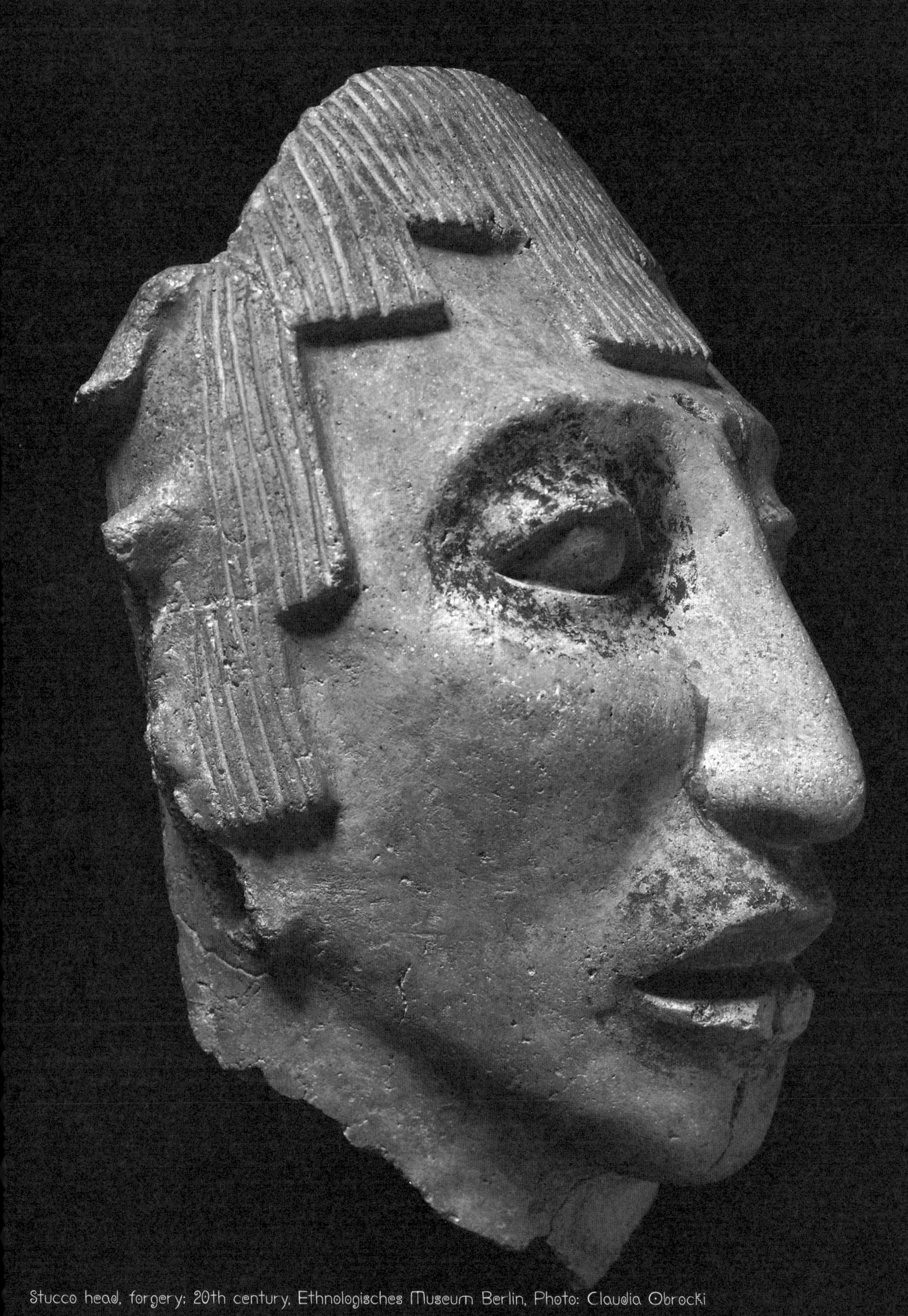

Stucco head, forgery; 20th century, Ethnologisches Museum Berlin, Photo: Claudia Obrocki

"misunderstanding." Is it possible to reconstruct the factors responsible for the museum's failure in terms of expertise, or self-understanding when it comes to expert knowledge?

The Classic Maya civilization flourished from 250–900 CE in the present-day Mexican states of Chiapas and Tabasco, the Yucatan Peninsula, Guatemala, Belize, and parts of Honduras and El Salvador. In Mexico during the last quarter of the nineteenth century, collector Florentino Jimeno amassed a large collection of classic archaeological objects from the Maya culture—predominantly clay figures—which were subsequently acquired by the then Königliches Museum für Völkerkunde (Royal Museum of Ethnology) in Berlin. This collection formed the basis of the Maya Collection in Berlin, which eventually came to include cut and polychrome painted pottery, greenstone objects, stelae fragments, stucco heads, and much more.

In 1960, the museum (then known as the Museum für Völkerkunde) was invited to purchase an impressive but fake stucco head from the "Classic Maya" period, and at a price considered steep by any standards. This story begins, logically, with the forger and his ability to create the illusion of authenticity in the sculpture. The forger is anonymous, and his commissioner remains obscure. In a letter dated December 5, 1960, the art dealer specified the sculpture's provenance as: "Found in the State of Chiapas as an offering in a tomb built into an oyster mound in the Sierra de Palenque."(SMB-PK, EM, 1 B/60/15, 05.12.1960). What we cannot know is whether the dealer himself had been fooled by the suggestive power of the so-called original or whether he knew that the piece was a forgery.

With a purchase of this magnitude, it was (and continues to be) a matter of course to consult with experts in advance, and to have certified specialists testify to the object's authenticity and provenance. The process began with a commissioned report from Konstandt Laboratories in New York, which "confirmed" the authenticity of the piece. Their report stated that "The top surface layer is part of the original sculpture. The variation in efflorescence indicates that the sculpture was exposed for a considerable time to the elements. This variation is indicative of an 'oxide' or weathered layer being present. The colors found are identical to those found on authenticated pieces. The colors are not of recent origin and do not, in our opinion, approximate present day paints. We are of the opinion that the sample is genuine and authentic."(SMB-PK, EM, 1 B/60/15, 31.08.1960). Though we cannot be sure whether it was the dealer himself who suggested this laboratory for the examination, this was presumably the case. So much for scientific assessments.

Likewise, a number of specialists responsible for the stylistic authentication came to similarly positive, if not downright effusive conclusions as to its authenticity. In a letter from Hans-Dietrich Disselhoff, at that time the American Studies scholar at the Berlin Völkerkundemuseum, Disselhoff opines that the Classic period portrait head of a Maya king is a

> "very lovely and valuable piece . . . One can, without exaggerating, speak of a masterpiece of world art that would be a particular highlight and a unique asset to the Berlin museum. As a museum director, I consider myself almost obliged to pursue the purchase . . . I would also add that the world-famous Ancient American collection at the Berlin museum lost its most precious pieces

> in the last days of the war, namely the exhibits stored in the Friedrichshain flak tower . . . purely irreplaceable pieces . . . The object has thus far been evaluated by Dr. Kutscher . . . and by the relevant expert Mr. von Kleist."

Disselhoff's predecessor, Walter Krickeberg, was also asked for an assessment, but was unfortunately bedridden at the time. "Nevertheless, I am sure," Disselhoff continues, "that Prof. Krickeberg would also enthusiastically support the decision to purchase this unique piece. A material authenticity report from Konstandt Laboratories in New York is available as well." The request to the Director General to apply for purchase funds from the Berlin Lottery is followed by another series of sentences expressing his profound admiration: "As it involves . . . a precious piece of world art, the ownership of which would certainly be in the Berlin Völkerkundemuseum's best interests. The attached photographs do not come close to showing the real beauty of the piece, which I, as an American Studies scholar, would not hesitate to say is equal to that of Nefertiti." (SMB-PK, EM, 1 B/60/15, 05.10.1960).

Today, the collection at the Ethnologisches Museum is considered the most important public collection of classical Maya pottery in Europe. This was not always the case. The institution suffered serious losses during the Second World War. The best known objects lost to date include two items from the Mesoamerican cultures: the so-called "Humboldt Disc" and "Humboldt Axe." Since then a number of other, outstanding pieces of classical Maya culture, among them the well preserved "Lintel 56" from Yaxchilán and the famous Chama vessel, have gone missing. It was not until the 1960s that the institution attempted to rebuild the war-decimated Maya collection by purchasing a number of important objects. One larger -than-life-sized "Maya" head (at a height of thirty centimeters), made of stucco with remnants of red and blue paint, was one of the first post-war acquisitions from the art market. (Ident. Nr. IV Ca 44330; SMB-PK, EM) Using funds from the lottery, the head was purchased in 1960 for twenty-three thousand US dollars (equivalent to ninety-two thousand German marks). Remember that at that time—more than fifty years ago—ninety-two thousand marks was a very hefty sum.

What is remarkable about the quotation above, penned by Disselhoff in a letter to General Director Kurt Reidemeister, is that the museum director, an American Studies scholar, assessed the "Maya" head to be as valuable as the bust of Nefertiti in the Egyptian Museum—perhaps the most famous single work of art in the Staatliche Museen zu Berlin. How should we interpret this statement? Aside from the eagerness to acquire the old, traditional object for what his letter describes as "the world-famous Ancient American collection,"(SMB-PK, EM, 1 B/60/15, 05.10.1960) and the pressing desire for added value considering the lamented war losses mentioned in the letter, this request should also be considered in connection with a spectacular archaeological discovery in the 1950s.

In 1949, four years after the end of the Second World War, archaeologist Alberto Ruz Lhuillier was excavating the ruins of Palenque in Chiapas, Mexico—one of the largest and most important city-states of the Classic Maya period—when, in the "Temple of the Inscriptions," he discovered a downwards-leading tunnel in the floor of the rear room of the building. In 1952, he reached a hidden grave chamber at the base of the pyramid and subsequently opened it. To this day, one can readily say that Lhuillier stumbled upon one

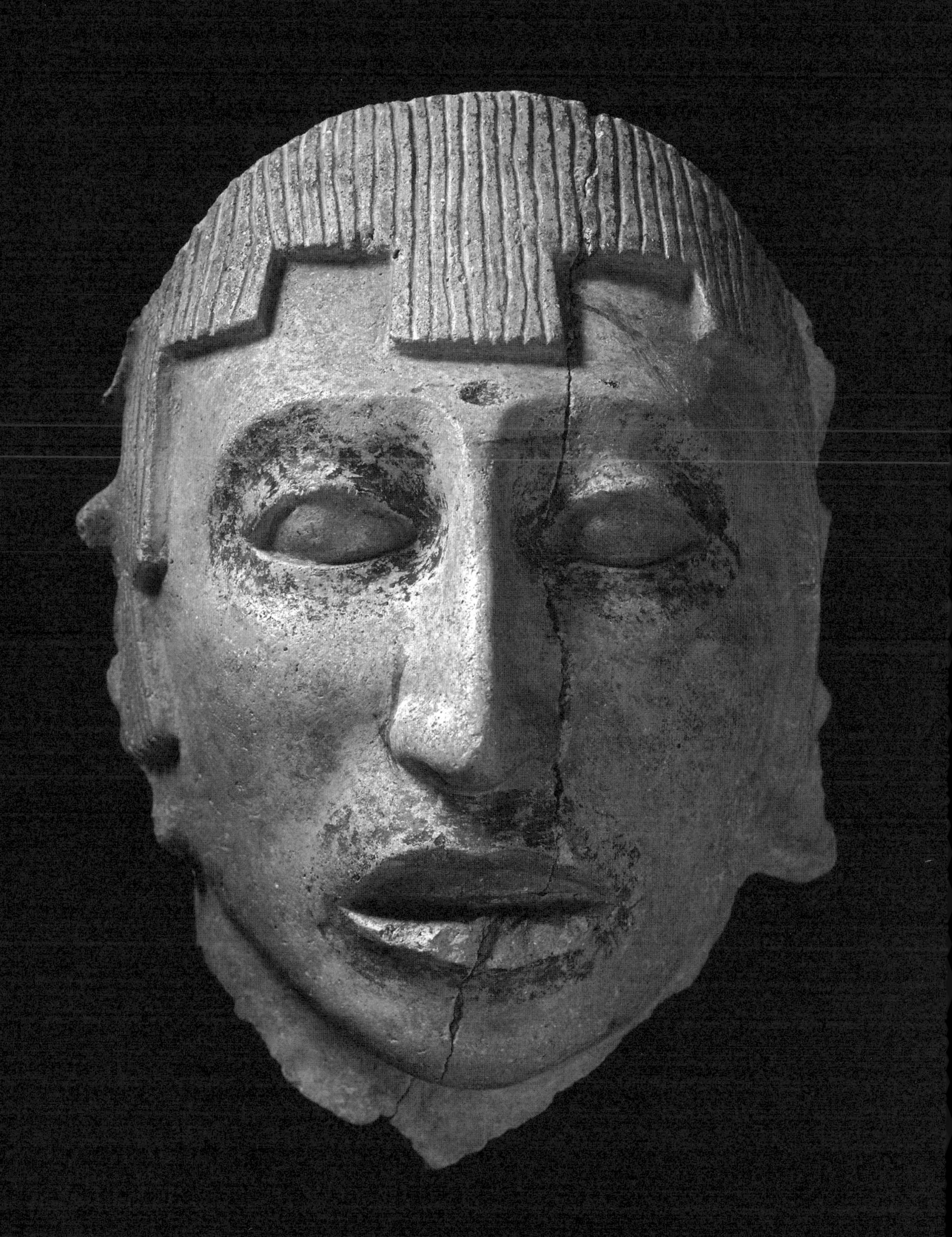

Stucco head, forgery: 20th century, Ethnologisches Museum Berlin, Photo: Claudia Obrocki

of the two most important archaeological discoveries in the Maya territory: along with the murals of Bonampak, the grave chamber with the now world-famous relief sarcophagus and final resting place of Pacal the Great, King of Palenque, was an absolute sensation. News of the sensational discovery spread like wildfire around the world. Even before this discovery, Palenque and the archaeological finds at this location were known for being of the highest quality, but nothing could compare to the spectacular sight of this unexpected treasure. It was an absolute revelation.

One can easily imagine how alluring and fantastic it must have been, just eight years after this unique discovery, to acquire a Nefertiti-equivalent stucco head from the fabled epicenter of the Classic Maya period—to some extent as a substitute for the "purely irreplaceable pieces" lost during the war. The subconscious mind seems to have been at work here as well. Enchantment with the Palenque findings, coupled with the urge to restore the collection to its prewar significance, appear to have been so powerful that the experts allowed themselves to be thoroughly deceived.

The letter refers to "a masterpiece of world art" and similar praise, going on to emphasize that "The object has thus far been evaluated by Dr. Kutscher from the Ibero-American Institute and by the relevant expert Mr. von Kleist . . ." (SMB-PK, EM, 1 B/60/15, 05.10.1960) Finally, on October 15, 1960, the museum director was able to supply a copy of a letter from Heinrich Ubbelohde-Doering, the former director of the Staatliches Museum für Völkerkunde in Munich to the Senat für Volksbildung, which stressed the rarity of this sculpture as compared to other masterpieces of world art. "Top class Maya art of international standing, especially stucco sculpture of this size and quality, are rarer than almost any other world art objects that appear on the art market, including Chinese Shang bronzes . . . But Maya stucco sculptures are rarer still, a fact well known to those who offer such an item for sale." (SMB-PK, EM, 1 B/60/15, 04.10.1960)

The forger and art dealer were of course very aware of this. The forger certainly knew that, given the rarity of such objects, it would be difficult to conduct a thorough stylistic comparison. We can only imagine the entrepreneurial skill needed to convince experts that the piece was in fact a genuine article.

"Top class," "international standing," "rarity"—these words shed light on the guiding wants and ambitions of the postwar generation. Even the reference to the (at that time) absolute rarity of these kinds of stucco sculptures—the reason that so little comparative material was available—should have raised a red flag with experts. "Whatever the case," Ubbelohde-Doering continued, "I believe, by your description of the head, that it is one of these magnificent works of ancient American art and think every effort to acquire it for the erstwhile Berlin State Museums is justified . . ." The phrase "by your description of the head" raises concern that this consequence-heavy expert opinion was based on descriptions and photographs rather than on direct visual observation.

What is more, Disselhoff declared that he was now in a position to include an assessment "from Professor Krickeberg, the internationally renowned, outstanding connoisseur of ancient Mexican cultures."(SMB-PK, EM, 1 B/60/15, 15.10.1960) Walter Krickeberg was charged with collecting exhibits that had been gathered in so-called "Art Collecting Points" during the war. "When the war was over, the Allies transferred the inventory housed in Grasleben and Kaiseroda to the Art Collecting Point in Wiesbaden

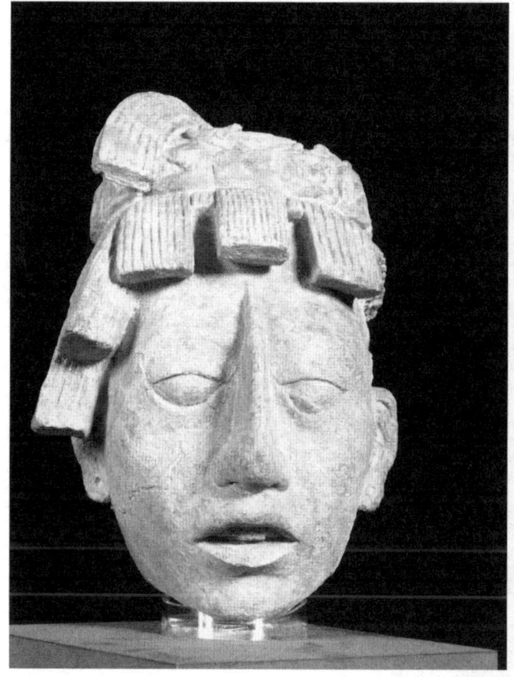
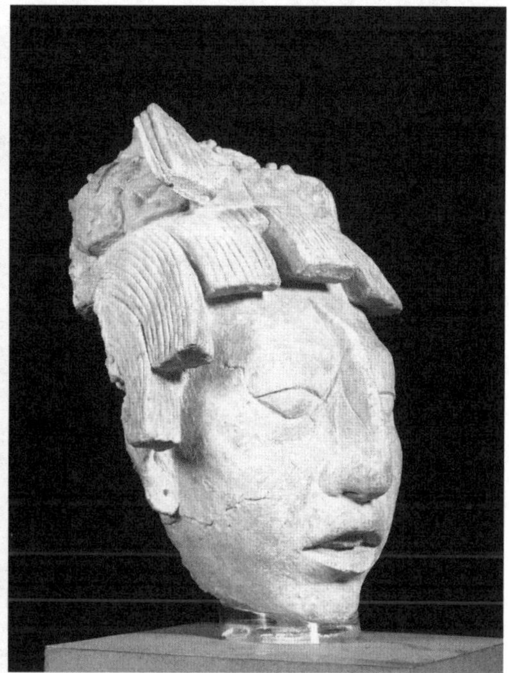

Stucco head, Palenque/Mexico, Maya Classic (7th century AD), Museo Nacional de Antropología, Mexico, Photo: Francisco Ruiz del Prado, MNA, INAH, CONACULTA

and to Schloss Celle, where they remained until 1948, in care of the American and English art protection departments . . . among them irreplaceable originals." (Eisleb 1973, 198). As soon as the war ended, Krickeberg tried to retrieve the evacuated inventory and bring it back to Berlin, but even these actions resulted in losses. In his report dated October 14, 1960 Krickeberg writes: "The . . . head is among . . . the most outstanding works of early Maya art of the seventh century CE, when stucco sculpture flourished in the vast, ruined city of Palenque, located in the Mexican state of Chiapas . . . an apex that stucco statuary never reached again in Palenque art, as we know since Alberto Ruz's 1952 discovery of the royal grave in the crypt of the 'Temple of the Inscriptions' at Palenque . . . " Two of these heads were found under the sarcophagus, "that resemble this object so much in size, face shape and paint residue that I am inclined to attribute to it the same origin . . . Were the rich headdress (which was most certainly part of the original) not broken, the similarity between the three heads would be even more evident." (SMB-PK, EM, 1 B/60/15, 14.10.1960)

Stucco, either fully or partially modeled in three dimensions, was an important means of expression for the Classic Maya. Stucco was easy to mold and thus particularly well suited to rendering individual features and physiognomic characteristics. The realistic portrait heads from the late Classic period, such as the ones from Palenque, serve as impressive examples of this (Fig. 2).

A detailed stylistic analysis comparing this head to the Palenquean stucco heads known to scholars at that time (which are indeed comparable to the Nefertiti in terms of fineness, expression, and perfection) should have raised doubts among the Berlin experts—as it did in Copenhagen.

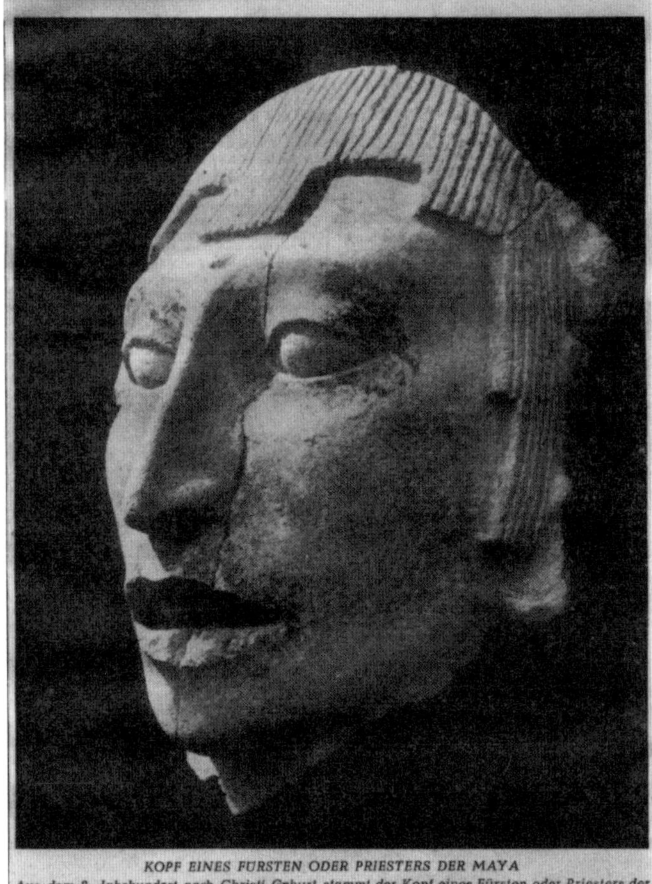

ILLETON SONNABEND, 10. DEZEMBER 1960

KOPF EINES FÜRSTEN ODER PRIESTERS DER MAYA

Aus dem 8. Jahrhundert nach Christi Geburt stammt der Kopf eines Fürsten oder Priesters der Maya, der in einem Grab in der Umgebung der Tempelstadt Palenque (Chiapas) gefunden wurde. Die Plastik im klassischen Maya-Stil wurde jetzt mit Hilfe des Berliner Zahlenlottos für 84 000 DM für das Völkerkundemuseum erworben. Photo: Zenker

Presentation in Berliner Tagesspiegel

Parallel to the events surrounding the purchase of the (alleged) Maya stucco head in Berlin, the dealer approached the Etnografisk Samling at the Nationalmuseet in Copenhagen with two more heads. The director Jens Yde was also very interested, but noted that his final decision depended on information "that we are still looking for at present." (SMB-PK, EM, 1 B/60/15, 25.10.1960)

The head was delivered to the Museum of Ethnology in Berlin on November 21, 1960. Three weeks later, they informed the public with a photo of this sensational purchase in the *Der Tagesspiegel* newspaper. (Tagesspiegel, December 10, 1960)

But unlike Berlin, Copenhagen declined the offer. A letter that has unfortunately disappeared seems to have cast serious doubt on the authenticity and provenance of the stucco head, or at least the ones offered to the institution in Copenhagen. On April 10, 1961, Disselhoff responded to this letter as follows:

> "I will of course handle your letter with the strictest confidence. Our head [the Berlin head], which is much less sumptuous than 'yours,' has been examined with regard to its material and assessed from various different perspectives. If your findings are correct, then the information that both heads come from a single grave cannot be accurate. I think Mr. Stolper [the dealer] is actually quite trustworthy. Let us hope that if this is indeed a case of deception, that he himself was deceived! Thank you very much for your confidential communication." (SMB-PK, EM, 1 B/60/15, 10.04.1961).

Despite doubts in Copenhagen about the stucco heads offered to them there (which allegedly came from the same complex of finds as the one at the Ethnologisches Museum), there were no such reservations in Berlin. After all, several experts had already positively confirmed its material and origins. The Berlin stucco head was exhibited in the museum and respectfully admired by many people, including the then-incumbent German Federal President. It is not necessarily the norm that a President would personally be introduced to an acquisition of the Staatliche Museen zu Berlin, thereby proving the political dimension of the event. The added value that such a (supposedly) significant archaeological piece brought to the institution was a matter of national interest. For better or for worse, they wanted to link themselves to the importance of prewar collection.

The newly acquired head was of course a prominent object in Disselhoff's article "Neuerwerbungen mexikanischer Altertümer" ("New Acquisitions from Ancient Mexico"), written for the museum journal *Baessler-Archiv*. To quote a few sentences from the article: "The most important acquisition by far is a larger than life-sized head from the Classic Period of Maya art." After thanking the German Lottery, the author uses the word "supposedly" in his description of the provenance. The object

> "supposedly comes from a grave in the 'Sierra de Palenque,' where it [the piece] is said to have found been along with a second head made of stucco . . . If the indication of origin is accurate, then there is a parallel to the two completely three-dimensional heads from the same material that were found in 1952 by Alberto Ruz Lhuillier, as grave goods in the crypt of the pyramid at the Temple of the Inscriptions at Palenque . . . The Berlin head was, to all appearances, originally completely three-dimensional. It was allegedly found broken into two halves. The chisel marks seen on the back side suggest that a modern metal device was used as a tool."

What follows is a detailed description that ends with the sentence: "Almond-shaped eyeballs bulge from beneath the lids. The eyes are large and more meticulously modeled than any Maya portrait that I am aware of." (Disselhoff, 1961, 5–7)

It is natural to ask oneself, in hindsight, whether the museum director and author was not perhaps a little unsettled by the doubts expressed by his colleague in Copenhagen, even though, in his reply, he saw no reason to transfer these doubts to the Berlin piece.

Nevertheless, several expressions in Disselhoff's article (which was published just a few months later) are striking in his choice of words—and clearly unconvincing if the director intended to show his firm conviction as to the object's authenticity: words such as "supposedly," "is said to have been found," "if the indication of origin is accurate," "to all appearances," "modern metal device," and "maybe," for example. It was not until 1964, just four years after the presentation at the museum, that serious questions about the authenticity of the Berlin stucco head came to the fore, and these from the illustrious scholar and then curator of the American Museum of Natural History, Gordon F. Ekholm. Dieter Eisleb, who by then worked at the Berlin museum in the institution's American Archeology Department, did the only right thing and subsequently asked Ekholm to reexamine a sample of the stucco. Here, the texture of the plaster turned out to be absolutely atypical for the alleged area of origin, but very similar to the other objects that had appeared in recent years and had, for some reason or another, turned out to be forgeries. The sample contained, for example, copious amounts of calcium sulphate, something that had never been found in hundreds of chemically analyzed samples from Palenque. As if that were not bad enough, Ekholm found a piece of hair ("perfectly fresh and pliable") while looking at the stucco sample of the head under a microscope. The follicle was that of a domestic pig[1]—and there were certainly no domestic pigs in pre-Hispanic America. The proverbial "hair in the soup" had been found, the negative judgment confirmed, the forgery unmasked. The findings, in other words, were clear: "The above considerations combined with the general appearance of your head lead me to believe without any doubt that your head is not a genuine piece." (SMB-PK, EM, 1 B/67/13, 15.10.1964)

There had to be a response. First, the dealer was notified. Then the General Director had to be informed of the new situation. (SMB-PK, EM, 1 B/67/13, 29.06.1967) He was told that, in addition to Ekholm's scientific and stylistic examination, José Luis Franco, an expert from Mexico, had also been consulted. Both experts objected—independently of one another—to essentially the same stylistic features. The seller of stucco head (who still believed the head to be authentic) was nolens volens prepared to swap the stucco head for a Mexican art object of the same price.

A stele from the pre-Hispanic Huaxteca culture was offered in its place. After the embarrassing experiences, Eisleb sent the photograph of this stone relief to Ekholm and asked for an assessment of its authenticity. The response was positive: "In my opinion the piece you are considering is definitely genuine and I think its acceptance would be an excellent solution to the problem of the stucco head." (SMB-PK, EM, 1 B/67/13, 26.10.1964) Naturally, after the disgrace to both the museum and the external evaluators, a number of voices continued to challenge the authenticity of the traded stele. But a mistake or error of judgment can be ruled out in this case. An August 1967 report from Mexican expert José Luis Franco C., who was already mentioned in connection with the assessment of the stucco head, confirmed Ekholm's view that the stele from the Huaxteca culture, in the Mexican state of Veracruz, is indeed authentic.

Any last apprehensions about the stele were finally put to rest by a papier-mâché copy that renowned Berlin "Mexicanist" and pre-Columbian American Studies scholar Eduard Seler sent to the museum some sixty-five years before the trade (SMB-PK, EM, Seler, E No. 651/1904). The Ethnologisches Museum had preserved Seler's imitation, which he created in 1902/1903 on his last trip to Mexico, and it appeared completely congruent to the stele acquired in 1967, down to the somewhat convex vein in the stone material, thereby allaying any lingering doubts as to the object's authenticity.

Conclusion

The specialist knowledge attributed to the relevant museum curators and other consulted experts did not bear out during the acquisition of the alleged Maya stucco head. The starting point for this disastrous transaction was the knowledgeable, anonymous forger and his ability to create the illusion of authenticity with the work. The stucco

1 Eisleb, oral communication, 1997.

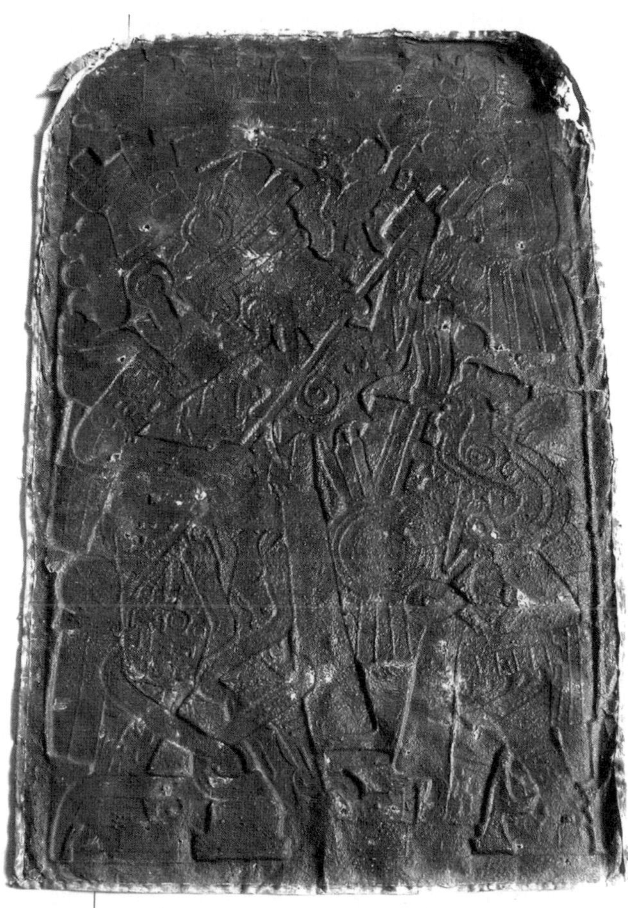

Paper mold from the Stelae from the Huaxteca culture Ethnologisches Museum, Berlin

head is, unquestionably, a perfectly strong sculptural work whose creation presupposes a combination of artistic talent and stylistic knowledge of Classic Maya period stucco art. One cannot help but attest to the forger's intelligence, which imbued the work with enough "typical" marks of quality that it developed a suggestive power. Nevertheless, the following questions will have to go unanswered. From which milieu did the forger come? Was he a Maya? Was it a commissioned work? Was the stucco head made in a forgery workshop or is it a one-off? What percentage of the purchase price did the forger receive?

The unfortunate circumstance of an erroneous initial analysis, carried out using the scientific standards available at the time, triggered a domino effect of several factors, and the objectivity of the test procedures should have been questioned right from the start.

Supporters of the purchase were eager to make up for losses incurred during the Second World War through spectacular new acquisitions, and to build on the significance of the collection before the war. We can assume that it was precisely this motivation that led to an uncritical and overconfident self-appraisal by the experts who attested to its authenticity, some of them on the basis of mere descriptions. They did this although a scarce few comparative pieces were known at that time. Any references to doubts were ignored. Instead, it appears that the respective experts based their opinions on the quality of the experts before them, and even tried to out-do each other in their opinions.

One tried to "top" the other's enthusiasm, which of course led to an appreciation in value. Detached from the object, its value seemed to increase as the serial chain of experts grew, creating an unintentional complicity. Only the later, responsible young curator Dieter Eisleb was able to see the process with professional distance.

The explicit comparison of the supposed Maya head with other icons of world art such as the valuable and rare Chinese Shang bronzes or the unique Egyptian Nefertiti bust underscores the desire to raise the collection's international profile. Thus the psychology of positive prejudice seems to have played a role in the all-too-enticing opportunity to acquire a head from the famous Maya city of Palenque, a site already world-famous for its magnificent artworks. Against the background of all this, there was the influence of a sarcophagus discovered just a few years before in the grave chamber of the Temple of the Inscriptions, in the same city. Through the power of suggestion, the alleged Palenque stucco head might be misleading.

On the first pages of his book "Die deutsche Literatur" (published in 1828), Wolfgang Menzel penned the familiar catchphrase describing Germany as "Das Land der Dichter und Denker" ("the land of poets and thinkers"). Since then, the German-educated elite have cultivated a self-concept as representatives of a nation of poets, thinkers, writers, philosophers, and artists. After years of Nazi barbarism, the fledgling Federal Republic of Germany was even keener to reconnect with the old, cultural values of pre-Nazi Germany. As an institution that preserves much of the material treasures of cultural heritage, museums played an important role here. Young West German society had to redraw its self-concept, and its cultural custodians strove to restore postwar Germany's reputation as a cultural nation. It was therefore of the greatest cultural and political importance to close war-damage gaps in the national collections as quickly and completely as possible, preferably through precious acquisitions. World audiences had to know that the new republic had renounced the culture-annihilating barbarism of its predecessors.

Given the serious losses to the Ethnologisches Museum's collection of American archeology, the offer to purchase the alleged Maya stucco seemed well timed. Purchase negotiations began in the late 1950s. Viewed from the perspective of research history, the event clearly fits into German postwar history at large, and not just into the history of the Ethnologisches Museum.

Translated by Amy Patton

Sources

Staatliche Museen zu Berlin – Preußischer Kulturbesitz, Ethnologisches Museum, Archive (SMB-PK, EM)
SMB-PK, EM, 1 B/60/15 (05.12.1960). Letter from the art dealer to the museum
SMB-PK, EM, 1 B/60/15 (31.08.1960). Expert report from Konstandt Laboratories.
SMB-PK, EM, 1 B/60/15 (05.10.1960). Disselhoff to General Director Reidemeister.
SMB-PK, EM, 1 B/60/15 (05.10.1960). Disselhoff to General Director Reidemeister.
SMB-PK, EM, 1 B/60/15 (15.10.1960). Disselhoff to Oberregierungsrat Günther.
SMB-PK, EM, 1 B/60/15 (14.10.1960). Expert report from Krickeberg.
SMB-PK, EM, 1 B/60/15 (25.10.1960). Yde to Disselhoff.
SMB-PK, EM, 1 B/60/15 (10.04.1961). Disselhoff to Yde.
SMB-PK, EM, 1 B/67/13 (15.10.1964). Ekholm to Eisleb.
SMB-PK, EM, 1 B/67/13 (29.06.1967). Eisleb to Reidemeister.
SMB-PK, EM, 1 B/67/13 (26.10.1964). Ekholm to Eisleb.
SMB-PK, EM, Seler, E No. 651/1904
Erwerbungsakte (acquisition records) 1B/1960/15
Erwerbungsakte (acquisition records) 1B 1967/13
Acta betreffend die Reise des Direktors Prof. Dr. Seler nach Amerika in den Jahren 1890 bis 1907 (Files concerning director Prof. Dr. Seler's travels to America in the years 1890 to 1907), I B 26, E 651/1904

Bibliography

Batres, Leopoldo. *Antigüedades mejicanas falsificadas, falsificaciones y falsificadores.* Mexico City: Imprenta de Fidencio S. Sorio, 1909.
Blom, Frans. "More Fakes." In *Maya Research 2* (1935): 251–252.
Disselhoff, Hans Dietrich. "Neuerwerbungen mexikanischer Altertümer." In *Baessler-Archiv, Neue Folge* vol. 9, ed. H. D. Disselhoff and K. Krieger, 5–7. Berlin: Dietrich Reimer Verlag, 1961.
Disselhoff, Hans Dietrich. *Geschichte der altamerikanischen Kulturen,* 2nd ed. Table 20. Munich: Verlag R. Oldenbourg, 1967.
Eisleb, Dieter. "Hundert Jahre Museum für Völkerkunde Berlin: Abteilung Amerikanische Archäologie." In *Baessler-Archiv, Neue Folge,* vol. 21, ed. K. Krieger and G. Koch, 175–217. Berlin: Dietrich Reimer Verlag, 1973.
Ekholm, Gordon F. "The Problem of Fakes in Pre-Columbian Art." In *Curator: The Museum Journal,* vol. 7, no. 1 (January 1964): 19–32.
Holmes, William H. "The Trade in Spurious Mexican Antiquities." In *Science,* vol. 7, no. 159 (March 19, 1886): 264.
Kelker, Nancy L. and Karen O. Bruhns. *Faking Ancient Mesoamerica.* Walnut Creek, CA: Left Coast Press, 2010.
Lehmann, Walter. *Altmexikanische Kunstgeschichte: Ein Entwurf in Umrissen.* Berlin: Wasmuth, 1922.
Menzel, Wolfgang. *Die deutsche Literatur.* vol. 1–2. Stuttgart: Gebrüder Frankh., 1828.
Ruz Lhuillier, Alberto. *El Templo de las Inscripciones, Palenque.* Mexico City: Instituto Nacional de Antropología e Historia (INAH), 1973.
Seler, Eduard. "Die Monumente von Huilocintla im Canton Tuxpan des Staates Vera Cruz." In *Gesammelte Abhandlungen zur Amerikanischen Sprach und Altertumskunde,* vol. 3, 514–521. Graz: Akademische Druck und Verlagsanstalt, 1960.

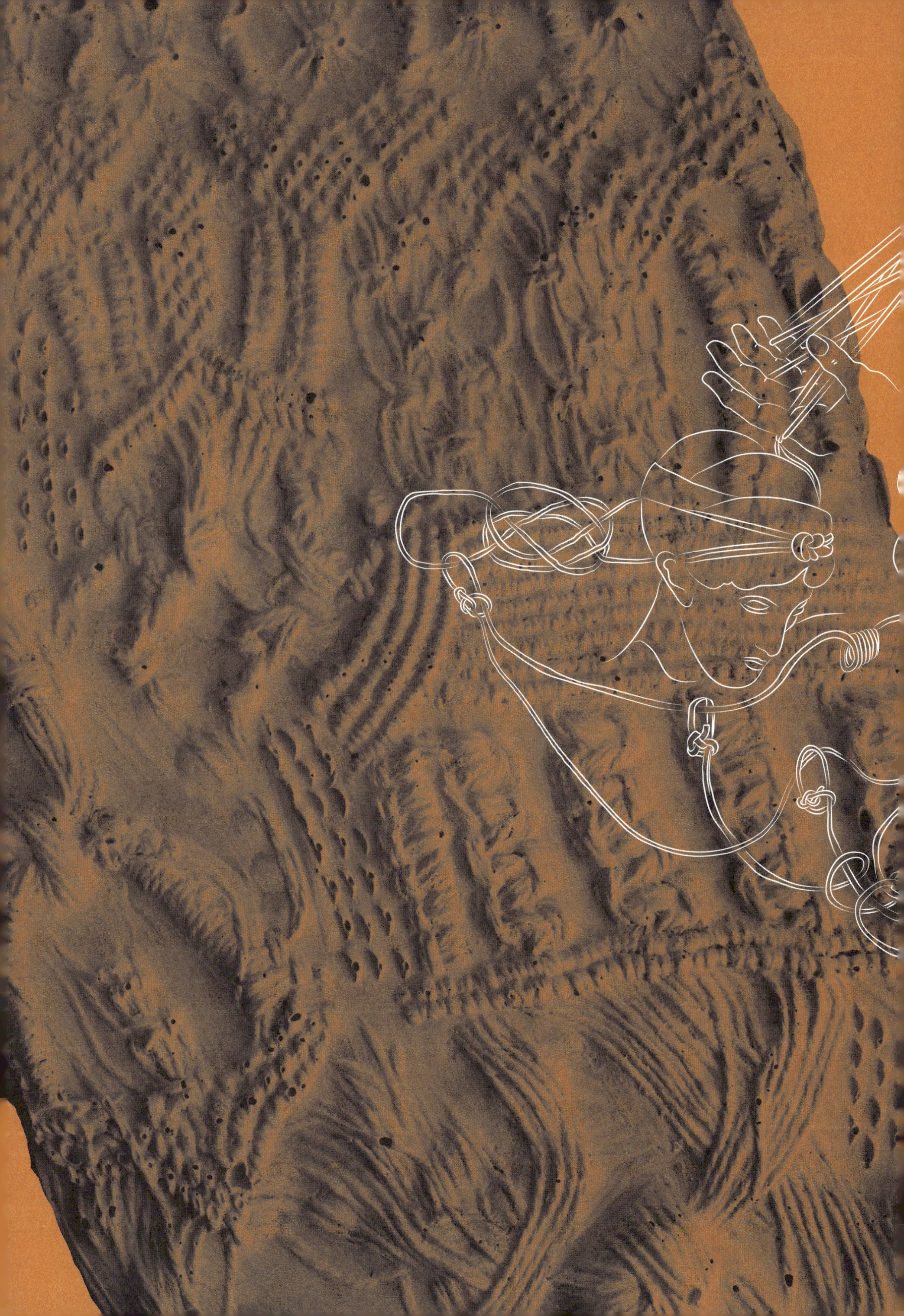

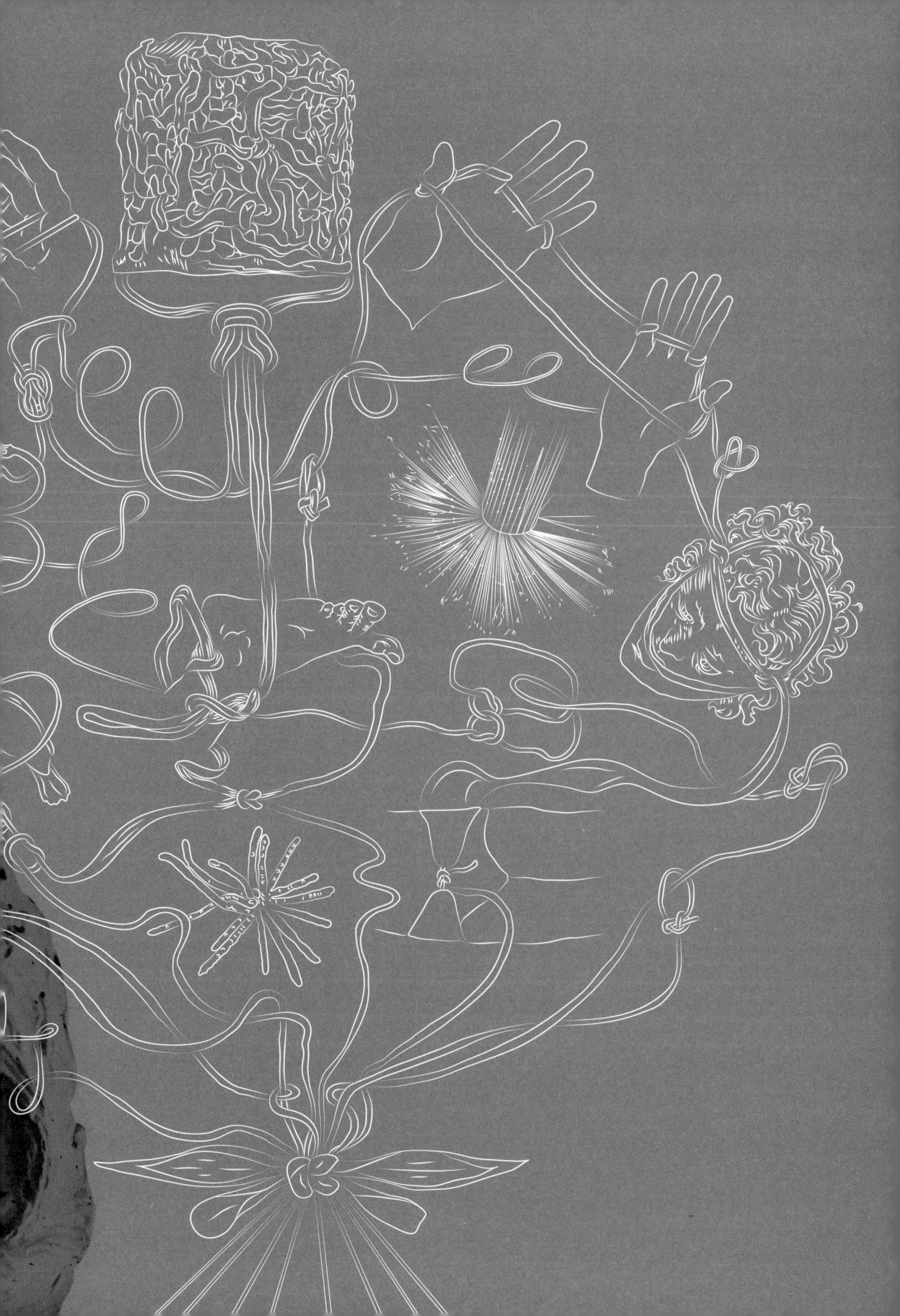

Starting from the top, spiralling inwards clock-wise: Omphalos (or navel of the earth) 5th century BC Greece / beginning Plinthios brokhos noose surgical knot, Italy / Bowline knot / "Eskimo" knot / "Eskimo" running bowline 1 / "Eskimo" running bowline 2 / Running bowline / Diplous Karkhesious, Greece c. 1500 BC / the head of a Greek bride, the Hercules knot was associated with virginity, 5th century B.C. Greece / mid-process of plinthios brokhos noose / the handle of an ancient Roman vase / Quipu 14-3866, Chulpaca, Ica, Peru, AD 1425-1532. Talking knots or recording device / Lykos brokhos, Latin, 1540 / the torso of a youthful votary and his "Cypriote belt", Cyprus 600 BC / the bacteria Leucothrix mucor are able to form true knots under the right conditions / True lover's knot / The Ploceidae, or weaver bird / Mercury's caduceus or wand. The knot in the center symbolizes the union of Jupiter and Rhea / Jug sling / "Eskimo" bowline / surgical leg knot, Italy 1544 / Hercules knot, reef knot or square knot / Hercules knot design from a silver bowl in the Hildesheim collection in Berlin.

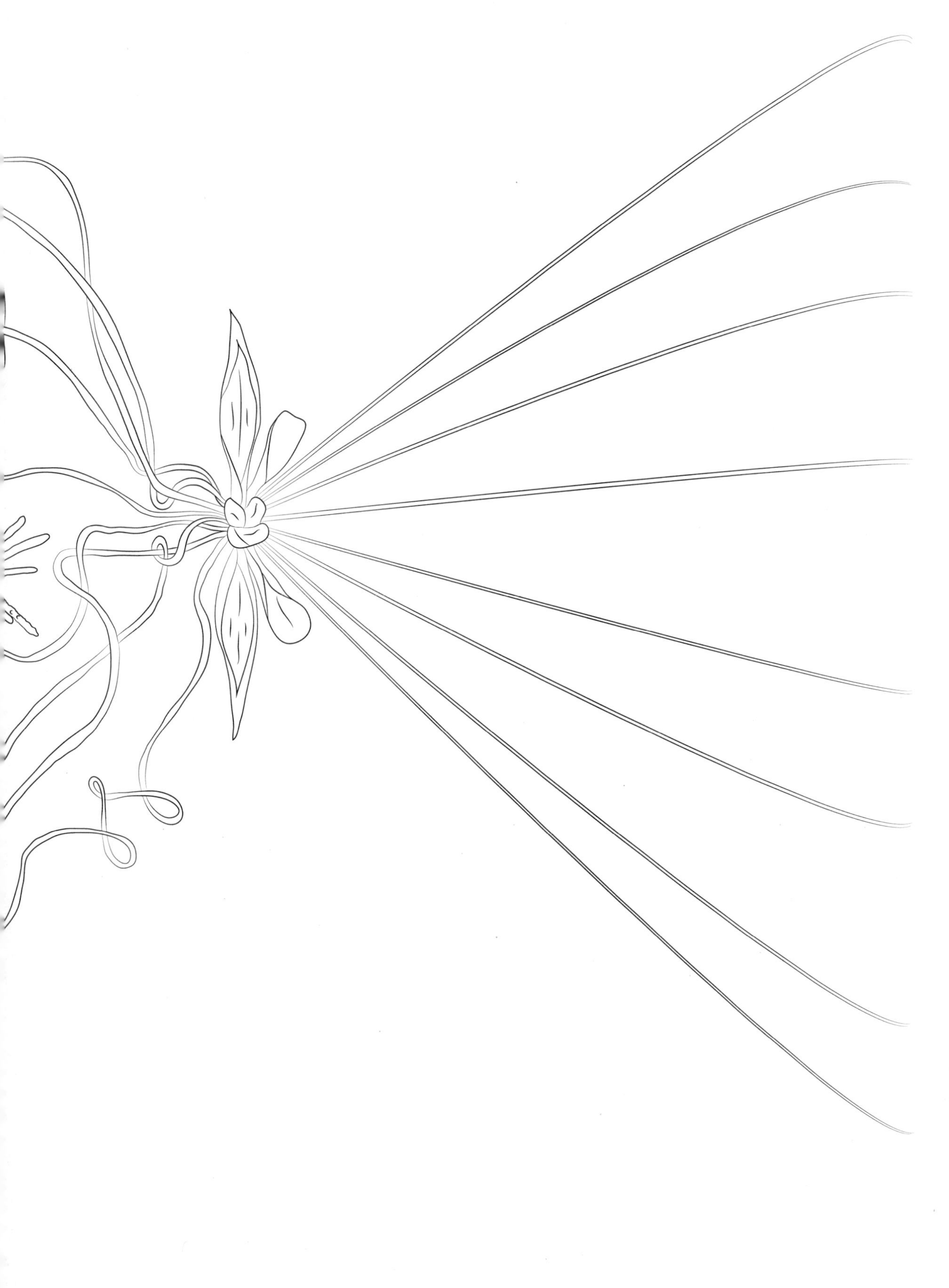

QUE HACER
PABLO KATCHADJIAN[1]

1 Book excerpts from "Qué hacer". Buenos Aires, Bajo la luna, 2010

1

Alberto and I are teaching in a classroom at an English university when a student asks us, in an aggressive tone: when philosophers speak, is what they say true or is it some kind of double? Alberto and I look at each other, a little nervous because we don't understand the question. Alberto reacts first: he steps up and responds that this cannot be known. The student, unhappy with the response, stands up (he is eight foot two), moves close to Alberto, grabs him, and starts to put him in his mouth. But though this seems dangerous, it's not just the students and I who are laughing, but Alberto also laughs, with half his body inside the student's mouth, and says: it's okay, it's okay. Afterwards Alberto and I appear in a plaza. An old man is giving food to a group of about ten pigeons. Alberto comes up to the old man and I sense something and want to stop him, but for some reason I can't. Before Alberto reaches the old man, the old man somehow becomes a pigeon and tries to fly, but he can't. Alberto makes splints for his wings and tells him he'll be healed very soon, that his problem is very normal. The old man seems pleased. Then we appear in the bathroom of a club. For some reason, we're in the women's bathroom. A group of five very pretty well-dressed girls comes in, sweating from dancing so much. One of them seems very drunk or high and Alberto closes in on her with clear intentions and throws himself at her; from what I can see, she lets him do what he wants, though it's not clear what he wants, because he's only rubbing against her as if his body were itching; she responds in the same way, which makes it look as if they're scratching each other mutually. The other four girls come up to me and suddenly all five of us are doing something that's not quite clear. It's as if the scene were being censored. So I notice that the girls are old, and at the same time I hear that Alberto is talking to the drunk girl about Léon Bloy. He tells her that he wanted to be a saint and that he suffered because he couldn't. He tells her about the scene where Véronique pulls out all her teeth, and though Alberto is calm, it seems as if he wants to pull out the girl's teeth. He grabs her by the hood of her sweatshirt and drags her out of the bathroom. Alberto seems to be made of rags, he's very light.

14

Alberto and I sense that our heads are getting smaller; Alberto says to me: what are we going to do with our hands when we don't have heads anymore? I respond with difficulty, because my jaw is locking; I tell him I don't know. At that moment we feel something like a balancing in the atmosphere, but just the same our heads keep getting smaller. Alberto says to me: this is what I call balanced terror. He tells me it's brutal—that is, that it's bad and good at the same time. I correct him: you wanted to say positive and negative. In response, he makes a harsh "tch-tch" sound and gestures toward me with his hand to shut me up. Suddenly the thing with our heads ceases to have a presence and we're in a bank. Alberto wants to exchange a broom he has in his hand for a sheaf of dollars. The girl tells him he can't, but Alberto insists. At that moment I look at the people who are in the bank. There are some tourists, a person who's poor in spirit, some old women, some immigrants, and some fascists. First I begin to suspect the tourists; then the immigrants; then the old women; then the fascists; then the person who's poor in spirit. But at that moment I become certain of yet another thing: we ourselves are terrorists, though not because we're *doing* anything terrorist, because neither we nor the others are doing anything at all. I ask Alberto if he feels like a terrorist, and he says he does. I feel the same way. I ask the tourists and they say they feel the same way; I ask the immigrants and they say they think they feel the same way; I ask the old women and as a response they show me the palms of their hands; the fascists don't respond and close their eyes; and the person who's poor in spirit tells me he doesn't know and covers his ears. We're all afraid of ourselves. What might we do? We don't know, and that is the problem: Of what might we be capable? I ask Alberto what we're capable of and he tells me that he doesn't know, and that he also doesn't know what to do with his hands. We calm down when we appear in a plaza and there's an old man who is simultaneously a pigeon. The old man has broken wings and Alberto heals them using his hands. He tells me: I use my hands for this. I give him a thumbs up to show my approval, but Alberto doesn't see me because he's very busy. When I decide to try to help him, the old man is already flying. The sky grows very luminous and we appear at an English university. I propose that we speak about the apocryphal correspondence between Seneca and Saint Paul the Apostle but Alberto, so as not to boast, wants to talk about plumbing, about the principle of water valves. We come to an agreement and decide to analyze the apocryphal correspondence between Seneca and Saint Paul the Apostle according to the logic of water valves. The students are extremely pleased and applaud so much that they can't hear us.

23

Alberto and I are together teaching a class at an English university. The class doesn't have a clear focus, though it seems to be an attempt to engage the subject of war (it seems to be about a war that is *currently taking place*). Alberto first says that war is latent, that is to say, present and invisible. Then I add that war is not the fact of war, but rather the sensation it produces. The students, the majority of whom are fascists (for some reason we are certain that they are) don't want to understand. We start to try to engage the subject using as our point of departure a phrase and its possible variations; for example:

- war is being nervous
- to be at war is to be nervous
- to be nervous is to be at war

And many others like that until we reach a phrase that seems perfect to us at that moment: war is a nervous state. The phrase remains, resonating until one of the students, who is eight foot two, asks us: is war a state of the soul? And an old woman asks us: could it be a mysterious war relationship? That's when we realize that we should have clarified that war, despite everything, exists independently of nerves, but we didn't do that so we wouldn't seem contradictory. Alberto tells me: we should have said the following: the nervous state is one of the ways of experiencing war; the other is to act in the war, but in order to do that it's crucial to know what to do. I tell him that it sounds good to me but that I'd add the following: to know what to do is the only way of canceling out nerves or transforming nerves into action. Alberto tells me that it sounds good to him, and when we're about to explain all this to the students, we appear in a forest where all the trees are burnt and healthy simultaneously. In the background a beautiful though tense and dissonant melody is heard; that is to say, a beautiful but not relaxing melody. And in the background, eight hundred drinkers who repeat: war can be/the only thing you see. Meanwhile, though we are not running, we have the sensation of running very swiftly. From faraway, like a desired goal (that is, a goal that plays the role of a desired thing), we see a person who's a failure who is simultaneously a person who's poor in spirit. On both sides, eight hundred old women applaud us.

24

Alberto greets me from the end of a road that leads downward. I seem to take a number of hours to reach him; when I get to him, we appear in an English university talking about things we know nothing about. The students notice that we don't know what we say we know and they stand up: they are eight foot two. They all grab us and it seems as if it were just one single enormous student with dozens of arms, but that's just a feeling, because we know there are a number of students. Suddenly we appear on a boat talking with an old woman. The old woman says that we are geniuses, but for some reason it bothers me that she should say it *like that*, and I respond that if we were geniuses we wouldn't have to decide anything. At that moment we discover that what we have to do on the boat is teach a class, and that's what we do. While we're teaching the class (which has no subject) we notice that the students don't understand what we're telling them and they're asking questions that have nothing to do with the subject (because even if there isn't a fixed subject there is the feeling of a subject, and what the students are saying feels different). Everything continues like that until one student asks a question: which of you is going to help me? The student is one foot seven inches tall and seems like a baby. Alberto goes up to him and lifts him in his arms, and at that moment three things happen at once: Alberto is an old woman, I see him mummified and the baby student has the head of a cow that is *clearly* medieval. For some reason, the situation becomes tense; Alberto blinks and that makes me think about war. The image that appears at that moment is of a trench filled with soldiers.

27

We're on a boat and we can glimpse, far off, an island where Alberto wants to go. He tells me: everything is on that island. Suddenly we notice that the boat, which is also a bridge at the same time, is full of dead fat people; Alberto tells me: they died, *but* because of an obesity problem. I ask him, a little surprised, what he means to say with that "but." Alberto, somewhat irritated, makes a harsh "tch-tch" sound at me and makes a gesture with his hand to shush me, because he's very focused on looking at the island and repeating "everything is there." Alberto wants to jump, but I have a better idea; I tell him: if the boat is also a bridge at the same time, then it can take us to the island. But this situation disappears and we appear in a bathroom in an English university that is also the bathroom of a club at the same time and also at the same time the kitchen of a church (we are certain of this triple condition). Alberto wants to go out into the street, but something stops us. An old woman is making a soup from which smoke is rising; when we move closer to look inside the pot, a kind of rebuke appears that makes us think about an old rag. A very tall student tells us: the problem is that the rag is made of loosely woven cloth; half the things can't be seen. And as if the student's words were waiting to be fulfilled, suddenly we only see half of the things that are there. Alberto tells me: everything is there but only half can be seen. The argument that broke out at that moment between Alberto and myself, on the one hand, and some students from an English university, on the other, is the following: how could it be known that what is being seen is half of something, that is, that it isn't simply something complete that gives the appearance of being half of something? Alberto and I want to believe that the other half is hidden, yet in some way available; the students say that these are appearances of halves that, in reality, are complete things and not halves. The conclusion we reach is the following: whether they are halves of something or complete things, the fact that they present themselves as halves causes the other half to come into existence. That conclusion fills us with happiness. Everything that follows has the air of a party that is interrupted when we realize that the students are still arguing about the particular type of existence of the half that's not visible.

33

Alberto and I are on a boat trying to read a book together, but we can't because on deck there are eight hundred drinkers sipping wine that smells like an old rag and singing: it's the war / that makes me roar with terror / and that's why I'm nervous. The melody they're singing is so happy that Alberto and I join in with them, though for some reason we're only pretending to sing: we insert ourselves among them and move our mouths. Everything goes on like that for a while until one of them realizes that we're not really singing and shouts: these guys aren't singing. Alberto looks at me and tells me: this is the moment to go to that island. Which island? I ask him. He points his finger toward a spot that's quite far away and tells me: everything is there. And without saying anything more, Alberto jumps off the boat. I stay there, doubting: I see Alberto down below, in the water, waiting for me, and I see the drinkers above, threatening me with their fists though they don't seem resolved to do anything to me. This situation lasts a long time until we appear at a cantina painted black. There are eight hundred drinkers drinking and toasting us as they shout: let's drink to them! We join them and all together we start to sing something sort of like the following: those who terrorize / doubt their own eyes / but as for me / I like what I see / because I don't believe / anything like that could be alive. And we go on like that for a long time, with a very happy spirit.

47

Alberto and I are trying to talk to a man with no eyes about what's around us, though it's quite difficult for us to identify the objects. This lasts a while until we appear in front of a mirror that reflects us in a way that horrifies us: Alberto is a mummy and my head is growing. We see in the mirror that behind us are eight hundred drinkers and an old woman. When we turn around to see them directly they're not there anymore, but when we look at ourselves in the mirror again we notice that they're still there and now our image is the image of us without deformities. So Alberto tells me: they are in the mirror and we are as much here as there. I posit a doubt to him, however: Are we here and there, or just here and that is our reflection, as would be normal? Alberto laughs and answers me: if they are there and not here it's because that is a place and not just an image. And just at that moment we see that in the background of the mirror there's an island that is not on our side. I tell Alberto: we should be able to go over to that side. The old woman, from the mirror, answers me: you can't, because you are there and you have an image here, and what for you is an image is real for us, which is why it doesn't make sense that you'd contemplate being in one place two times; I'm trying to say that you are already there, but in a way that doesn't serve you at all. After that we appear in a toy store; a naked old woman is helping us and asks us what we want. Alberto tells her he wants to buy something for one of his nephews, and that he's thinking of a broom; he thinks for a bit and adds: a broom made of gold. The old woman tells him that she doesn't have gold brooms and Alberto, nervous, starts to clean his little black boots. Then we are walking through a forest full of trees; in each tree are eight hundred drinkers who generate an unbearable smell of old rag, and that smell ruins our stroll.

Translated by Jen Hofer

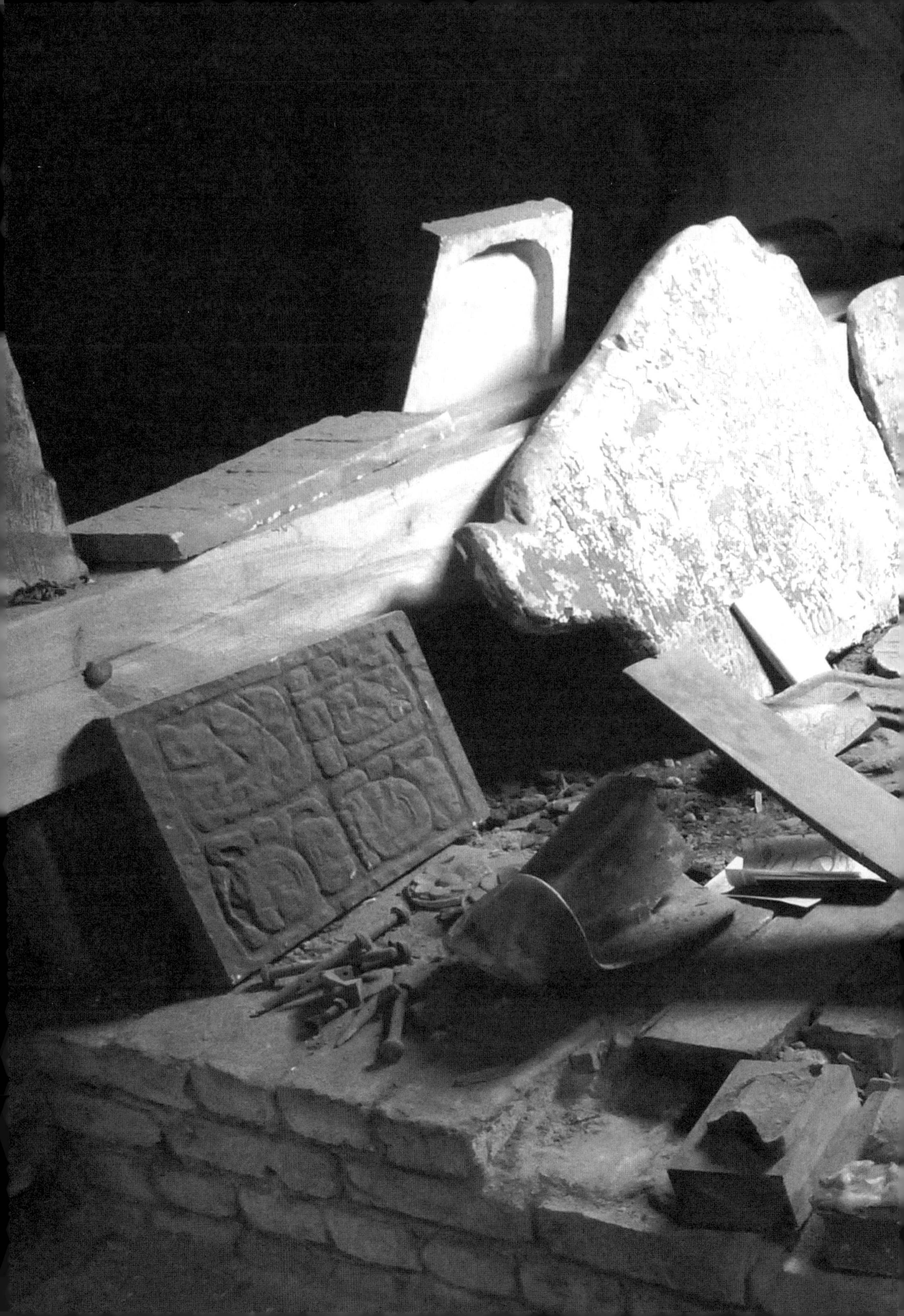

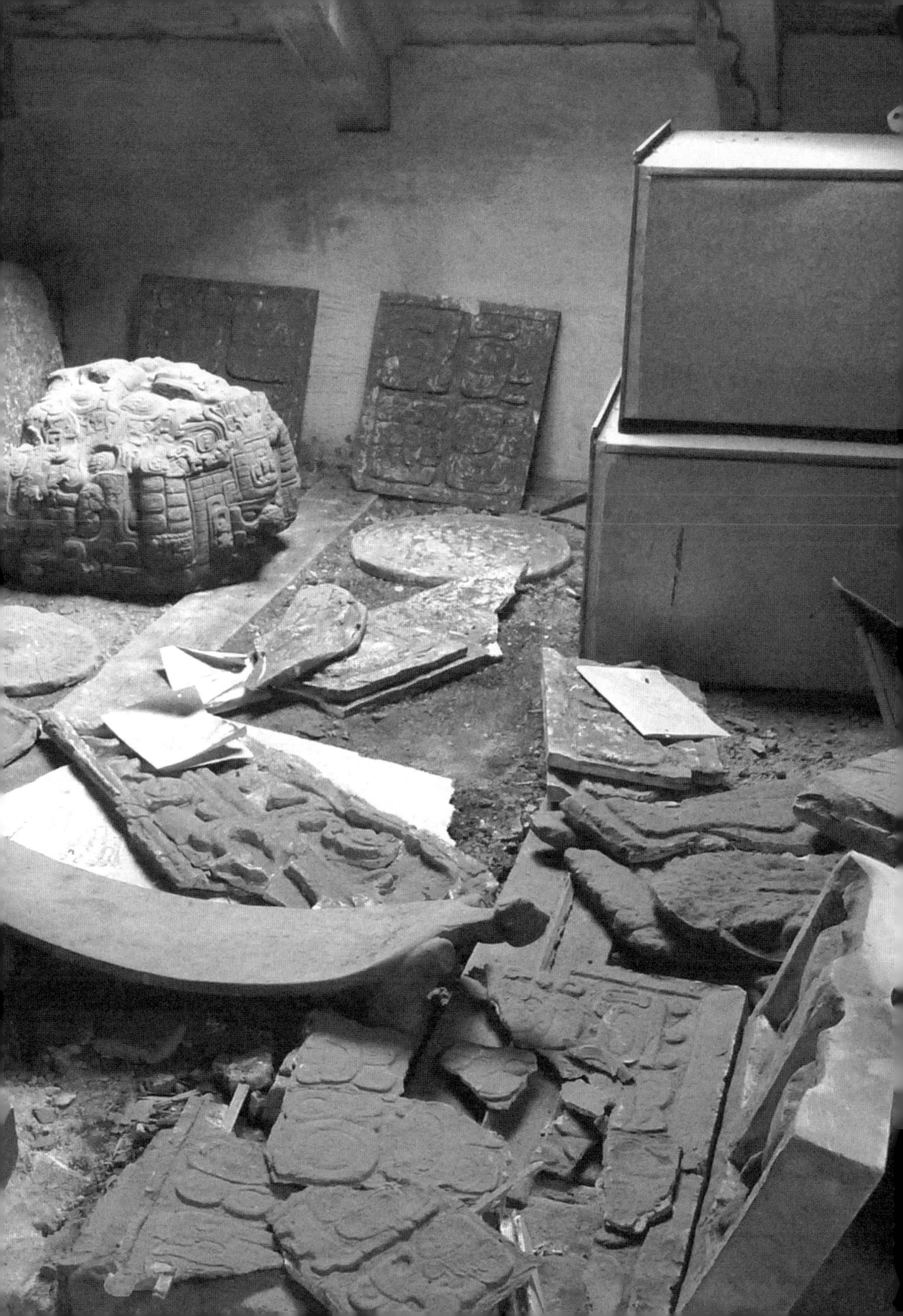

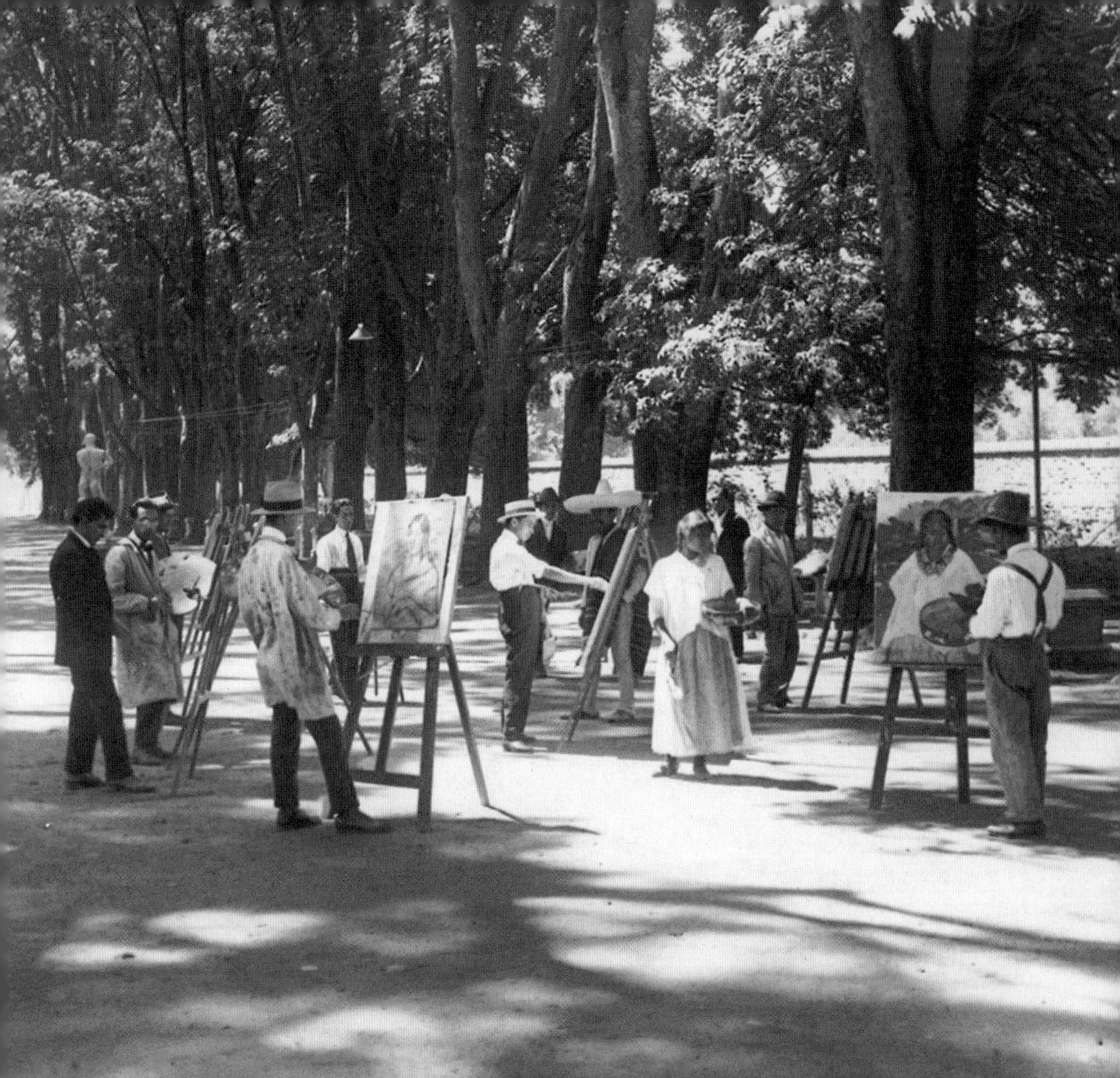

Luz Jiménez at the Art School in Coyoacán, ca. 1920.
Andrés Blaisten Collection

ARTISTS, MODELS, AND SCIENTISTS IN THE PRODUCTION OF INDIGENEITY: MILPA ALTA, TWENTIETH AND TWENTY-FIRST CENTURIES[1]

PAULA LOPEZ CABALLERO
CEIICH/UNAM

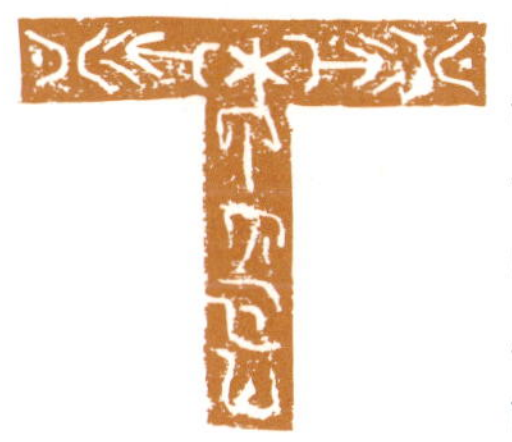

he end of November 2003. A cool, damp breeze descends from the forest surrounding the town of Santa Ana, known by locals and visitors as "the most traditional" of the twelve towns that make up the Milpa Alta district in Mexico City, called delegación Milpa Alta.[2] On this November morning, men and women of all ages—as families with their children or grandchildren, or at times in small clumps—wait in the main plaza, in front of the little parish church and behind the market. I recognize many from running into them previously in the street or in other public events. In a few minutes, the opening ceremony will begin for a poetry-reading contest in Nahuatl, the mother tongue of the majority of the population until about thirty years ago.

Each year, a group of residents who actively promote the Nahuatl language handle the organizing. All of a sudden, under a huge yellow tarp covering the plaza, a number of *conchero* (shell) dancers take possession of the space and, to inaugurate the event, begin to perform what they present as "a greeting to the four parts of the universe . . . like our grandparents did." The initiative comes from a young man from the urban area of the Valley of Mexico, one of the most committed students at the Nahuatl language course held every Saturday morning in Santa Ana. His group of dancers includes men and women, young and old, dressed in a rather free—and lyrical—interpretation of pre-Hispanic outfits: feathers, loincloths, shells, and bells on their ankles. They perform a dance that—according to the explanation they offer—was part of the rituals of "our ancestors," the Aztecs. Faced with these half-naked characters, many of them with long, flowing hair and no shoes, crowned with impressive, multicolored plumes, repeatedly jumping to the rhythm of a drum, it isn't long before I hear muffled laughter, half-whispered comments, and general surprise in the audience. Around me, reactions shift rapidly from a bit of disdain to condescension to feeling embarrassed for the dancers. "Why do they put on those feathers like Apaches!" "And those girls! Dressing like that, showing their whole bodies!" "Did you see those long-haired guys?" The comments that people make to each

1 This text is a re-worked translation of an article published in French in *L'Homme* (López Caballero, 2012).

2 I carried out fieldwork as part of a doctoral thesis in Anthropology for fourteen months in three periods between 2002 and 2005. See López Caballero, 2012.

other and that I'm able to catch make me understand that for the residents of Santa Ana, represented and self-identified as Nahuatl indigenous people, heirs to the Aztecs, these dances only evoke barbarity and immorality; for them, those dances belong to a world to which, without a doubt, they are not the heirs. In fact, the dancers are forced to end the ceremony before they'd planned, because the public begins to disperse. A call to order by the master of ceremonies, and we continue on with the flag ceremony and the national anthem; these are conventions that begin the majority of public activities in Milpa Alta, even events commemorating the campesino struggle of the 1970s, a powerful local movement that seriously challenged the authority of the State in the region. The public sings along to the flag presentation ceremony while the flag bearers—children from the elementary school—march along. When the children stop halfway across the plaza, the attendees sing the national anthem; some sing a version in Nahuatl, and everyone stands as a sign of respect. Once the flag bearers have made another turn around the plaza to leave, the atmosphere relaxes again, and the first person to recite Nahuatl poetry gets ready for his or her moment on stage.

Throughout the day, I had the opportunity to continue talking with different people about the Nahuatl heritage of Milpa Alta and about the way it continues to be lived by its residents. "We have a lot of traditions here, señorita, old customs from before the Conquista," Doña Amalia, a vendor from the market, tells me. Also, César, a student, explains with pride: "Here, the language of our grandparents is the same as the one from before the Conquista . . ." This way of presenting themselves and their own culture locates the Nahuatl language as the most valuable symbolic good, followed by stories, legends, customs, and ancestral sayings, which most of the time are still recounted in Nahuatl and associated with the pre-Hispanic world. Like a treasure that was able to escape the vagaries of time and history to remain alive till today.

Nonetheless, unwittingly, during the opening ceremony, an "incident" had occurred. The pride that many inhabitants of Milpa Alta often show for their "Aztec" or Nahuatl origins was met face to face with another presentation of that same past—that of the *conchero* dancers. But rather than leading to a sense of unity, the result was a confrontation between these two representations. A clash that left everyone confused: on one side, the inhabitants of Santa Ana, for whom those distant origins are fused with a sense of belonging which is expressed more simply through patron saint celebrations, the Nahuatl language, and a number of images of the pre-Hispanic past that are very close to those mobilized by official culture and official festivities (fiestas patrias); for that reason, they did not recognize themselves in those "pre-Hispanic" dances. On the other side, the dancers—according to what they told me afterwards—left the scene disppointed, questioning the authenticity of those residents who seemed more identified with the national anthem—of the descendants of the conquerors—than with the dances of their "real" ancestors. (Extracts from my field notes, November 24, 2003).

This episode is meaningful, because—in order to understand the incomprehension and disconnection produced between the two groups—many of the parameters typically used to analyze these phenomena end up being insufficient. New questions are needed. Indeed, the clash in this situation is not between the dominant group—in Mexico usually identified as mestizo—and a subaltern or minority group—indigenous—since here both groups present themselves as bearers of that heritage. This is also not an opposition between institutionalized representations—like those of a museum, for example—and vernacular representations of indigenous identity, since both can be considered "counter-cultural" or popular. Further, in this collision of representations of indigeneity, what is more easily associated with indigenous identification—the heritage of the pre-Hispanic world—is expressed and claimed by the group of urban visitors. The inhabitants of Milpa Alta, for their part, practice their identity through cultural expressions that are not usually classified as "authentically" indigenous (the anthem, saints, etc.).

But then, who is indigenous? The dancers or the inhabitants of Milpa Alta? What makes indigenous people indigenous in this situation? Or, put differently, what does "indigenous" means? The far-off, pre-Hispanic past or the saints? The dances or the national anthem? Both of the versions defended by the groups interacting in this situation? Neither of them? Which is worth more? Why? Do we have to choose between one or the other? Or should we throw both of them away? Because of course, some might say that neither of these expressions or practices are actually authentic, or "really indigenous," and that authentic indigenous culture is found further away, deeper inside . . .

We have learned to think that the "otherness" that indigenous people supposedly manifest is a radical difference, a distinct ontology, with an essence all its own, something innate and inherited. All of these terms—essence, ontology, etc.—have a naturalizing undercurrent; the racializing sediments therein are quite clearly visible. Nevertheless, an almost obligatory first conclusion of the occurrence I have narrated is that if—as was seen here—there are two versions of what it is to be indigenous, many more have probably existed and still exist today with multiple and varying forms and contents. I don't want to say that "being indigenous" is equivalent to putting on and taking off an identity as if it were a suit or a hat. Indeed, not just anyone can claim this heritage, nor can just anyone deny it. What I am suggesting is that we should be interested, precisely, in the conditions that allow for the adoption or expression of this form of identification, more so than in evaluating its level of authenticity or its historical depth. And if this is so, perhaps we will be able to let go of the more ontological dimension of this form of identification, the naturalizing substrate that associates "indigenous" with an essence transmitted from generation to generation, even if that might seem counterintuitive to common sense.

More than an ontological question (knowing who is or is not indigenous and why), my question is a sociogenetic one, that is, an investigation of the genesis of each version of indigenous identity. Insofar as it is possible, I aim to reconstruct the historical process through which being indigenous has been endowed with certain content in specific situations. In the case of Milpa Alta, this question entails a long history that can be documented at least since the end of the sixteenth century.[3] In this text, I will focus exclusively on the social relations that, throughout the twentieth century, determined the representation of the inhabitants of Milpa Alta as the heirs to the Aztecs. We will see that, throughout this process, scientific and artistic productions about the inhabitants of Milpa Alta played a central role. Specifically, we will see the strong interactions between

3 For a more complete analysis and for a reconstruction of this process since the sixteenth century, see López Caballero 2012.

scientists, artists, and their models and informants. Finally, in the conclusion, we will systematically—as this example allows and as is suggested by the editor of this volume—unsettle the distinction between essence and matter, between original and copy.

The State, the Indigenous, the Anthropologist: The Three Threads of the National Regimes of Alterity

It is well known that, while still aligned with the nineteenth-century, evolutionist, racial paradigms (Powell 1968; Staab 1959), the ideas of Manuel Gamio (1917) systematize an "integrationist" approach to populations categorized as autochthonous. Gamio argues that "la raza indígena" (the indigenous race) could and should be thought of as a contribution to the nation instead of simply dissolving away. If this had not yet happened—still according to Gamio—the reason should be sought in the profound lack of knowledge about these groups, which impeded their effective governance and integration. The populations categorized in this way were converted into "objects of study," into subjects of state intervention and modernization, prerequisites for their more efficient and rapid "assimilation." This doctrine would allow for anthropological thought in post-revolutionary Mexico to establish close ties with a project of national construction and to become a "governmental anthropology" (Castañeda 2003, 243), of which M. Gamio would be one of the primary creators and promoters. This policy has received the generic name of "indigenismo" ("indigenism").

It is an oft-repeated story that Manuel Gamio met Franz Boas at the Escuela Internacional de Arqueología y Etnología Americanas, founded in Mexico by the German anthropologist between 1911 and 1912. There, the young Gamio was likely intellectually influenced by Boas, primarily with regard to his ideas about cultural relativism. However, what is less known is that among the first generation of students at the Escuela Internacional de Antropología, in addition to M. Gamio there was a woman, probably the first Mexican woman to study archeology and ethnology. Her name was Isabel Ramírez Castañeda. The information available to us about this anthropologist is limited. She spoke Nahuatl fluently (called "Mexican" at the time); she was educated to be a schoolteacher, and she had taught in Milpa Alta, which perhaps was her birthplace. How did she discover the world of anthropologists? No clue is available in this regard. Was she the one who had the curiosity and initiative to enter this scientific community? Or was she "discovered" by anthropologists in one of their visits to the region? Is she the person who initiated the long series of exchange between academics and natives of Milpa Alta? Did she begin the list of Nahuatl speakers who would look to negotiate as best as possible their status of "informants" with anthropologists?

We know that Isabel Ramírez took courses at the Escuela de Antropología until its closing in 1914. We also know that she was survived by two publications, one of which speaks about her region of origin, "El folklore de Milpa Alta, DF, México" (The folklore of Milpa Alta, Mexico City, Mexico) (Ramírez Castañeda 1912), and comprises a story in Nahuatl and its translation with an introductory note. It is the first bibliographic mention of Milpa Alta, which she wrote for the eighteenth session of the International Congress of Americanists (London, 1912), and which was probably presented by Boas at the event, since Ramirez was not able to attend the meeting.[4] This contribution is part of a larger research project on "Aztec" language and folklore directed by Boas and other students and professors at the Escuela Internacional de Antropología, which led to a number of publications about Milpa Alta (Boas 1920; Boas and Haeberlin 1924; González Casanova 1920). As is the norm with Boasian research, these compilations rarely include any analysis. Only the article by I. Ramírez—though it does not offer documentary proof—explains the origins and the cultural wealth of Milpa Alta, whose towns had been founded by "Aztec noble families who escaped the siege of México-Tenochtitlán with their riches and their servants after the conquest by Cortés . . . They remained safely in the same place until the arrival of the Franciscan monks" (Ramírez Castañeda,1912, 352).

Implicated in the formation of the post-revolutionary State, the institutionalization of anthropology—which began with the Escuela Internacional de Antropología—coincides chronologically with the (re)presentation of Milpa Alta as an enclave of preservation of Aztec culture. This representation was first articulated in writing by Isabel Ramírez. Born at the same time, Milpa Alta and anthropology developed alongside one another throughout the century as "complementary sisters," mutually feeding each other, taking shape together, and influencing each other.

Giving the Town a Face

"In one house, there was a nice young woman [Isabel Ramírez?], who knew how to read papers and write . . . I learned how to recognize one, two, three letters and also to read and write at this school . . . In 1908 when I went to school . . . the children had to be standing in front of the school by seven thirty in the morning, when the bell rang. It was then that all the boys and girls ran to take their places . . . We studied twice a day and the girls who went to school wearing dirty shoes, unwashed and unkempt, were sent to the boys' school . . . It was embarrassing for the boys to wash and comb our hair . . . All this took place in the year of 1908 when we were first taught to live properly" (Horcasitas 1965, 24–29).

We find ourselves in 1908, during the pax of Porfirio Díaz, the dictator-president who governed Mexico for more than twenty years. In Milpa Alta, a nice young woman labors to teach the campesino children to read and write in Spanish; their mother tongue is Nahuatl, perhaps also her own as well. This young woman embodies the efforts of a government that could only imagine modernity as the abandonment of "primitive" customs, beginning with language. Among her students, this one little girl—avid to learn and keenly excited by the order offered by national educational programs (the uniforms, the official ceremonies where children would line up and salute the flag)—bequeaths us this testimonial in Nahuatl fifty years after the event. Her name is Julia, but she is more widely known as Luz Jiménez. Not only did she not give up her mother tongue, but her memoirs and stories, published in the 1960s in Nahuatl, will be celebrated as a "classic of contemporary Nahuatl literature" (León-Portilla, 1993, 358).

4 For a concise biography and information on her scientific career, see Ruiz Martínez (2003, 2006) and Rutsch (2003, 2007, 2010).

Actually, before the modernizing and Hispanicizing policies of the Porfiriato could attain their goals, armed uprisings broke out across the entire country beginning in 1910.[5] In Milpa Alta, no one could imagine the years of war, death, and violence that would follow. First, they faced the abuse of the Carrancista army as they stole, burned houses and harassed the young women. Milpa Alta would soon be in the line of fire between the Zapatistas and the federal government; conflict in the region would become more and more common. Later, in 1916, a terrible massacre would decimate the majority of males in the region, among them Jiménez's father and uncles. Milpa Alta would finally be abandoned completely for a number of years. The women and children would first flee to Xochimilco, then later to the capital. These events are narrated in Luz Jiménez's memoirs; she decides to end her story with her departure from Milpa Alta, when her campesino childhood ends as well, "just when her adult life begins." (Karttunen 1994, 195).[6] From that moment, little by little, she became an icon of Indian-ness, exalted by post-revolutionary artists. Because when Jiménez joined the impoverished masses of the capital, revolutionary and nationalist fervor—the "Mexican renaissance"—was beginning to emerge. The search for an authentically Mexican art and the search for an indigenous soul to discover, explore, and exhibit gave Jiménez the opportunity to augment her options, otherwise likely limited to jobs as a maid or cook. There are no accurate accounts of these years of her life, but according to the commemorative biography written following her death, the artists at the outdoor art schools established beginning in 1913 would have met her in approximately 1917 or 1918 at a beauty contest in Santa Anita—one of the promenades for capital-dwellers, near Lake Xochimilico.

As Mexican anthropology continued its slow process of institutionalization, young and revolutionary artists—still engrossed with the utopia the new regime embodied and particularly with the mission of "forging the nation" (*forjando patria*)—discovered Jiménez, the woman who, for them, represented "mother earth" (Jean Charlot) and the essence of Indian-ness. It was right at this moment when Indian-ness began to mean "Mexican-ness" as well This was how she became a model at the Academia de San Carlos, the school of fine arts, and later at the outdoor art schools in Coyoacán and Chimalistac, where the post-revolutionary artistic avant-garde was studying. Two painters—the Mexican Fernando Leal (1896–1964) and later the French artist Jean Charlot (1898–1979)—shared her as their favorite model.[7] They visited her town and marveled at the pilgrimage to the neighboring town of Chalma, which they saw as the expression of a resurgence of the pre-Hispanic past.[8]

5 In 1910, the wars of the Revolution broke out and in 1914, the tiny Luz was witness to the arrival of Emiliano Zapata to Milpa Alta, where he was received with enthusiasm by the population (Horcasitas 1989 [1967], 104–105).

6 This account of Luz's life draws from Karttunen 1994 and 1999.

7 Jean Charlot explains in an interview with his son John: "She had been already a model, a special model, we could say of Fernando Leal, and she certainly was my favorite model" (Interview with Jean Charlot, August 7, 1971 consulted August 14, 2009 : http://libweb.hawaii.edu/libdept/charlotcoll/charlot.html).

8 Until the end of her day, Luz would maintain close, lasting relationships with these two artists. Jean Charlot became her daughter s godfather, and he introduced her to all of his artistic and intellectual circles. For more on Luz s life, see: CONACULTA (2000); Karttunen (1994, 1998, 1999); León-Portilla (1993).

One of the first frescoes in which Jiménez appears is "La fiesta del señor de Chalma" (The Feast of the Lord of Chalma) painted by F. Leal in the Escuela Nacional Preparatoria in 1922, in which she appears as just one of the women participating in the ceremony. She also appears in "La Creación" (The Creation), Diego Rivera's first fresco in that establishment (1923) and later in a series the artist painted for the Secretaría de Educación between 1923 and 1928. Finally, around 1929, she would work for Rivera for the Palacio Nacional frescoes. Meanwhile, José Clemente Orozco painted her, Edward Weston and Tina Modotti photographed her, and artists like Roberto Montenegro sculpted her for the majority of the national monuments erected during the period.

Through these works of art (paintings, murals, photographs, sculptures), an increasingly clear profile would begin to take shape, not so much of Jiménez's personality, but rather of a kind of "universal and monumental indigenous person." Fernando Leal expressed as much when he spoke of his indigenous models, in particular of Jiménez: "I liked to give their racial type a monumentality that was not diluted by Western standards" (cited in Karttunen 1994, 201). For Anita Brenner, Jiménez became "the classic native woman" in contemporary painting.[9] Years later, for his part, Jean Charlot would describe her in this way:

> There is a whole image there that she projected. Now, many of the other girls could put their village clothes on and pose with a pot on their shoulders, but they didn't do it, so to speak, to the manner born. And Luz [...] could do it both naturally, as the Indian girl that she was, and know enough so that she could imagine from the outside, so to speak, what the painters or the writers saw in her, and she helped both see things because of that sort of double outlook she could have on herself and her tradition." (Charlot 1971)

Luz Jiménez's success resided then in her ability to "stage" something (herself) that the painters could (or imagined they could?) recognize as "Indigenous," as autochthonous, emanating from the depths of a distant past. Apparently, Jiménez kept a necessary distance that enabled her to use her "culture" and extract recognizable features from it for the painters. In the words of one of her biographers, "Luz allowed herself to be a screen on which the painters projected their own concepts of the Indian woman" (Karttunen 1994, 201). During that short period, that ephemeral moment, the artistic, intellectual, and political avant-gardes were actually looking to understand who those masses of indigenous campesinos were: to assign them a profile that after a few decades would become a prototype, and to exalt them in an alterity composed of purity, essence, and timeless authenticity; an alterity that, extricated from history, could be contained, dominated, and suppressed both symbolically and physically.

Ten years later, toward the end of the 1920s, with her daughter and her mother in her charge, Jiménez found herself in a difficult economic situation. The artists closest to her (Charlot, Brenner, Weston, Modotti)had left Mexico. The high spirits linked

9 Political activist, anthropologist, journalist, and writer, Anita Brenner (1905–1974) was a key figure in the intellectual and artistic life of the period. She and Luz also maintained a long and close friendship. Luz frequently worked at her home. Brenner was also Luz's daughter's godmother, as well as a constant help in finding income. For more on Anita Brenner, see CONACULTA (2006), Glusker (1998).

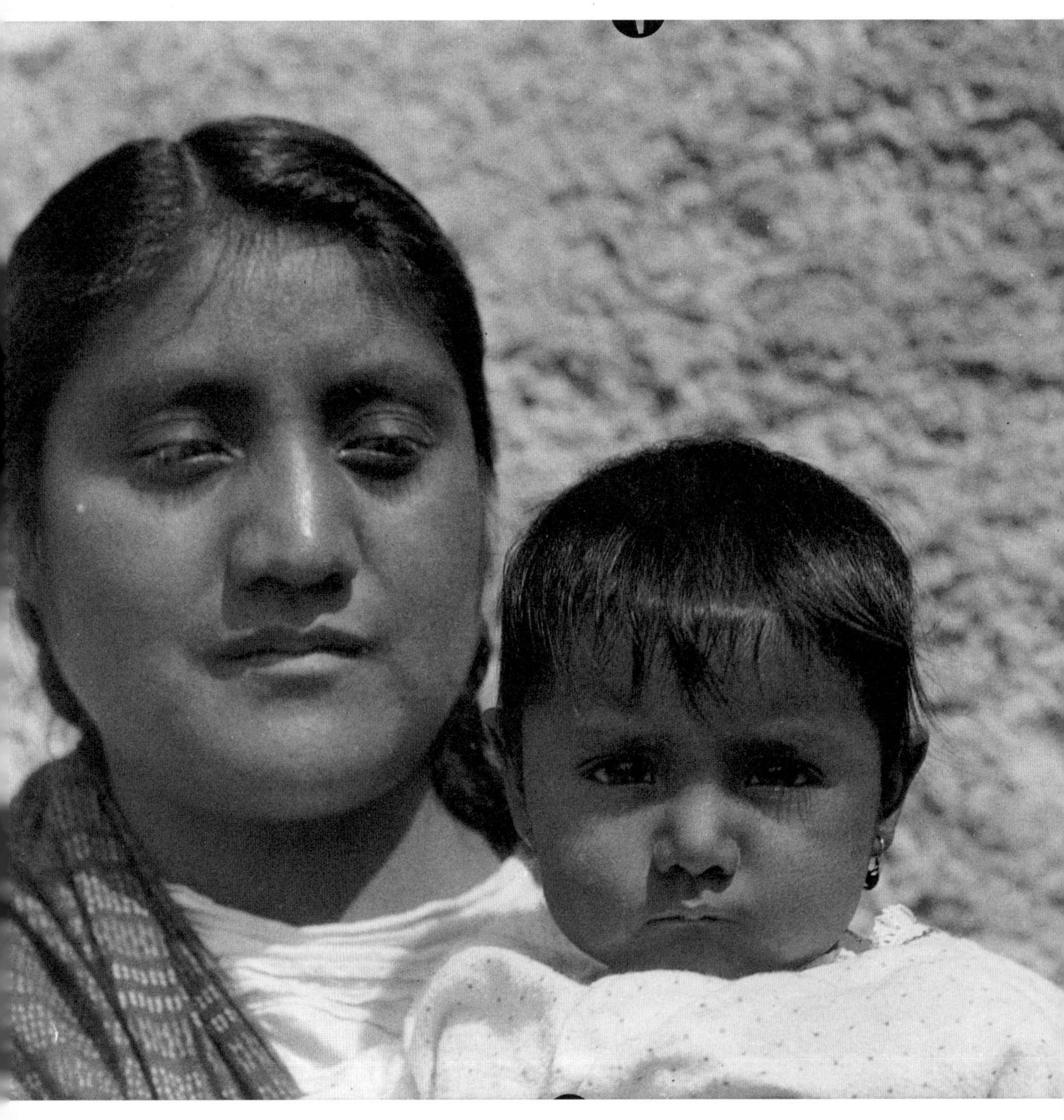

Tina Modotti, Luz Jiménez e hija, un retrato, 1925.
Photo archive INAH (35303) CONACULTA.INAH.SINAFO.FN.MEXICO.

to revolutionary utopia were in decline, just as was Mexican muralism as well. The political environment was changing, and the new regime was consolidating itself and institutionalizing. Brenner, was the one to come to her aid once again. Brenner had emigrated to New York in 1927 to publish a book about the "Mexican renaissance"; there, she met Boas and decided to begin a thesis with him. In that university setting, she met an American researcher interested in the Nahuatl language: Benjamin Lee Whorf (better known for his work with Edward Sapir on the relationship between language and perception), and she recommended Luz Jiménez to him as an informant. Jiménez then discovered a new facet of what was perceived as the "cultural wealth" around her—her cultural heritage and especially the Nahuatl language—that probably became for her a kind of socioeconomic resource.

The Work With Linguists: Reencountering the "Aztec" Language

Whorf, a linguist by training, and Alden Mason, a former student of Boas who was also part of the Escuela Internacional de Antropología in Mexico, had established a genetic classification of linguistic affiliations between oral autochthonous languages, following the comparative method of Edward Sapir. In this way, they connected the autochthonous language of the Mexico City area—which they called "Aztec"—with the language of the Coras and the Huicholes in northwestern Mexico, as well as with the Hopi language in Colorado.

Whorf dedicated two publications to Nahuatl; the first, from 1937, addresses the historical evolution of the language. In his second work, from 1946, in addition to the documentary evidence with which he usually worked, he added linguistic material collected "from living speech." In this work, he references the region where he worked on what he calls the "Aztec language," which comprises a set of similar and mutually intelligible dialects in central Mexico. The origin of this family of "Aztec" languages is found in the language spoken in México-Tenochtitlan and in the surrounding valleys prior to La Conquista. Whorf calls this language the "Classical dialect" and which, contrary to what might be thought, is not a dead language:

> "The language is not spoken any longer in Mexico City . . . but it is still the native speech of Indian towns in and around the Valley. The dialect of the village of Milpa Alta D.F. . . . is one of these survivals, in my opinion, one of those which are most like Cl [the Classical dialect]." (Whorf 1946, 368)

In 1930, Whorf lived for six months between Milpa Alta and the neighboring town of Tepoztlán, investigating the Classical dialect. He worked with individuals he describes as "excellent informants": Melesio Gonzales from Milpa Alta, Mariano Rojas from Tepoztlán, and none other than Luz Jiménez. The result of his research deals with the linguistic particularities of the "Aztec dialect" spoken in Milpa Alta due to its proximity to the Classical dialect (ibid., 368). Thus, the connection between contemporary Milpa Alta and the Aztec empire was extended by those scholars, with the contribution, albeit passive, of Luz Jiménez. The language spoken in Milpa Alta came to be understood as the one that supposedly traversed the century with no perceptible modifications. We must remember, nonetheless, that Whorf insisted that his interest in classical Nahuatl came above all from his Mexican colleagues (ibid., 368). It is possible, then, that the work of Mexican linguists and historians on autochthonous languages went hand in hand with a nationalist and indigenist ideological project for which the recuperation of an original classical culture—that of the Aztec empire—would be indispensable.

This political project culminated in the institutionalization and solidification of an understanding of pre-Hispanic cultures—and particularly of the Aztec empire—as original antecedents of the post-revolutionary regime. But, in a parallel way, the indigenous world ended up being attractive not only for scholars and artists but also for lovers of ancient traditions and esoteric knowledge. Byron McAfee arrived in Mexico from the United States in 1906, as an employee of a U.S. oil company. He was passionate about ruins and the ancient culture of Mexico, as well as about Nahuatl language. Along with other compatriots, he created a group of travelers whose hobby would be learning Nahuatl with a native of Tepoztlán, a town he visited regularly, in addition to Milpa Alta, beginning in 1925. Ten years later, in 1936, he typed and compiled approximately six hundred Nahuatl language lessons that he had personally taken. Luz Jiménez also collaborated with him on them.[10]

At the beginning of the 1940s, a young man from the United States joined McAfee's group to provide new momentum. Robert Barlow was twenty-two years old and since the age of nineteen, he had been the inheritor of the rights to the work of H. P. Lovecraft, with whom he had an intense correspondence, comprised of fantasies and fictions, until the writer's death. Barlow discovered Mexico and the pre-Colombian world as a new source for his creative imagination. He moved to Mexico in 1941 to learn classical Nahuatl. Out of the meeting with McAfee, they created—via their own means—the journal Tlalocan, in which they brought together all kinds of materials about Mexican native languages and autochthonous culture in general: articles about glyphs, documents transcribed and translated from Nahuatl, codices, myths, etc. This publication became a university reference for those interested in pre-Hispanic language and texts—both written and oral. At the end of the 1940s, Barlow took over as the chair of anthropology and Nahuatl literature at Mexico City College, an American university founded in Mexico City.[11] In addition to publishing several texts about Milpa Alta (Barlow 1960), Barlow taught Nahuatl with Luz Jiménez until his suicide in 1951 (see Mexico City Collegian, January 18, 1951).[12]

A bit prior to these events, around 1948, in Barlow's home, Jiménez met another anthropology student, Fernando Horcasitas, a North American born in Los Angeles to Mexican parents, with whom Jiménez established a long-lasting, productive collaboration during the following fifteen years. The two of them continued taking Barlow's Nahuatl classes and, once Horcasitas joined the editorial board of Tlalocan, they began

10 For more on Byron Lee McAfee's life and activities, consult: (www.oac.cdlib.org/findaid/ark:/13030/kt7489p0sj/).

11 Currently it is the Universidad de las Américas.

12 Barlow had William S. Burroughs as a student; in a letter, Burroughs told his friend Allen Ginsberg the story of his professor s suicide. See Burroughs 1993.

to publish texts in Nahuatl. In 1960, the journal published a story by Jiménez, arduously prepared by Barlow. But Luz and Horcasitas above all worked together on a collection of stories—*crónicas* (non-fiction chronicles) from Jiménez's town—that she dictated, he transcribed phonetically, and both translated. In 1963, Horcasitas began a job at the Universidad Nacional, and Jiménez accompanied him to teach there. When he returned to ask her for oral texts in Nahuatl, this time she chose to recount her memoirs: the story of her childhood from the moment in 1910 when she remembered her teacher, that kind young woman referenced earlier in this text.

In 1965, on her way to look for another job in Mexico City, Jiménez was run over by a car. She died the same day. For this reason, she did not get a chance to see her memoirs published, first in Nahuatl and Spanish (Horcasitas 1989 [1967]), and then in Nahuatl and English in 1972. It is significant that the preface was written by historian Miguel León-Portilla, the leading specialist in the pre-Hispanic Nahuatl world. León-Portilla establishes the association between pre-Hispanic origins and Jiménez's heritage explicitly: "We could say that the image of the events in the book at times reaches a level of expressive force comparable to that found in other indigenous texts from the sixteenth century, like those in which the Aztec versions of the conquest are conserved." (ibid., 9)

Eleven years later, Horcasitas published a new compilation of stories by Jiménez, in which he appears as editor, attributing to her the status of author this time, rather than simply informant (Jiménez 1979). In effect, despite multiple collaborations with different anthropologists, her role was always limited to "informing" the research, as the social and academic norms of the times dictated. The mediating role played by artists and researchers seemed unavoidable, although in the case of Horcasitas he limited himself to transcribing, organizing, and publishing the texts. The numerous subsequent editions of these works are testimony to the success of the stories, the liveliness of her memories, and the force of the images she transmits within them.

The Original Indigenous Woman, a Product of Contingency

This is how Luz Jiménez traversed the first half of the twentieth century: directly providing an image of indigenous beauty and authenticity, of idealized "Indian-ness" so successful as to become dominant even in our own time. In the same way, she fed anthropologists and linguists with her oral narrations and her Nahuatl language—refined and complex, a model of classicism and purity, as well. She is the voice and the face of the ancestral past, of the origins. Jiménez embodies what Daniel Fabre (2008) calls "the man-world," referring to that anthropological obsession with finding what anthropologists perceive as the "last" witness to a finite world, about to disappear and which must be rescued from oblivion. Her biographer seems to come to the same conclusion when she affirms that in her narratives, "though Luz is always present, her autobiography seems more like the history of a community than that of an individual (Kartunnen 1994, 195).[13]

13 Writing about Jiménez, Miguel León Portilla uses very similar terms: Jiménez's stories "are an autobiography in which her entire people is present." (León Portilla 1993, 357).

Slowly, with Jiménez, a definition of what it means to be indigenous would be sketched out and later stabilized, utilizing all those traits that were perceived as the most visibly different: language, rural life, geographical isolation, phenotype. In her story, the roles of model and author are constantly shifting and in flux. Jiménez embodies the source of indigenous authenticity that painters and linguists were looking for, and at the same time, she is its active producer: she is representation and author. Nevertheless, we cannot forget that this back-and-forth between representation and creation was always inscribed in hierarchized positions and that she never enjoyed the explicit and openly recognized authority to speak independently about her own heritage. The artists and scientists would only retain her ability to show and to "make audible" that which they perceived as her indigenous vein in order to transform it into national heritage.

Luz Jiménez's career illustrates one of the multiple elements that contributed to make Milpa Alta into an island of pre-Hispanic authenticity, as the never-ending list of anthropologists working in there —including myself—testifies. Milpa Alta is incorporated in this way into the national topography, imagined as a remnant from the pre-Hispanic world, with Jiménez as its witness. This process allows us to see that identification as indigenous, as heirs to the pre-Hispanic world, does not find its origins in a timeless, ahistorical essence, but rather through a series of interactions, encounters, and relationships that were integral in determining the stabilization of certain profiles and contents. These contents, today currently recognized as indigenous, are actually contingent and historical, products of social relationships and not their determinants. Instead of looking to reconstruct an "indigenous logic" that would underlie social practices, that would even be unconscious for the actors, here I have tried to restore a sense of the historicity of those cultural expressions. It is worth mentioning that being interested in the social and historical conditions of indigenous identification does not mean evaluating the authenticity of a specific culture, nor reaching a final conclusion about the identity of a specific individual or social group. This is a problem actually devoid of meaning if the analysis is centered on the lived experience of the actors. In my view, reconstructing the historicity of this form of identification is equivalent to renouncing to a "correct" definition of indigenous identity in favor of concentrating on the circulations, exchanges, and accidents that have allowed for its use as a marker of difference. The dialectical process in which both anthropologists and artists, as well as informants or models, participate—despite occupying very different positions—in order to elaborate a certain kind of identification is understood here neither as an imposition nor as an instrumentalization of the dominant discourses, but rather as the—necessary—use of nomenclatures to organize social experience.

What can be destabilized, then, is the basic opposition between essence and matter, original and copy, which can also be understood as the difference between being and doing, or between definition and use. The first term of all of these binaries refers to stability, to the innate, to that which remains; the second refers to variability, to contingency, to the superficial. Jiménez's story alters this opposition by showing that, contrary to what is usually accepted, the first term of these binaries (essence) is a product of the materiality of social action, practice, and use. That is, indigeneity, conceived as a stable, permanent, and invariable heritage that determines all its concrete realization—

which is the day-to-day expression of said identity—must actually be understood instead as the result of contingency and materiality. But if we accept that essence is the product of its material realization—that, in a certain way, the original is only actualized through its multiple copies—the distinction itself becomes inoperative. The goal of finding the essence, the base level of indigeneity against which social practices are contrasted, must then be set aside. Instead, we must focus on understanding the social and historical conditions that have allowed for certain forms of identification to acquire those contents and to occupy specific positions in a hierarchical field of identifications. Adopting this analytical strategy allows for the inversion of the more classical framework that supposes that indigeneity, either of a person or a group, determines their way of establishing social relations. What can be seen here is that it is in social relations themselves where the distinctions allowing for the identification of someone or something as indigenous are produced. Instead of the "core essence" or the "cultural logic" of a social group that might "explain" the members' modes of behavior, the case I have detailed enables me to formulate another perspective: it is about understanding and analyzing the challenges and the stakes involved for actors in the social realm. These experiences and interactions have made it possible for there to be gatherings of Nahuatl speakers in Santa Ana today, organized by inhabitants who seem to recognize the national anthem and the feasts of saints as more "indigenous" than certain countercultural manifestations like the "pre-Hispanic" dances of the *concheros*.

Translated by John Pluecker

DOCUMENTS

Archive of Byron McAfee: www.oac.cdlib.org/findaid/ark:/13030/kt7489p0sj/).

"Students and Faculty Mourn Passing of Professor Barlow," in : Mexico City Collegian, January 18, 1951.

Interview with Jean Charlot, on August 7, 1971 consulted on August 14, 2009: http://libweb.hawaii.edu/libdept/charlotcoll/charlot.html

BIBLIOGRAPHY

Boas, Franz. "Cuentos en mexicano de Milpa Alta, D.F., recogidos por Franz Boas y traducidos por José María Arreola." The Journal of American Folklore 33 (1920): 127.

Boas, Franz and Herman K. Haeberlin. "The Folktales in Modern Nahuatl." Journal of American Folklore 37 (1924): 345–370.

Burroughs, William S. The Letters of William S. Burroughs: Vol. 1 1945–1959. London: Penguin, 1993.

Castañeda, Quetzil E. "Stocking's Historiography of Influence: The 'Story of Boas', Gamio and Redfield at the Cross-'Road to Light.'" Critique of Anthropology 23 (2003) 235–263.

CONACULTA. Luz Jiménez, símbolo de un pueblo milenario: 1987–1965. Mexico: CONACULTA/INBA/Museo Casa Estudio Diego Rivera, 2000.

———. Annita Brenner: Vision de una época / Vision of an Age. Mexico: CONACULTA /Editorial RM, 2006.

Fabre, Daniel. "Chinoiserie des Lumières. Variations sur l'individu-monde." L'Homme (2008), 269–299.

Gamio, Manuel. Forjando patria. Mexico City: Porrúa, 1960.

Glusker, Susannah J. Anita Brenner: A Mind of Her Own. Austin: Texas University Press, 1998.

González Casanova, Pablo. "Cuento en mexicano de Milpa Alta, DF." The Journal of American Folklore 33 (1920), 188–200.

Horcasitas, Fernando. De Porfirio Díaz a Zapata: memoria náhuatl de Milpa Alta. México: Universidad Nacional Autónoma de México Coordinación de Humanidades, 1989 [1967].

Horcasitas, Fernando, ed. Life and Death in Milpa Alta: A Nahuatl Chronicle of Diaz and Zapata. From the Nahuatl Recollections of Doña Luz Jiménez. Norman: University of Oklahoma Press, 1972.

Jiménez, Luz. Los cuentos en náhuatl de doña Luz Jiménez. Ed. Fernando Horcasitas and Sarah O. De Ford. Mexico City: Universidad Nacional Autónoma de México, 1979.

Karttunen, Frances. "Images in Paint, Pictures in Words: Doña Luz Jiménez (ca. 1895–1965)." Between Wolds: Interpreters, Guides and Survivors. Ed. Frances Karttunen. Rutgers: Rutgers University Press, 1994, 192–214.

———. "Indigenous Writing as a Vehicle of Postconquest Continuity and Change in Mesoamérica." In Native Traditions in the Postconquest World, edited by Elizabeth Hill Boone and Tom Cummins. Washington, D.C.: Dumbarton Oaks Research Library and Collection, 1998, 421–447.

———. "The linguistic career of doña Luz Jiménez." In Estudios de Cultura Náhuatl 30 (1999), 267–274.

León-Portilla, Miguel. "Lecturas de la palabra de doña Luz Jiménez." In Estudios de Cultura Náhuatl 23 (1993), 361–363.

López Caballero, Paula. "Altérités intimes, altérités éloignées : La greffe du multiculturalisme en Amérique latine." Critique Internationale 51 (2011), 129–149.

———. Les Indiens et la Nation au Mexique: Une ethnographie historique de l'altérité. Paris: Karthala, 2012.

———. "La formation nationale de l'altérité : Art, science et politique dans la production de l'autochtonie à Milpa Alta (Mexico), 1900–2010." L'Homme 203–204 (2012): Anthropologie début du siècle, 239–264.

Powell, T. G. "Mexican Intellectuals and the Indian Question, 1876–1911." The Hispanic American Historical Review 48(1)(1968), 19–36.

Ramírez Castañeda, Isabel. "El Folklore de Milpa Alta, D.F., México." International

Congress of Americanists: Proceedings of the XVIII Session (1912), 352–361.
Ruiz Martínez, Apen. Insiders and Outsiders in Mexican Archaeology (1890–1930). Doctoral thesis. Austin: The University of Texas at Austin, 2003.
Ruiz Martínez, Apen (2006): "Zelia Nuttall e Isabel Ramírez: las distintas formas de practicar y escribir sobre la arqueología en el México de inicios del siglo XX," in: Cadernos Pagu (27), pp. 99-133.
Rutsch, Mechthild (2003): "Isabel Ramírez Casteñeda (1881-1943): Una anti-historia de los inicios de la antropología mexicana," in: Cuicuilco 10(28), pp. 1-18.
Rutsch, Mechthild. (2007): Entre el campo y el gabinete. Nacionales y extranjeros en la profesionalización de la antropología mexicana (1877-1920). Mexico City: INAH / IIAntropológicas, UNAM.
Rutsch, Mechthild. (2010): "'Vivir una vida nueva': Jorge Engerand (1877-1961), entre la antropología mexicana y la estadounidense de principios del siglo XX." in: Nueva antropología XXIII(73): 147-69.
Staab, Martin. (1959): "Indigenism and Racism in Mexican Thought: 1857 - 1911." in : Journal of Inter-American Studies 1(4): 405 - 23.
Whorf, Benjamin Lee (1937): "The Origin of Aztec Tl," in: American Anthropologist 39(2), pp. 265-274.
———. Linguistic Structures of Native America. New York: The Viking Fund Publications in Anthropology, 367–397.

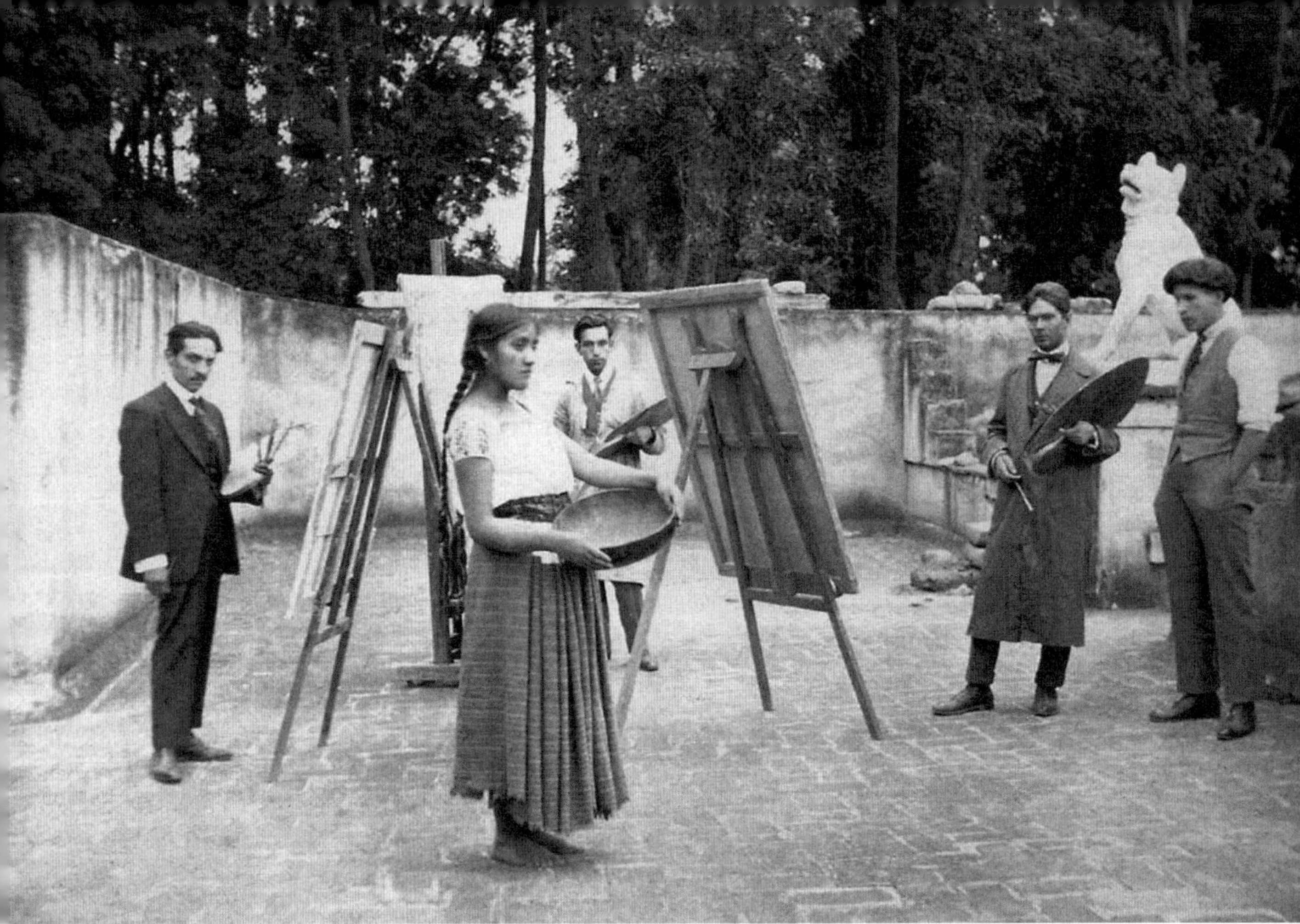

Luz Jiménez posing for Ramón Alva de la Canal, Fernando Leal, and Francisco Díaz de León at the Art School in Coyoacán, ca. 1920.

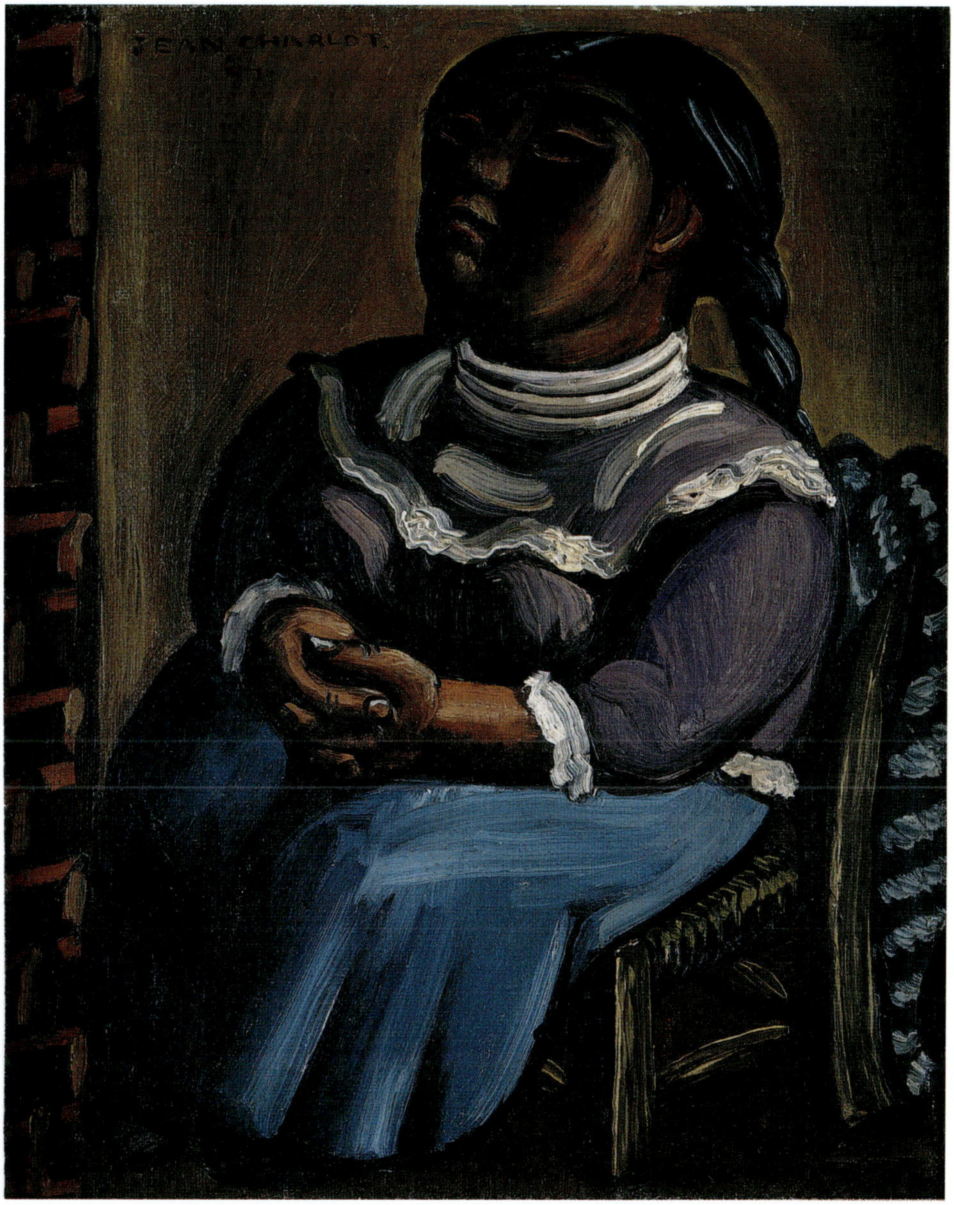

Jean Charlot, Luz, 1924.
Oil on canvas, 36 x 28.4 cm

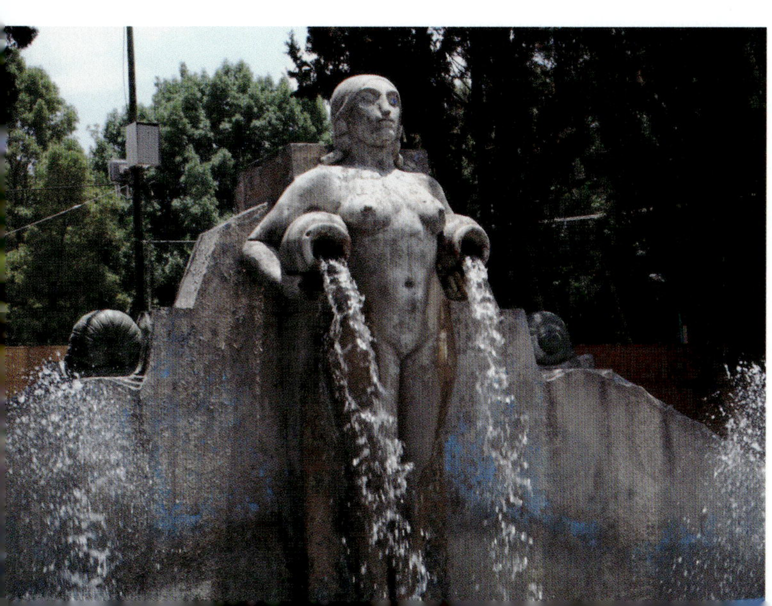

La Fuente de los cántaros, Mexico, 1927.

Exhibition catalogue cover Ocumicho : Arrebato del encuentro, curated by Mercedes Iturbe Argüelles, Museo de Arte de Moderno, Mexico City, 1993

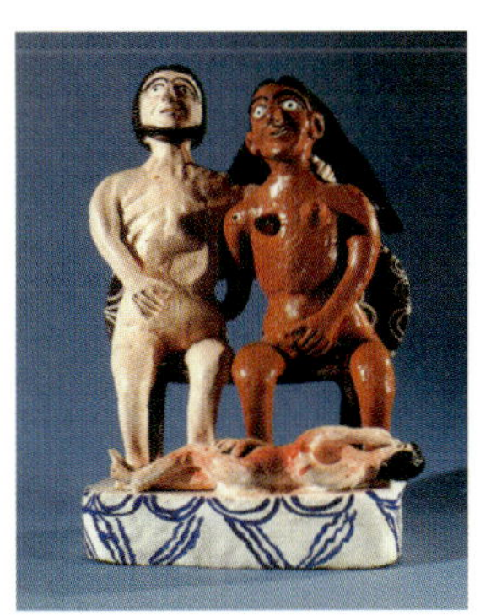

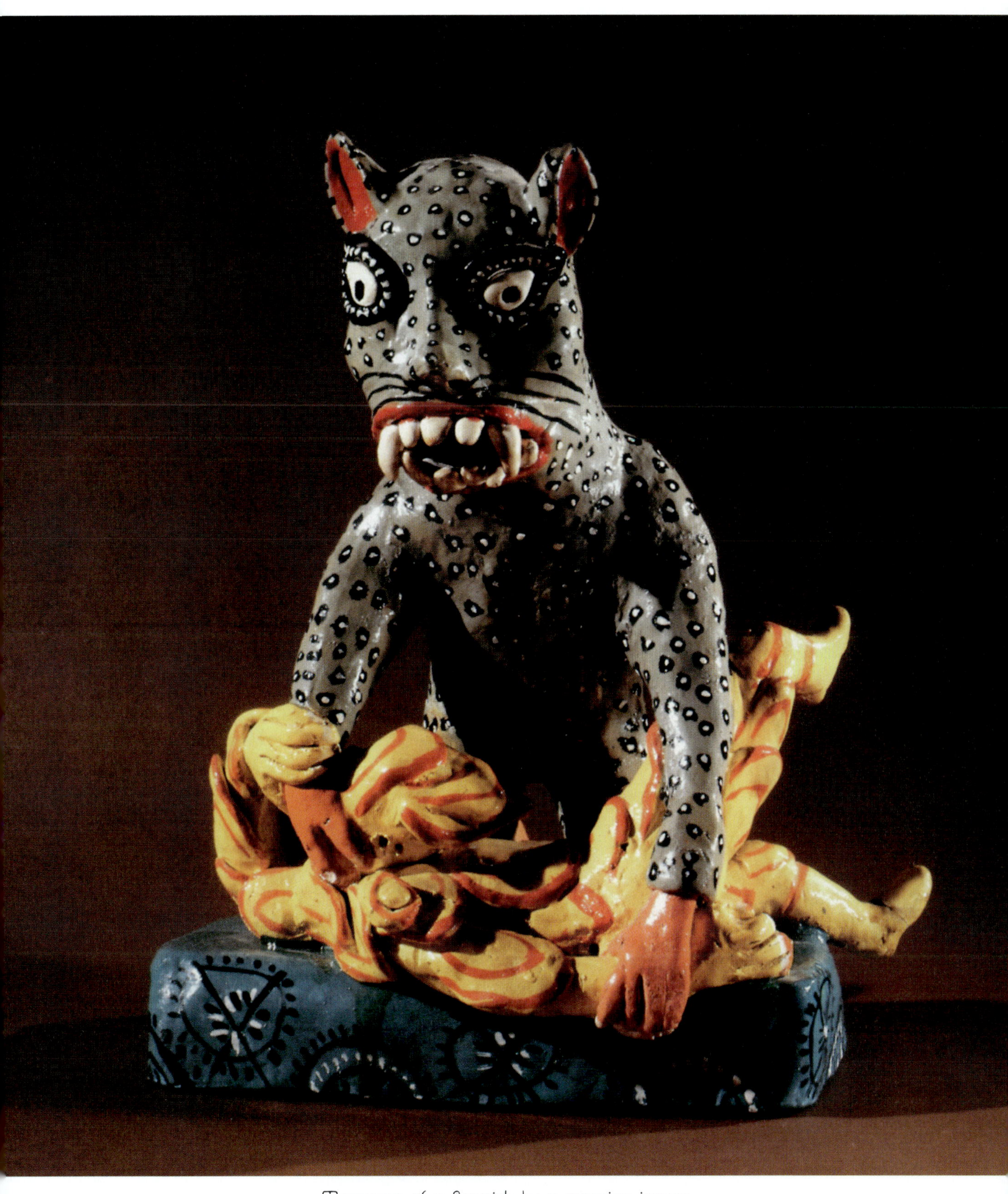

Massacre of a Spanish by a warring jaguar
Shown at the exhibition: Ocumicho: Arrebato del Encuentro, Museo de Arte Moderno, México, 1992
Photographer: Lourdes Grobet

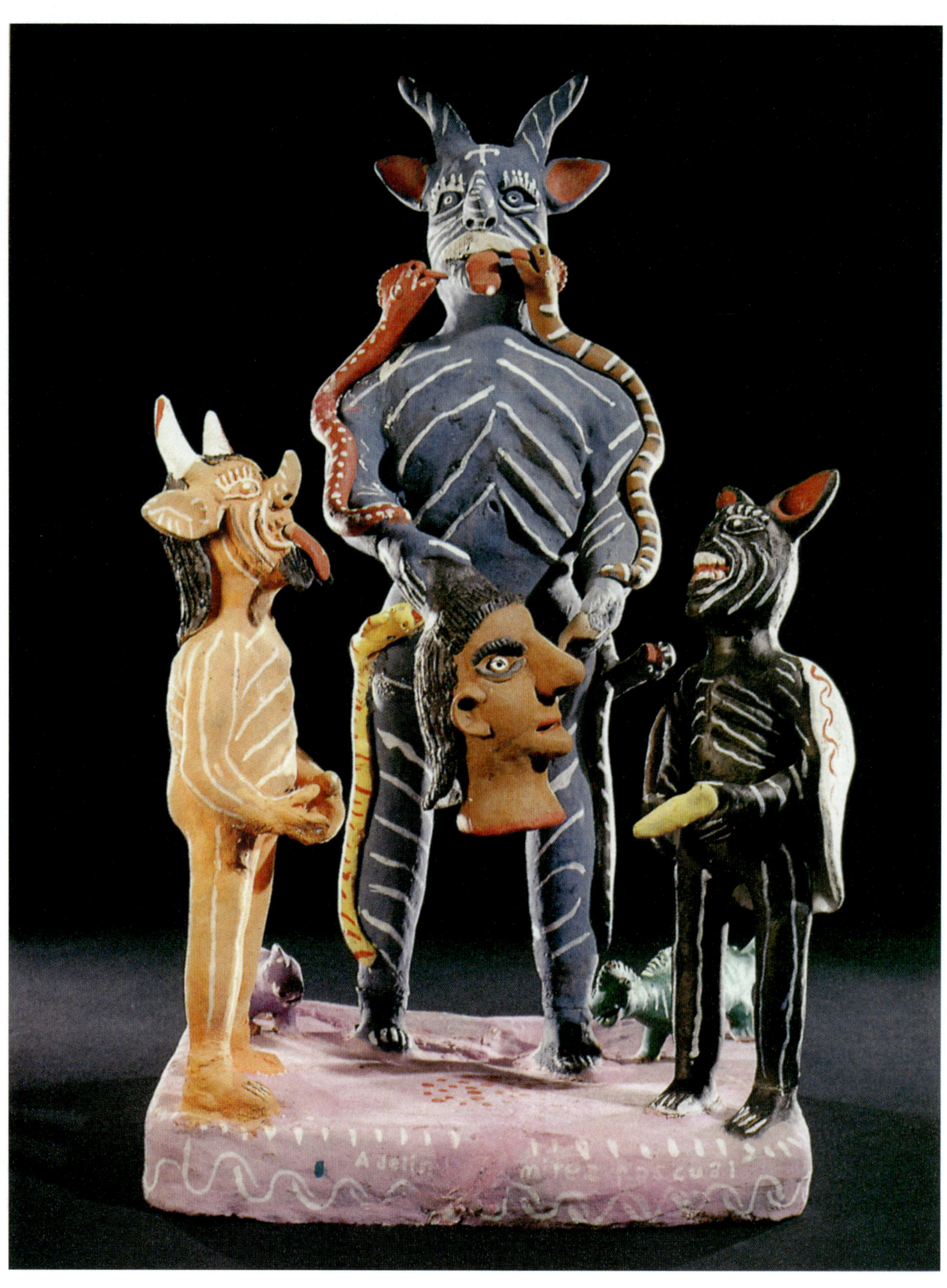

Qu'un sang impur abreuve nos sillons
Shown at the exhibition Les Trois Couleurs d'Ocumicho, Ambassade du México, Paris, 1989

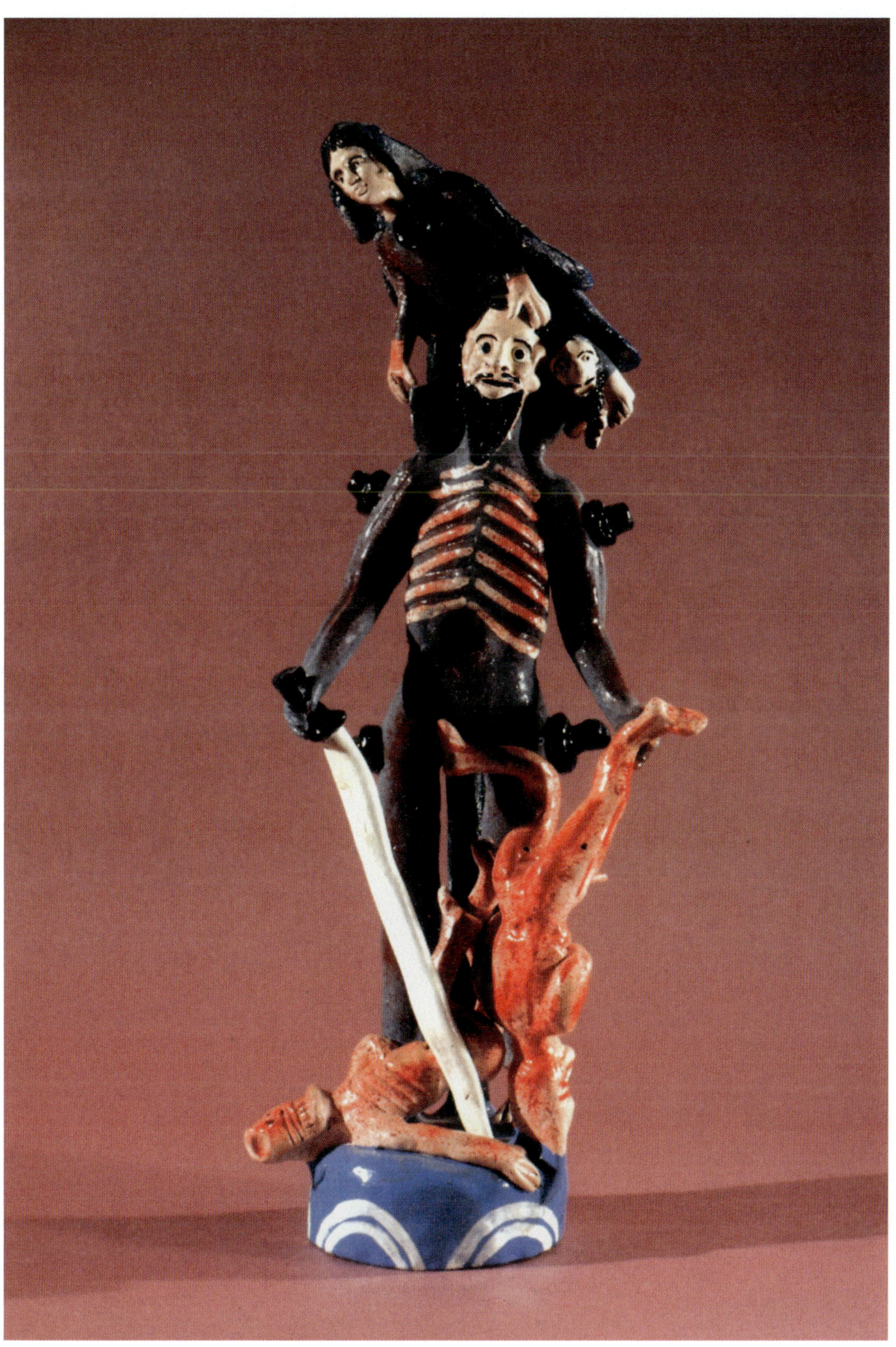

Hernán Cortés
Shown at the exhibition: Ocumicho: Arrebato del Encuentro,
Museo de Arte Moderno, México, 1992
Photographer: Lourdes Grobet

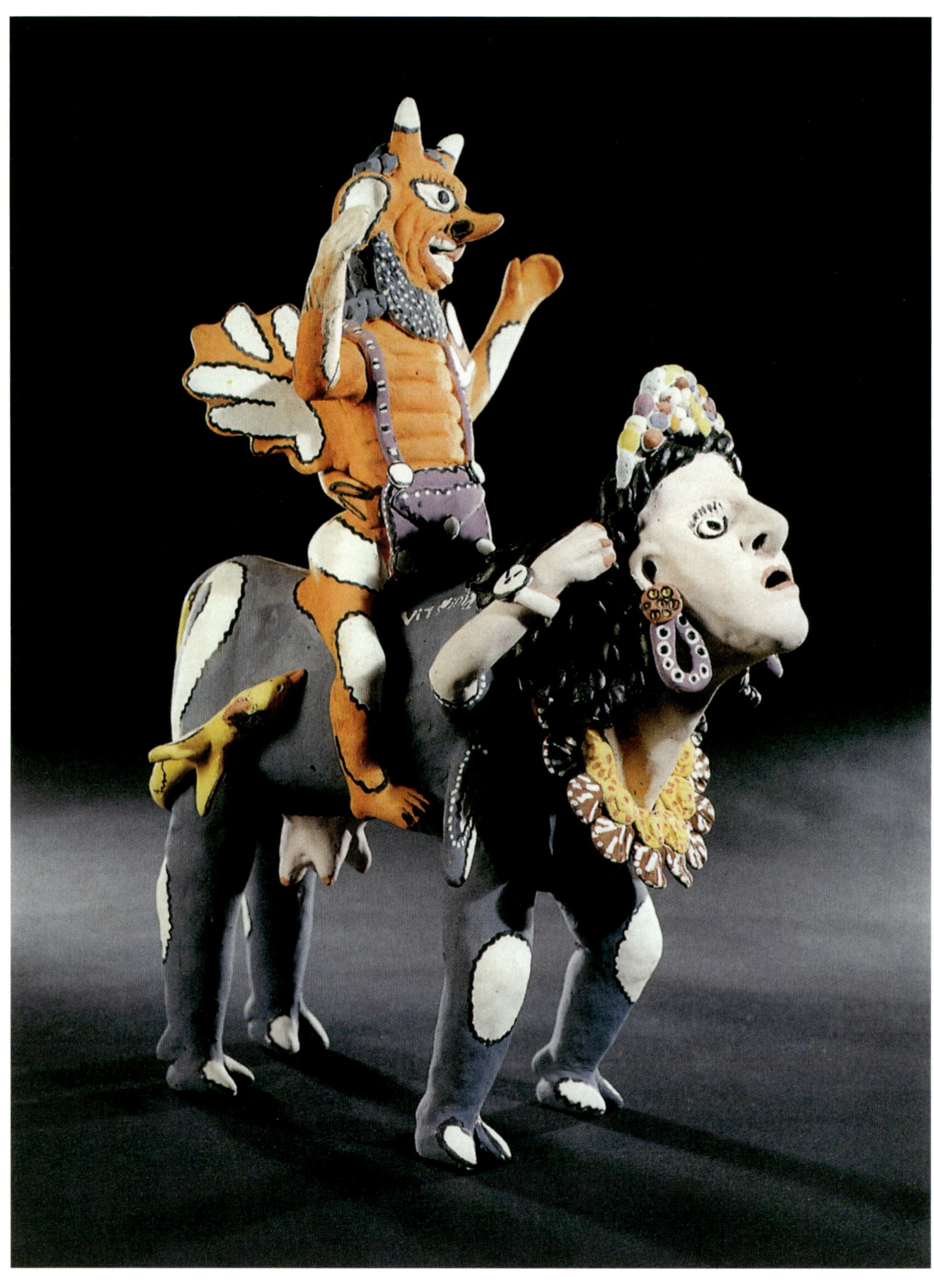

Caricature contre Marie-Antoniette / Marie-Antoniette's caricature
Shown at the exhibition Les Trois Couleurs d'Ocumicho, Ambassade du México, Paris, 1989

THE GOOD, THE BAD, THE UGLY AND THE BEAUTIFUL OF OCUMICHO'S DEVILS

VICTORIA NOVELO OPPENHEIM
CIESAS

It is said that Ocumicho— a rural Purépecha town a few miles from the city of Zamora—"is notable for its fantastic, polychromatic clay figures, which represent devils and strangely-shaped animals"(Martínez Marin 1981, 72). Also made in the town are miniatures and toys "among which stand out the grotesque figures of devils or multi-headed animals."(*Atlas Cultural de México* 1987, 38). Ocumicho is a place where the people speak and dress according to their cultural ways (combining ancestral traditions with the modern ways of migrants). It is said that in the playful tradition of Ocumicho:

> Fantasy and surrealism emerge in the Dantesque figures . . . in which the artist appears to recreate the nightmare of a lunatic or a desperate person in clay, copying the terrible image of monsters or demons, colored black, red, and yellow with white accents and golden horns. They are like offspring that devour each other, with serpents coiled or emerging from their mouths. In these figurines, the brilliant, aggressive colors finish off the terrifying and impressive impact the observer receives. (Sánchez Díaz 2006, 244)

It might seem that the topic of ceramics as they are made in this small town of Michoacán would fit within the specialization of psychiatry magazines and not in the visual arts, but, as will be seen, those first impressions are not necessarily objective. In this article, I will discuss the type of ceramic products that distinguish Ocumicho, locating them in their cultural and productive contexts, so as to be able to reach other possible conclusions with regard to the definition of these objects that are described with so many different adjectives that they might at first be frightening.

The Town and its Producers

Several studies undertaken in the field recount that the rise of ceramics in Ocumicho is subsequent to the Mexican Revolution, after which the town was left quite battered and could not continue with its customary trade in leather goods due to a lack of cattle and the high prices of the hides. Something led a number of people to go to Guadalajara, where they bought molds of small animals that possibly came from the ceramics of Tlaquepaque, and they began to produce clay toys.(Gouy-Gilbert 1987, 22) In light of the fact that the ancient leather-making trade, besides being masculine, is not at all similar to ceramics, the question of how they learned the new craft still remains to be researched. In addition, the question remains as to whether this craft—as many authors mention without offering sources—was traditionally practiced by women, who made whistles and figurine banks for children "for innumerable generations." The number of molds began to multiply and other subject matter emerged, inspired by local celebrations and dances; these were added to existing simple painted animals: rabbits, hens, pigs, and bulls. The figurines that the women made and still make with molds and modeling (the men only transport the clay) circulated in a local and regional market where "they were sold or traded in the celebrations of patron saints in nearby towns."(Miranda 1984, 26) These crafts can be seen in books on popular Mexican arts edited in the 1970s and 80s.

As far as hypotheses: the town of Patamban, near Ocumicho, has a long ceramics tradition, as does its other neighbor, San José de Gracia. The people of Ocumicho extract the clay from the area around the latter town. It might be possible that they learned the method—but not the subject matter or the finishes—from the ceramics makers nearby, though often neighboring towns do not get along well and are very protective of their "secrets." The fact is that by the 1960s there was a drastic change in models and work techniques at the same moment the production of the "devils of Ocumicho" blossomed. The invention of this new tradition is attributed to a man—Marcelino Vicente—an illiterate artist who died very young. His story—at times embellished with sensationalist details about his personal life—appears in all of the books, reports, tourist articles, and exhibition catalogues that can be found about the village. An author who is very well versed on the subject of the ceramic works of Ocumicho describes him in this way:

> The story of Marcelino Vicente has become a myth that is constantly repeated in the town to the delight of the buyers, anthropologists and the inquisitive; most notable in the story is his face-to-face encounter with the devil who told him "take a good look at me, I'm here so you can make figurines of me." From then on, Marcelino Vicente made models of devils that became a school in his town . . . he defined the style of a period. The constant innovations in subject matter, formats and personal styles developed in the 60s mean that the contemporary works are quite different from older ones: "previously they were very simple, not as perfect, just a simple, badly-painted standing devil, not the more refined ones of today." Nevertheless, they all have a family resemblance that allows us to affirm the existence of a shared style.(Garrido 2000-2001, 131)

Much has also been written with regard to the origin of the model of the devil that Marcelino began to sculpt: whether it was Purépecha or Spanish. One response that seems convincing to me is the one proposed by Cecile Gouy-Gilbert in her 1987 study. After observing the first devil pieces in the Pátzcuaro Museum, she concluded that the characters are modeled "on the criteria of representation of the Christian devil." (Gouy-Gilbert 1987, 28) I would add that if, as was said previously, the first ceramicists went to Guadalajara to buy molds—presumably at Tlaquepaque—various types are traditional and commonly found there: clay nativity scenes with sheep, shepherds, mules, donkeys, and the Holy Family, as well as devils, hens with eggs, caves with red devils on top and a hermit inside, roosters, and other animals. The drawings of devils, *Satanás*, are also common in books of religious education within various Christian denominations. That is to say that the Mexican devils are Christian in origin.

The fame of Ocumicho as a producer of devils began with the inclusion of Marcelino's works in exhibitions and fairs at a moment when agencies were founded to promote the craft production of Michoacán and Mexico more broadly. From there, the devils moved to the Feria del Hogar (Home Show) in Mexico City and then to The International Craft Fair in New York. This happened between 1962 and 1964. In his commercial undertakings, Marcelino was accompanied by a man who served as his Purépecha interpreter and who a little while later became the promotor of the new style of ceramics creation. This man was also president of a group sponsored by the Fondo Nacional para el Fomento de las Artesanías (National Fund for the Promotion of Crafts; FONART) (Gouy-Gilbert 1987, 28–29).

> My name is Teodoro Martínez Benito, and I represent the craftmakers of the town. Marcelino Vicente was the person who invented these handmade pieces: the devils of Ocumicho . . . I haven't studied anything besides clay. Marcelino Vicente didn't teach us anything; we just saw how he hollowed out the pieces . . . We make littles devils and we take them to Morelia, Mexico City and Pátzcuaro. And the Mexican, American and French women come here, also, how are the others called? From San Antonio, they buy the figurines. The pieces, the devils, we make them just because people want them. People don't want good pieces: we've made ones of *danzas de moros* [dance of the Moors] or *danzas de pastorelas* [dance of the Shepherd's Play], people do like those. But they like the devils more. The funnier they are the more they pay; the less funny, the less they pay... that's how it is. (Becerril and Ríos 1981, 15)

The way Ocumicho's ceramics circulated began to change when public and private distributors found new materials and symbols for the devil, which ended up being a big seller. The devils began to be modeled on scenes in which, at times, they were accompanied by mythical, fantastic, or monstrous animals (according to different points of view) such as serpents, lizards, dragons, or creatures with two heads, decorated with brilliant and shiny-colored stripes that either attracted or repulsed tourists at the fairs. I remember a famous model of that period: a small sculpture of a black devil with red and white lines on its body, standing on its head and with a white snake's head sticking out of its backside. There were also some in erotic positions and in humorous situations, doing sports and trades.

The origins of the new forms are rooted in cultural, material, and spiritual dimensions in which the creative imagination moves and is fed by innumerable sources, maintaining a particular local style that is recognizable in terms of modelling, decoration, proportions, adornment, and composition. The inspiration can be born out of book illustrations (I would swear that the creators were familiar with the work of José Guadalupe Posada); out of objects in museums, fairs and galleries; out of images constructed from stories heard repeatedly since childhood during the different indoctrinations through which members of a society pass during the inculcation of social and cultural norms; from the beings—real and mythical—that live in the natural and social environment; and out of the suggestions of craft buyers and promotors, as well as artists and gallerists. It all combines in different proportions in the experience of the maker-creator in order to make the stories emerge out of the clay.

Local Creativity, Subjects and Influences

The women ceramicists continued on the path opened by Marcelino. The ones who had the necessary talent continued to innovate with a growing awareness of the market. Anyone—if he or she has the gifts of virtuosity and mastery of a trade and also meet the conditions that enable him or her to experiment with the materials and their techniques—is capable of creating, innovating and initiating new subject matter and formats: in this case, in clay sculpture. But in a community with close to a hundred ceramicists (out of a population of nearly 3,200 inhabitants), the ones who stand out and who are thus recognized by their own people—and who also have been able to enter the international art market—are not the majority, as happens in other towns made famous by their so-called popular art.

Nevertheless, the more serious studies on the subject of Ocumicho signal the importance of the intervention of external agents in the aesthetic perspective developed in the sculptures, which led to an art "for others." That is to say, the figurines the women produce are alien to them, since it is not likely that "we would find one of these sculptures decorating a house in Ocumicho."(Garrido 2000–2001, 131)

The forms of the devils and their companions have been considered monstrous, terrifying, and have even been compared with devils that adorn the gargoyles of medieval cathedrals.(Miranda 1984, 43) This perspective is in line with the meaning and significance attributed in dictionary definitions to any being that presents generally negative characteristics, outside of the normal order of nature. The term is reserved for a being that inspires fear or repugnance (deformed, aberrant, counterfeit, grotesque, horrible, hideous). Thus, the obligatory question is: how did Ocumicho's women ceramicists select this aesthetic attitude in their works? We find the answers in the process of construction of the ceramic tradition of the devils.

Cecile Gouy-Gilbert (Gouy-Gilbert 1987, 30–32) lays out three stages in the evolution of ceramics in Ocumicho: In the first stage, which spans from the 1940s to the 60s, traditional molded ceramics were of a festive and religious character that was sold locally. In the second phase, beginning with Marcelino's work and the first Fonart intervention, ceramics were focused on the production of the production of animal figures —real and mythical—in line with Marcelino's models. In the third phase, beginning in 1974, Fonart clearly drove ceramic production, "suggesting [that the women ceramicists] take their celebrations or the Bible as references" to update their models. Perhaps the person who devised this recommendation thought of it as a strategy to disseminate the notion of the existence of a source of images full of transgressive characters, especially Satan, with his collection of temptations that could be fearsome for God and his human creations. Then, the women ceramicists began to introduce new sculptural groupings, including the Last Supper. Others related their work to Holy Week or town celebrations in which devils appear as companions or figurines challenging the sacredness of the subject matter. The sports or erotic scenes with devils and humans are "suggestions" of collectors and traders, usually from the United States. The human figures in this type of piece have their skin painted pink (in a clear symbolic demarcation between the color of the figures and the color of the local population). The suggestions also included the use of colors. The glossiness of the oil paint used previously was done away with and substituted with vinyl paints and natural colors and dyes. This type of "innovation" defined a period of interventions by agencies promoting crafts in the ceramic and textile trades, equally or even more widespread than the *ad nauseum* use of Diego Rivera's calla lilies in any craftwork promoted by the traders.

Another type of "suggestion" came from bureaucrats in visual arts offices or museums in Mexico. The most well known case is the initiative by Mercedes Iturbe, who made two proposals to a group of Ocumicho craftswomen. The first, in 1989, was the production of figurines related to the French Revolution, which resulted in an exhibition that traveled across Europe. The second was Arrebato del encuentro (Rapture of the discovery), an exhibition inaugurated in the Museo de Arte Moderno in Mexico City in 1993 that dealt with the Conquista. In both cases, the women were asked to make interpretations out of clay of the images provided to them about the selected topics, with scenes of the French Revolution on one hand and scenes from the Conquista on the other. It goes without saying that these were events the women were previously entirely unaware of.

In the words of Iturbe, the projects sought to "remove the figures from their purely artisanal context, situating them within the category of contemporary art, without distorting their own character." The goal was to stimulate the creativity of the craftswomen. The women complied with the request and, with the skills of their trade and with their usual style of modeling and painting, they elaborated characters very different from the normal ones. It's difficult to say that they gave their imagination and creativity free reign when the object of the design was provided to them, though their ability to move the flat illustrations to three dimensionality was successful and the use of color ended up being very attractive. Always using the local style, they recreated the murals of Orozco, the drawings of Huitzilopochtli, the engravings of Cortés with Moctezuma, etc. The reactions of intellectuals who enjoyed the exhibitions and wrote reviews and catalogues showed the asymmetrical relationships between the new artists and their new clients, who also invented a mythical context as the Ocumicho craftswomen's source of inspiration, faciliting their consumption by hopelessly romantic admirers of the delirious naiveté of the production of "the others," the same poor people as always.

With regard to this point, allow me to clarify some concepts related to popular art. "Craft object or craftwork" refers to a product that emerges out of a distinctive and longstanding way of working that dates back to the medieval trades and that—despite changes, adaptations, and transformations—continues to produce objects, primarily in series but also as unique pieces (a series of cooking pots for mole, a Paracho guitar or a painting on *amate* paper, for example). The distinctiveness of the craftwork process is that the producer-craftsperson has a command of all phases of their trade. It is one person with skills they make use of, in some cases, with mastery and virtuosity acquired through apprenticeship and living customs.

In Mexico, we find the common conception that identifies craftwork with popular art, implying a separation from the concept of "art" in and of itself. From the pioneer Gerardo Murillo, also known as Dr. Atl, to famous painters, anthropologists, critics, and other researchers, craft objects are defined as "manifestations of the ingenuity and skill of the people of Mexico," which have the stamp of an innate and deep aesthetic sentiment in their forms, technique, decorative spirit, harmonies, and colors. It has even been said that in popular art, the works are "unconscious creations of pure artistic purpose" (Toussaint 1982, 199–222). There is more or less agreement that popular visual arts are works that have a practical and utilitarian meaning and that respond both to the need to adorn objects and daily activities as well as to the celebrations of the ritual calendar. But it has also been said that the authors of these objects have not attended a "cultured" academy where certain techniques and ideals are prescribed and where one is up to date with the artistic movements in the world (Reuter 1982, 187–198)In addition, the objects are still identified by the locations of their origin and not by the names of their authors—they remained quite anonymous, though very well known in their communities, for which reason they did not need to sign their works.

It remains to be said that popular art—as conceived by institutions legitimating what art is—is sheltered fundamentally in rural areas of the country and is produced mainly by *campesinos, mestizos,* and indigenous people, even though there are also urban craftspeople who inherited colonial traditions. Both are located in the politico-social subalternity of society and make up part of the working classes; that is to say that the classist connotation of the concept "popular art" is clear. But there are also other problems of definition. Western culture—which has separated life from art and whose industrial way of life has divided the moment of creation or design from the moment of its execution—has given rise to the distinction between "pure" art and "applied" art with its corresponding authors: the artist and the craftsperson. This removes aesthetic value from objects of daily life or classifies them as a lesser, primitive, naive art, which devalues the objects of craftspeople, who bring talent, sensitivity, and skill to their trade, thus becoming artists, though they do not recognize themselves in that category.

These conceptions are at the base of an entire age of construction and consolidation of nationalism—the original post-revolutionary sort and today's outmoded form—with its trite discourse about the identity of Mexicans mixed with the "virtues" of the tourist industry. Within said industry, the praise for craftwork or popular art has not yet been coupled with an interest in the quality of life of their creators.

The Meaning of Taste for Ocumicho's Craftswomen and People

Eva María Garrido's cogent analysis elucidates and explains how the women ceramicists see the issue of production "for others." To do this, she uses her skills as a field anthropologist and complements her observations and interviews with the support of masters-level university linguists and native speakers of the local language in order to understand the aesthetic concepts from the perspective of the Purépecha language and culture.

In the Purépecha language, Garrido says, there are words that encompass a wide array of meanings linked to the positive and the negative. One, *ambákiti*, is the positive, the good, and from this term come expressions that mean to live correctly, cleanliness, health, delicateness, something of quality, well made, luminous, and beautiful (pretty or pleasant). *No ambákiti* is the negation of the former and "is used primarily to define what is bad, rotten, unhealthy, cruel and a character related to all these qualities, like the devil, a being which in Ocumicho is the epitome of ugliness."(Garrido 2000–2001, 132) Although there are more specific words to classify things that are visually beautiful or ugly—from whose roots are derived other terms related to dirtiness, bad odor, or negative attitudes—one word for ugliness is the same word with which the devil is often named. Also, that which is badly made is also ugly. The meaning of the words—positive and negative—has, as can be seen, an ethical-aesthetic dimensionality. Things can be morally or visually ugly or beautiful, and these aesthetic patterns are shared and are expressed in the spoken language. But in addition, Garrido's research enabled her to conclude that the ceramic works that are made with the intention of pleasing the local community are primarily objects associated with ritual and celebration. And when the beauty of a work stands out, one notes that it has a lot of decoration—primarily the flower—and that it is ornate, *"bien doble"* (many drawn and modeled forms), in addition to the brilliance of the colors. The pieces that are not pleasing and that are rejected as ugly are such because of the iconography used, because of the presence of the devil character that brings together everything unpleasant. They will be ugly independent of the aesthetic treatment they receive. The especially ugly ones with lots of unpleasant characters—lizards, snakes, small lesser devils, or the scenes of sexual content—are the *ikichakua*, the disgusting, horrible, impossible monsters, although they can also be the objects of mockery or humorous commentary.

And so, how can the observer understand that art "for others" can be very well made (good fabrication, technique, materials, finishes, coherence, proportion)? Very simply. In the local value system and according to the feeling of people from Ocumicho, those pieces are the "ugly, yet beautiful" works. This sublime contradiction is quickly resolved, since the recognition of it being well made does not entail or contemplate its local consumption. The pieces a Purépecha buys, "the ones they place on the altar of their home or to decorate the central beam of their barn along with other mementos," or the ones they would give as a gift to another *paisano*, are the dolls, whistles, banks, and bulls and other animals blessed in the celebration. (Garrido 2000–2001, 142) The ugly works are for the others, the outsiders the tourists, the store buyers, whose tastes are well known by the craftswomen since that is the market where they place the vast majority of their products.

Where Did the Grotesque End Up?

If the grotesque is a mixture of incompatible elements, distortions, or unpleasant extravagances, it is possible to use this adjective to refer to the ceramics of the Ocumicho devils, and not only for the diabolical subjects of the clay figurines. Placing the grotesque in the framework of the social relations involved in ceramics production, we find several situations that contradict the oft-repeated statements of official and intellectual discourse about Ocumicho's successful producers.

One-third of the town's population over fifteen years of age is still illiterate, with an average schooling of three years. There is now a high percentage of residents that have running water at home (though even in the 1980s and 90s, water only "fell" two or three times a week); there are also paved highways and houses with telephones, in addition to a *Colegio de Bachilleres* (high school) and a fragile health service with one primary care clinic. Even if the craftswomen fall ill, they cannot stop working. Even now, sales do not provide an increased opportunity to save money for the women; this goes hand in hand with the high rates of migration *"al norte"* (to the north) by members of many families. Perhaps the leaders of groups with monopolies in the markets organized by institutions are doing a bit better. The diplomas that some women have received as prizes in contests were until recently kept in bags in the kitchen; that is, if they didn't burn them in an emergency to keep the stove on, they show them to buyers to increase the price of their work by a few pesos.[1]

As producers with a skilled trade, as members of an artistic community, and as citizens with social rights established by a variety of laws, they still do not have access to social security, to the recognition of work-related illnesses, or to formal artistic education. What is more, they do not even know—unless they patiently surf the Internet—in which museums and galleries their work is found. They do not know what has been written about them, the prices that stores and galleries are charging for their work, or why external recognition has not been translated into a higher quality of life.

The relationships with buyers and promoters who admire Ocumicho's art—yet "suggest" changes meant to increase sales—reproduce this sort of production "for others." These works could be classified as *intrusive* due to their adverse relationship with the local aesthetic and ethics, or in other words, due to their fundamental cultural difference. The outsider's aesthetic and ethics—of "the others"—is overlaid with a commercial relationship to which the producers must submit and subordinate themselves, though this relationship is dressed up as an indigenist ideology of "benefit" to the artist. *Intrusiveness* is also visible in the separation between the mental design of the work, the form it takes at first, and the demand to make works around a particular subject matter. In this process, their creative freedom is restricted, or more accurately, appropriated

1 Personal communication from Eva María Garrido, July 2013.

from them as artists, which supposedly the clay craftswomen of Ocumicho should have. In my opinion, this is where we find the grotesque within Ocumicho's production: in those relationships with the capitalist market that keep the women inside of the peculiar Mexican interethnic and intercultural relationships defined by the prevailing classist, hierarchical, and authoritarian system. To top it all off, the town lives within a social context in Michoacán that is overrun by violence, and completely surrounded by the demented nightmare of crime assaulting our entire country.

Translated by John Pluecker

BIBLIOGRAPHY

40 siglos de arte mexicano, arte popular, Mexico: Editorial Herrero, 1981.

Atlas Cultural de México. Artesanías, Mexico: SEP-INAH-Planeta, 1987.

Becerril Straffon, Rodolfo and Adalberto Ríos Szalay.*Los artesanos nos dijeron...* . Mexico: Fonapas, Fonart, 1981.

Dr. Atl. *Las artes populares en México*. México: Editorial Cultura, 1922.

Florescano, Enrique. *El juguete michoacano*. México: Gobierno del Estado de Michoacán, Secretaría de Turismo y Santillana Ediciones Generales, 2006.

Garrido Izaguirre, Eva María. "Categorías del gusto en la escultura de Ocumicho, un pueblo purépecha," In *Bulletin* Societé suisse des Americanistes, 2000–2001.

Gouy-Gilbert, Cecile. *Ocumicho y Patamban, dos maneras de ser artesano*. Collection de Estudes Mésoaméricaínes, Series 11–10 (Mexico: Cemca), 1987.

Miranda, Francisco "Ocumicho, una comunidad en fiesta," in *Relaciones* (4:16, 1983)

Martínez Marín, Carlos "La alfarería," in *40 siglos de arte mexicano, arte popular* (Mexico: Editorial Herrero, 1981).

Sánchez Díaz, Gerardo "En busca de las historias de los juguetes michoacanos," in *El juguete michoacano*, ed. Enrique Florescano (Mexico,:Gobierno del estado de Michoacán, Secretaría de Turismo and Santillana Ediciones Generales, 2006),

Novelo, Victoria. "Ser indio, artista y artesano en México." In *Espiral. Estudios sobre Estado y Sociedad* (4:25, 2002). Mexico: Universidad de Guadalajara, 165–178.

Ocumicho: arrebato del encuentro. Exhibition catalogue. Mexico: Conaculta, INBA, SRE, Gobierno de Michoacán, 1993.

Reynoso, Louisa. *Ocumicho*. México: FONART-SEP Cultura, 1984.

Sayer, Chloë. *Arts and Crafts of Mexico*. San Francisco: Chronicle Books, 1990.

Reuter, Jas "Arte Popular," in *Textos sobre arte popular*. Mexico: Anthology, Fondo Nacional para el Fomento de las Artesanías, Fondo Nacional para Actividades Sociales, 1982.

Toussaint, Manuel "El arte popular en México," in *Textos sobre arte popular*. Mexico: Anthology, Fondo Nacional para el Fomento de las Artesanías, Fondo Nacional para Actividades Sociales, 1982.

www.mexicodesconocido.com.mx/ocumicho-donde-al- diablo-se-le-moldea-michoacan.htlm.

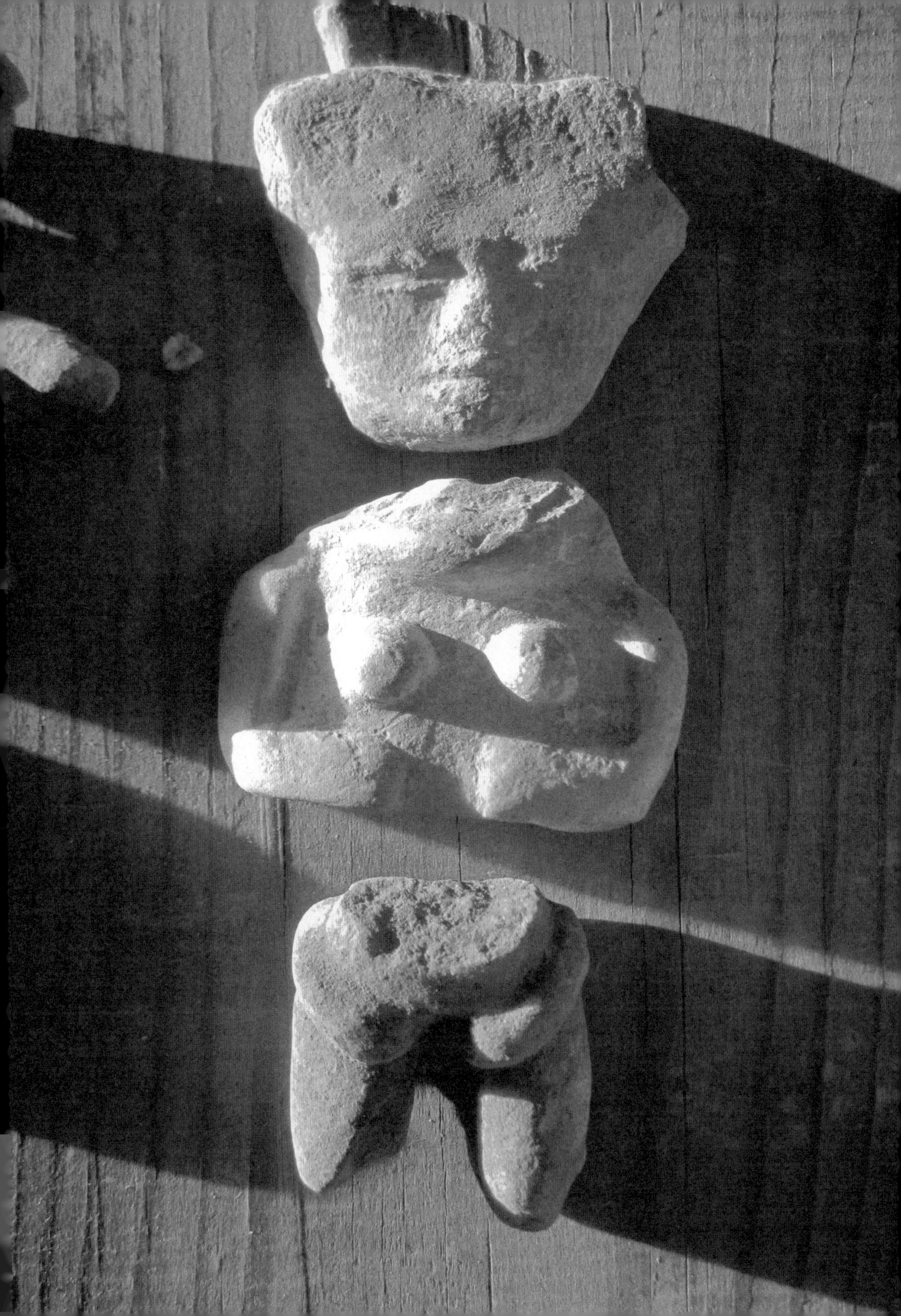

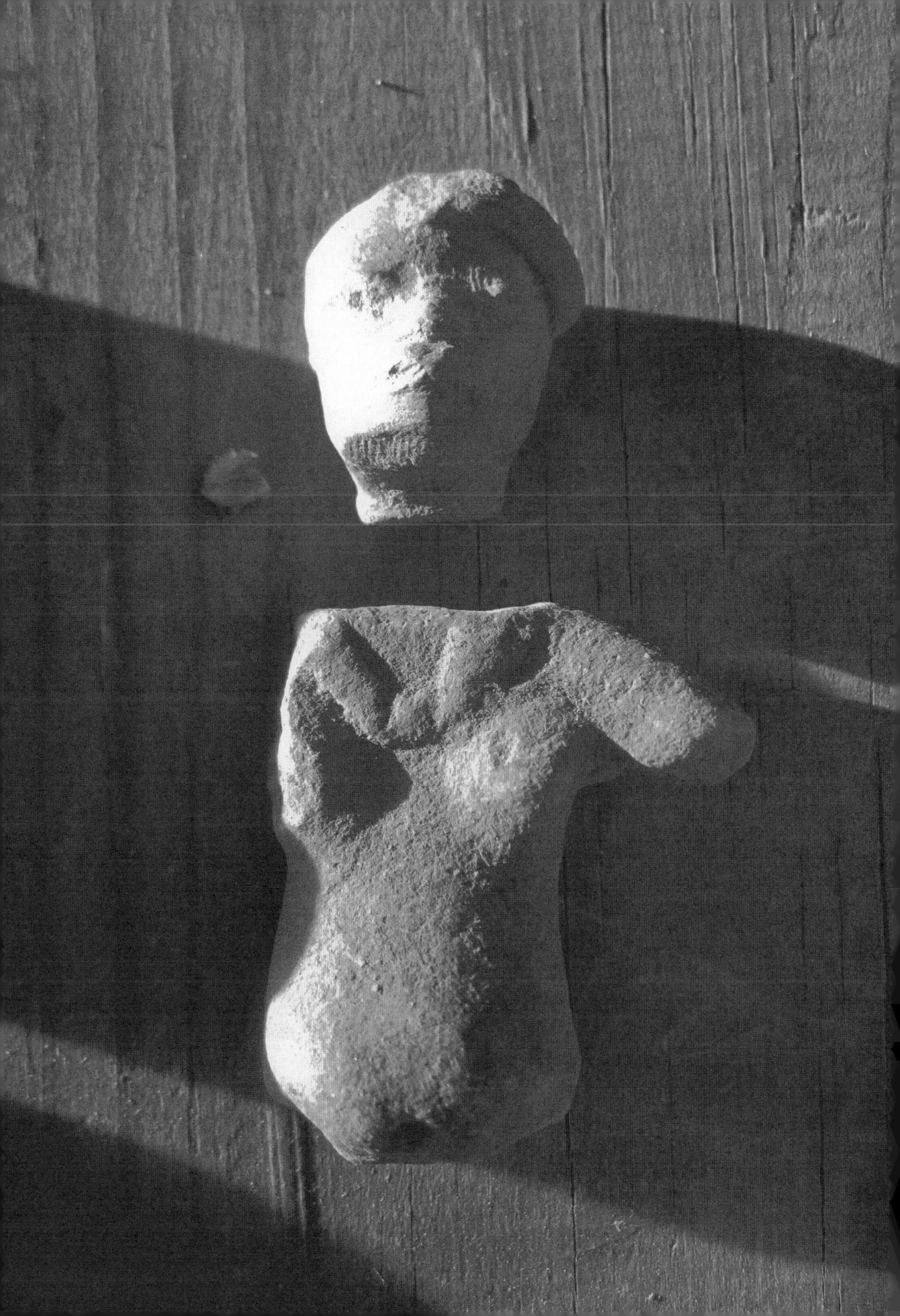

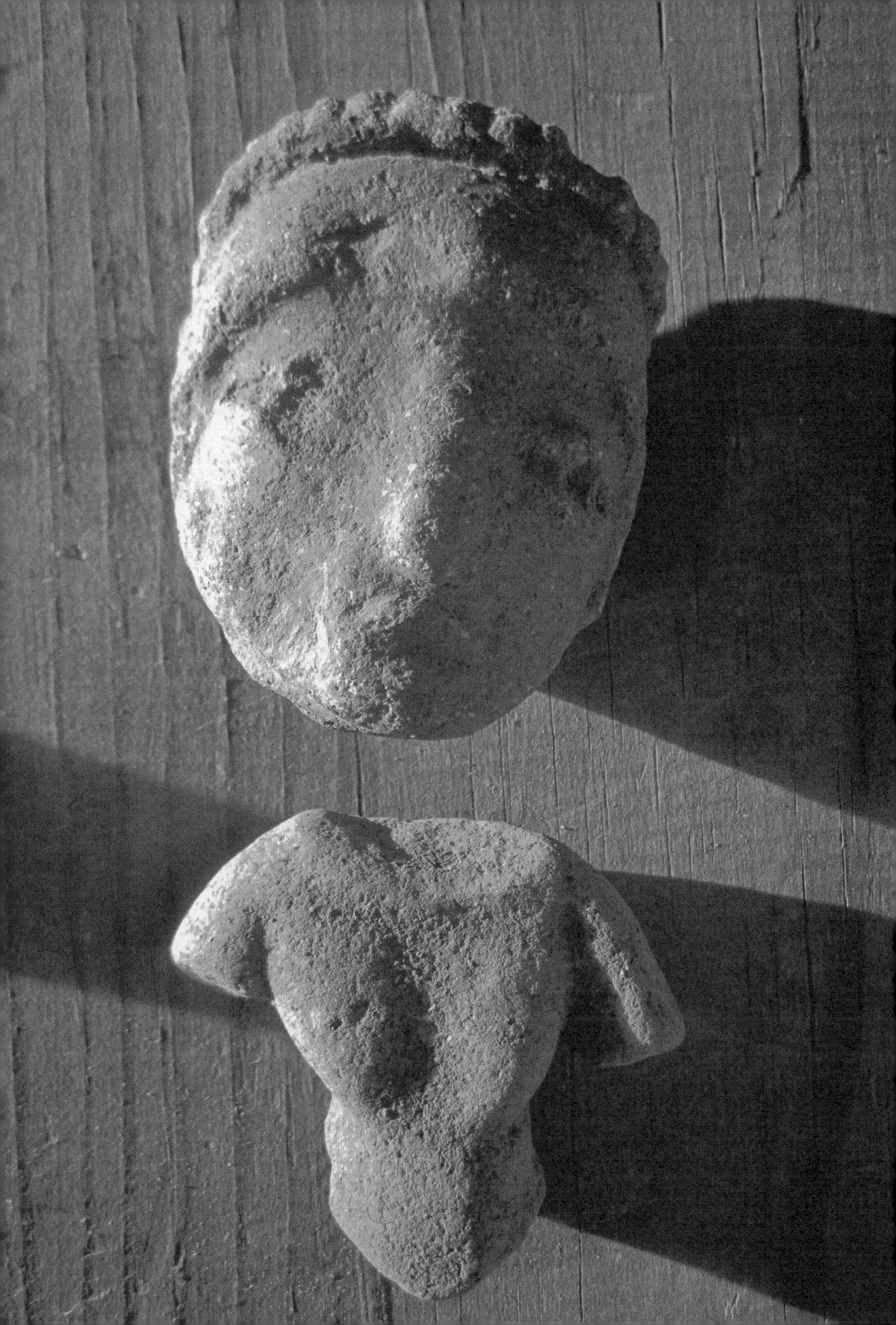

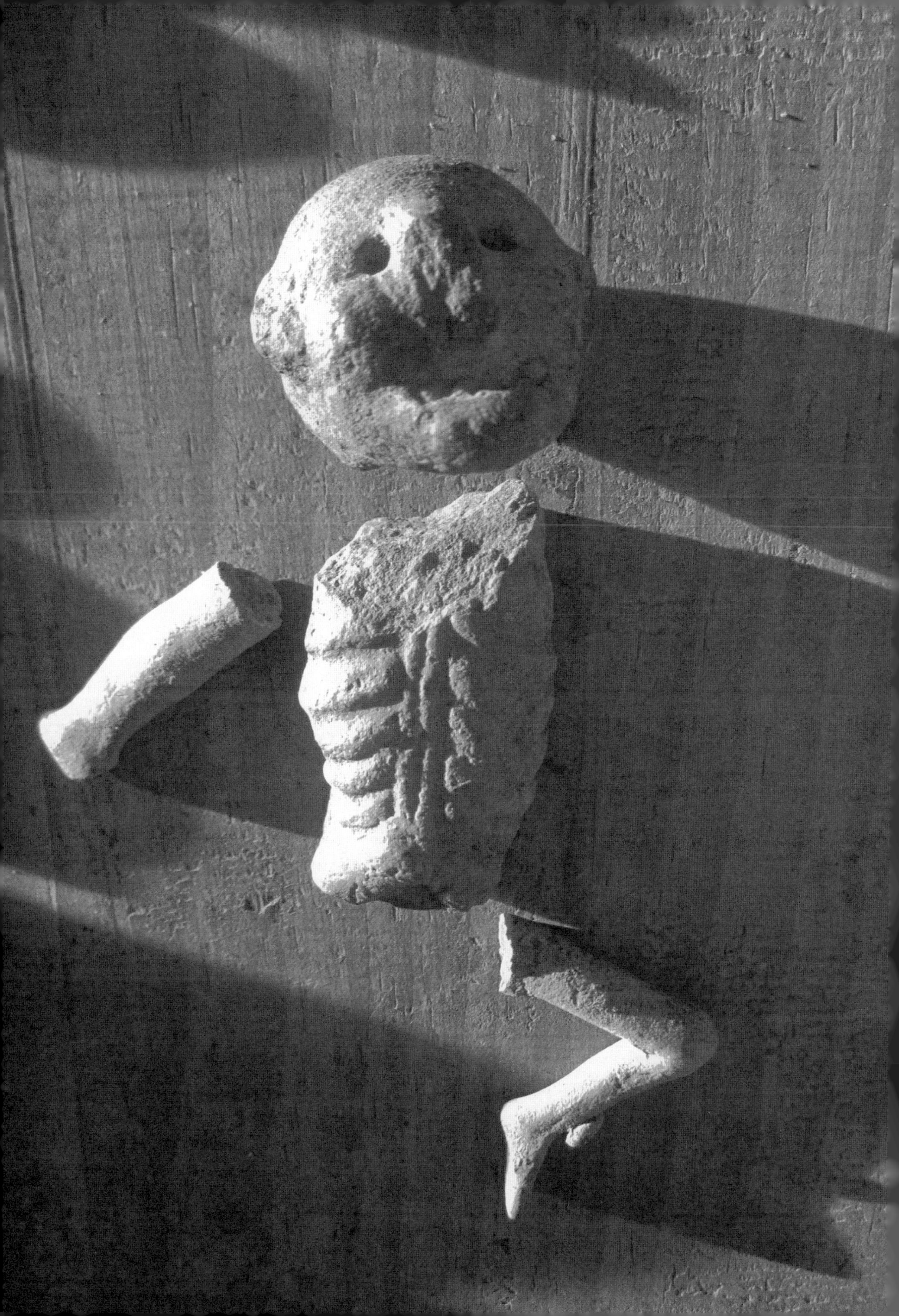

ANATOMY OF A FAKE

ADAM T. SELLEN
CEPHCIS, UNAM

When we visit a museum dedicated to archaeology, we expect to see artifacts that date from antiquity, original works that will tell us something about the ancient cultures that produced them. Sometimes, however, even the most expert eye is fooled by a contemporary creation, and a museum may end up acquiring and displaying a misrepresentation of that history: a fake. We are all intrigued by fakes, perhaps because we imagine that these creations are the result of a deceptive and desperate mind, but also because successful hoaxes and frauds expose the limitations of experts. Intrigue, however, can quickly turn into indignation when we consider how much chaos this material can cause for research, because undetected fakes in museum collections invariably distort our carefully constructed models of the ancient past.

For historical, economic, and aesthetic reasons, certain types of pre-Columbian artifacts have been faked on an impressive scale and can represent a significant portion of a museum's collection. For example, Zapotec urns—a type of ceramic effigy vessel from southwest Mexico—have been ubiquitous in museums since the turn of last century, and many institutions with a focus on Mesoamerica possess at least one fake, if not dozens. The development of objective tests such as thermoluminescence (TL) has played an important role in identifying these fakes, and the systematic testing of large collections has exponentially increased the fund of our knowledge about these creations. Nonetheless, it is often not practical to test every object because of the costs involved. Furthermore, as a learned friend of mine once pointed out, this exercise is often equivalent to "shooting fish in a barrel." To truly comprehend fakery and how it comes about, one must delve into the historical contexts that defined them, because the process of creating fakes follows particular traditions. Moreover, ceramic fakes have specific anatomies, and like bodies they can be copied, modified, added to, and grafted upon, operations that can be studied through an autopsy of their imagery. Thus, even in the age of objective tests, art-historical approaches still provide useful tools for assessing authenticity, such as detailing the history of provenance or employing comparative iconographic studies; the trained eye, of course, is still a standard in separating the proverbial wheat from the chaff.

Despite the notable advances in the field of identifying fakes, many remain in the public domain and are exhibited as ancient artifacts. The purpose of this study is to shed light on a fake currently on display in the National Museum of Anthropology in Mexico City, by considering its history and particular anatomy. By following the trajectory of this object and others, we may map the web of social networks surrounding them. The artifact, a large Zapotec urn in a seated position and with designs incised on its chest and extremities, is displayed on a central plinth in the Culturas de Oaxaca exhibit in the Museo Nacional de Antropología in Mexico City (Figure 1).

According to the explanatory label, the urn represents *Pitao Xicala,* a Zapotec deity associated with summer, love, music, flowers, dance, and games. Inscribed on its chest is a stylized butterfly that is reportedly one of the attributes of this god, an insect that evokes summer and the heat of the sun, and another symbol of this season is an unidentified vegetable that the deity holds in his right hand. The figure is reportedly from the Central Valleys of Oaxaca and dates to the Classic period, which spanned 200–800 CE.[1]

The object's identification and interpretation comes from Paul Westheim (1886–1963), a German art critic who was an early proponent of German expressionism and an Oskar Kokoschka scholar. His Jewish heritage demanded that he flee Nazi Germany in 1933, and he spent the rest of his life exiled in Mexico, writing books on pre-Columbian art. The urn was a particular favorite of his, and appeared on the cover of his 1950 edition of *Arte antiguo de México,* where he gave the provenance as San Lorenzo Albaradas, Oaxaca. Rather than refer to it as a Zapotec deity, he used the Nahuatl designation of *Xochipilli,* or "The Prince of Flowers" (Westheim 1977, 219). How did this object come to form part of the collections of the Museo Nacional de Antropología? The urn was donated by a Swedish businessman and avid collector, August Edwin Paulson (1869?–1954), who lived in Puebla, Mexico. According to Sigvald Linné (1938, 10)—a compatriot and author of a catalogue of the collection—Paulson acquired much of his holding from Oaxaca, where he was involved in business in around 1890. About 30 percent of his collection came from the engineer C. V. Chisholm, who worked in Oaxaca during the region's railway boom, and Paulson stated that many objects were collected with the assistance of an "Indian friend" whom he employed to help him identify artifacts (Brunius 2002, 49–50). The donation, however, is a more complicated story. In 1924 Paulson wanted to export his entire collection (some eleven hundred objects) to his native country, and while the Mexican government was willing to allow the extraction, they required that one particular object stay behind. Sigvald Linné explains:

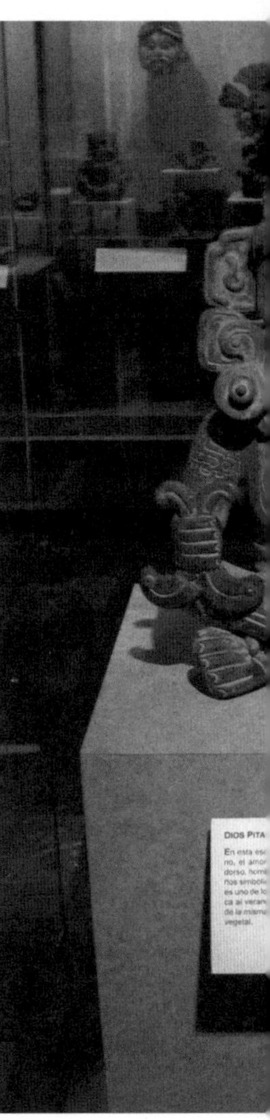

Figure 1
Dios Pitao Xical
on display at the M
Nacional de Antropo

1 Dios Pitao Xicala. En esta escultura en arcilla, se representó a la deidad del verano, el amor, la música, la danza, las flores y los juegos. En el dorso, hombros y piernas el personaje representa exgrafiados diseños simbólicos. En el pecho destaca una mariposa estilizada que es uno de los atributos representativos del dios, este insecto evoca al verano y el calor del sol. Como símbolo fertilizador propio de la misma estación, la deidad sostiene en su mano derecha un vegetal. Valles Centrales, Clásico 200-800 d.C. This text was written by the curator of the exhibit, Martha Carmona, who has published this view on other occasions (Carmona 1995, 168).

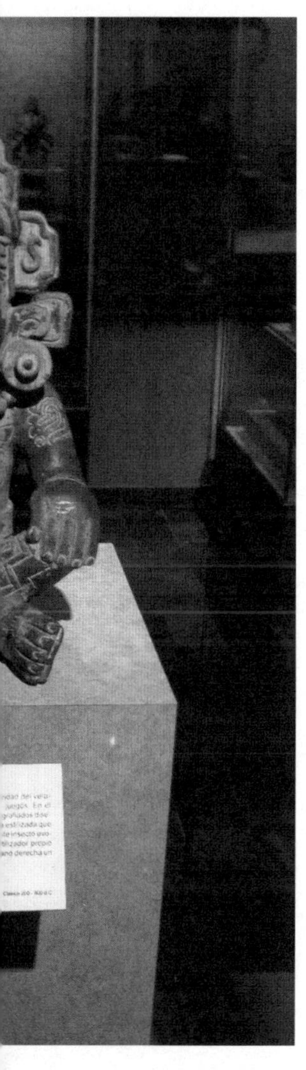

> As, according to the opinion of the Mexican specialists, this funeral urn must be regarded as unique, its taking out of the country could not be permitted. It was therefore handed over by Mr. Paulson to the Museo Nacional, Mexico. As will be apparent the figure differs in many respects from the majority of the urns, and, apart from possessing a number of interesting details, bears in its general character evidence of having been created by a real artist (Linné 1938, 126).

Perhaps, in hindsight, this was not such a good deal for Mexico, because, apart from the many fakes Paulson had in his collection—judging solely from the catalogue—several urns are of ancient manufacture.[2]

After Linné published the information about the urn and the first photo of the object (Figure 2), it would be reproduced in countless catalogues and books on pre-Columbian art, securing its place in the pantheon of masterworks from Mexico.[3]

The first to have serious doubts about the authenticity of the piece was Ignacio Bernal (1910–1992), an archaeologist and erudite Oaxacan specialist who became the director of the Museo Nacional de Anthropología in 1962. His objection was published in "Arqueología oaxaqueña," a reprint of an article that was originally published in English in the *Handbook of Middle American Indians* (1965: vol. 3, 788–813). The new version, edited by the archaeologist John Paddock, was better illustrated than the first and included a photo of the object with Bernal's comment:

> The aesthetic impact of this piece caused the government of Mexico to prohibit its inclusion in a lot of "urns" that are now in Sweden; but in 1964 it was identified as a fake, and is no longer exhibited (Bernal 1992, 34).[4]

The archaeologist gave no reasons regarding why it was thought to be a fake or indication whether he had some role in making this assessment. The visual aesthetics of the urn were often commented on, without particulars on why it was unique, but despite these observations the experts came to different conclusions regarding its authenticity.

2 Philippa Shaplin, a recognized expert on fake Zapotec urns, suggested that over 80 percent of the Paulson collection was false.

3 See, for example: Toscano 1943, 43; Westheim 1950, front page; Disselhoff y Linné 1960, 50, fig. 23 (drawing by Linné); Gendrop 1960, 139, fig. 160; Anton 1968, 116–121; Les richness de l Ancien Mexique 1994, 10, fig 12; Carmona Macías 1995, 168, fig. 8.

4 "Su impacto estético hizo que el gobierno de México prohibiera la inclusión de esta pieza en un lote de "urnas" que ahora están en Suecia; pero en 1964 se reconoció como una falsificación, y ahora no se exhibe"

In the absence of an objective test, such as TL, is it possible to determine whether it is an ancient or a recent creation? An understanding of where this type of pre-Columbian fake originates and a comparison of its iconography with known fakes in other collections can supply us with many clues.

A Faking Industry is Born

At certain times in history, enthusiastic collectors are plentiful, but the objects of their desire are scarce. Taking into account the rules of supply and demand, and that many collectors have more money than sense, it is easy to comprehend how a cottage industry in forgery can be born. It follows, then, that to understand the origins of this clandestine industry, an initial step is to establish the general time frame of forgery production. Conventional wisdom has held that the older a collection is, the more likely it will contain authentic pieces.

Early evidence for the *absence* of fakes in Mexico is contained in a letter dated from 1830 from Maximiliano Franck to the president of the French Geographic Society, Edme-François Jomard. Franck, a Bavarian who spent two years in Mexico producing meticulous drawings of antiquities, wrote that the Mexicans had only become interested in pre-Columbian artifacts within the five years prior to the date of his letter. This may be exaggerated, but in retrospect his comment coincides neatly with the results of expeditions by Alexander von Humboldt and Guillermo Dupaix that are often credited with generating interest in the subject. Franck goes on to assure Jomard that the appearance of "pastiche" objects had not been introduced into Mexico as they had in Italy or Egypt. Here we can understand a "pastiche" as synonymous for "fake," insofar as it is imitating another art style, though Franck was probably speaking more literally, referring to the process of pasting molded elements onto a base figure. He reasoned that the Mexican people were as yet unaware of how to make fakes, but predicted that over time it was bound to happen.[5] This was extraordinarily insightful thinking on his part, and a few years later it began to occur.

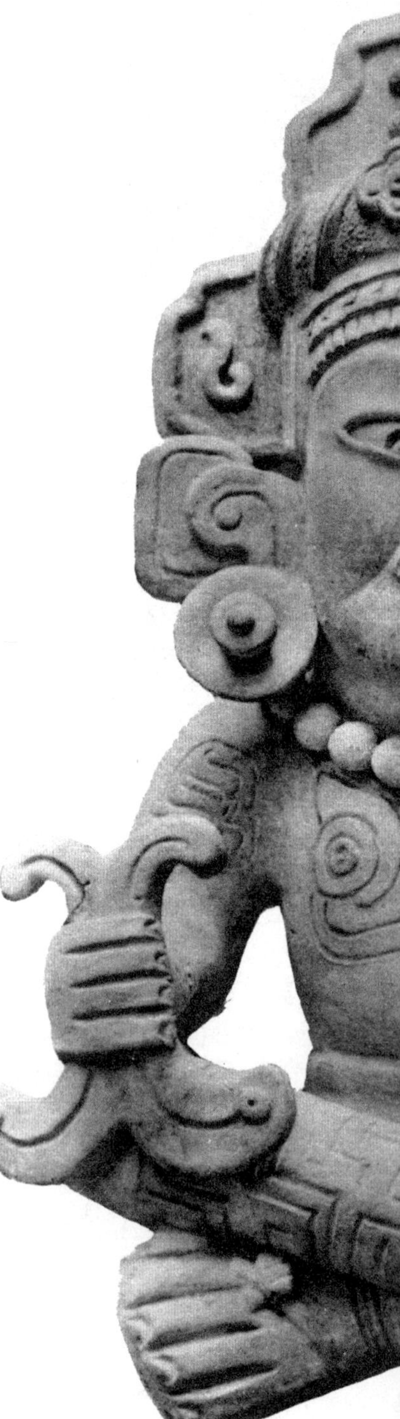

5 Maximiliano Franck to Edme-François Jomard, March 1831, in *Bulletin de la Société de Géographie* vol. 15, no. 93-98 (1831): 283.

One incident of pastiche fakes occurred in the mid-nineteenth century and is an often published story. It is rarely cited from the original work in which it appears—Paul Eudel's book *Trucs et Truqueurs* (1907)—but rather from Leopoldo Batres's study *Antigüedades mejicanas falsificadas* (1910), in which long passages have been translated from the original French into Spanish. It goes like this: during the period of the empire of Napoleon III, French troops occupied Mexico from 1862 to 1866, and a commission of *savants* was charged with putting together objects that represented the pre-Columbian past of Mexico. Vast quantities of ink were dispensed on descriptive essays of the objects that were documented with etchings and prints. An exhibition of the "antiquities" was presented at the Trocadero Museum in Paris. Apparently no one doubted the authenticity of the artifacts except a certain Mr. Perrier, who was vindicated one day when excessive humidity and the sun's glare caused various parts of the effigies to become unstuck, evidencing that a fraud had been perpetrated (Eudel 1907, 31–32).

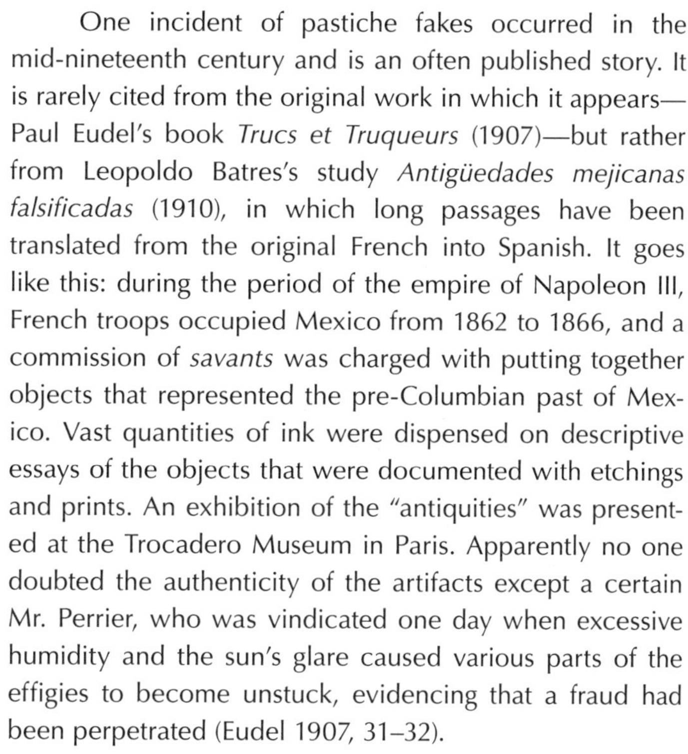

Figure 2
Paulson urn published in Linné (1938, 126).

While this episode is anecdotal proof of the early existence of fakes, the story has taken on an unusual pastiche life of its own, with bits added here and there. It started with Frank Boos, an American who has published various catalogues and studies of Zapotec urns. He changed the translation and omitted any reference to either Eudel or Batres, maintaining that the fakes were souvenirs manufactured for "French troops stationed in Mexico" (Boos 1966, 15), but in Batres's version no reference is made to souvenirs or to the French army having received anything. Compounding the problem are the numerous works that cite Boos directly without referring to the original source.[6] Consequently, Boos implied that fake Zapotec urns had been fabricated in the 1860s as souvenirs for the French soldiers, but there is really no proof for this position and we do not know the specific origin of the faux objects that ended up in Paris, or what they looked like.

6 In agreement with Boos are Philippa Shaplin in her master's thesis, "An Introduction to the Stylistic Study of Oaxacan Urns," 33; Pascual Mongne in "Les Urnes Funéraires Zapoteques: Collectionnisme et Contrefacon," 20; and Staffan Brunius in "A Greenstone Figure with Olmec Were-Jaguar Motif," 59. The exception is Esther Pasztory, who correctly cites Batres and Eudel on this issue. See "Three Aztec Masks of the God Xipe." In Falsifications and Misreconstructions of Pre-Columbian Art, ed. Elizabeth Boone (Washington D.C.: Dumbarton Oaks, 1978), 90-92.

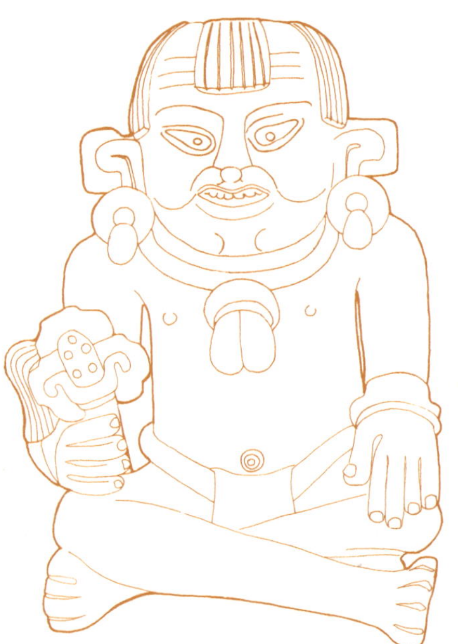

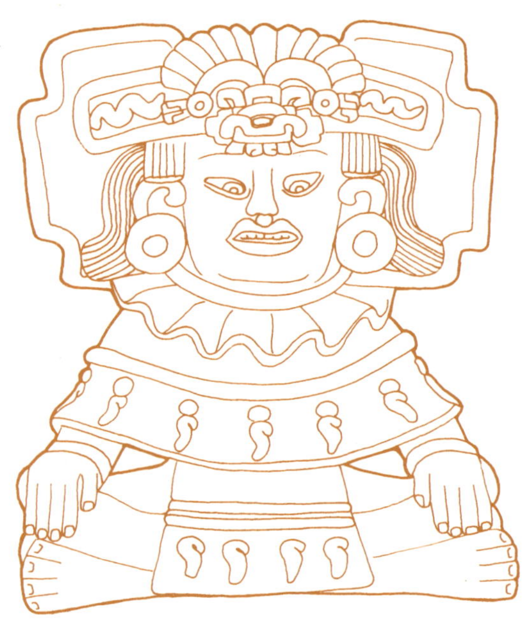

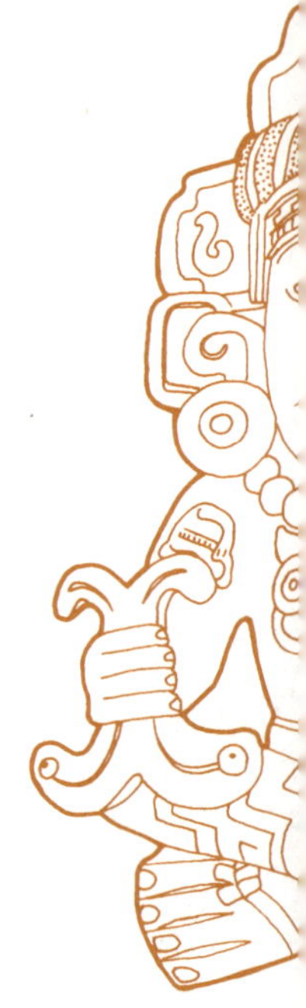

Figure 3. The Paulson urn (center) compared to four fake Zapotec urns from different museum collections a-b) Ethnologisches Museum, Berlin, cats. 40641 and 35269; c) Paulson urn, Museo Nacional de Antropología, Mexico City, Mexico; d) Royal Ontario Museum, Toronto, Canada, cat. 1892; d) British Museum, London, England, cat. AM 1946. All of these effigies except the Paulson urn were tested with TL and proved to be fakes.

In general the evidence suggests that wholesale fakery happened late in the history of Mexican archaeology, around the end of the nineteenth century. A few researchers have alluded to different forgers who were active in Oaxaca at the beginning of the twentieth century. Boos (1966, 15) alleges that a German forger had established a flourishing "fake factory" in Oaxaca in the 1920s, but without ever mentioning a name or giving more details. The archaeologists Ignacio Bernal and Lorenzo Gamio (1974, 8) implicated the "Pharmacist" of Tlacolula[7] as the perpetrator who sold fakes to Eduard Seler, curator of the Königlische Museum in Berlin (presently the Ethnographic Museum in Dahlem). Over several years, from 1907 to 1915, we know that Seler assembled a large collection of Oaxacan materials, including many Zapotec urns for his museum. A collection-wide test of those urns in the early 1990s showed that at least half the collection was manufactured in the twentieth century (Goedicke et al., 1992). Grouping the fake and genuine urns according to their acquisition years revealed that the fake materials began to arrive at the museum in 1907, and while the Berlin museum had acquired a number of Zapotec urns before that date, well into the nineteenth century, all were determined to be authentic by the TL testing. This strongly suggested that the fake industry started sometime at the beginning of the twentieth century and that Seler had been in contact with the forger. The prime suspect was a mine owner and British consul in Oaxaca, Constantine Rickards, who in 1919 sold a large collection of Zapotec urns to the Royal Ontario Museum in Toronto, many of which were later determined to be fake (Sellen 2000).

7 These researchers did not give a name, but it was probably Adolfo Martínez Bustamante, the pharmacist of "La Preladita" in Tlacolula, who with his wife housed an extensive collection of pre-Hispanic material behind his store, much of it looted from Yagul, a nearby archaeological site.

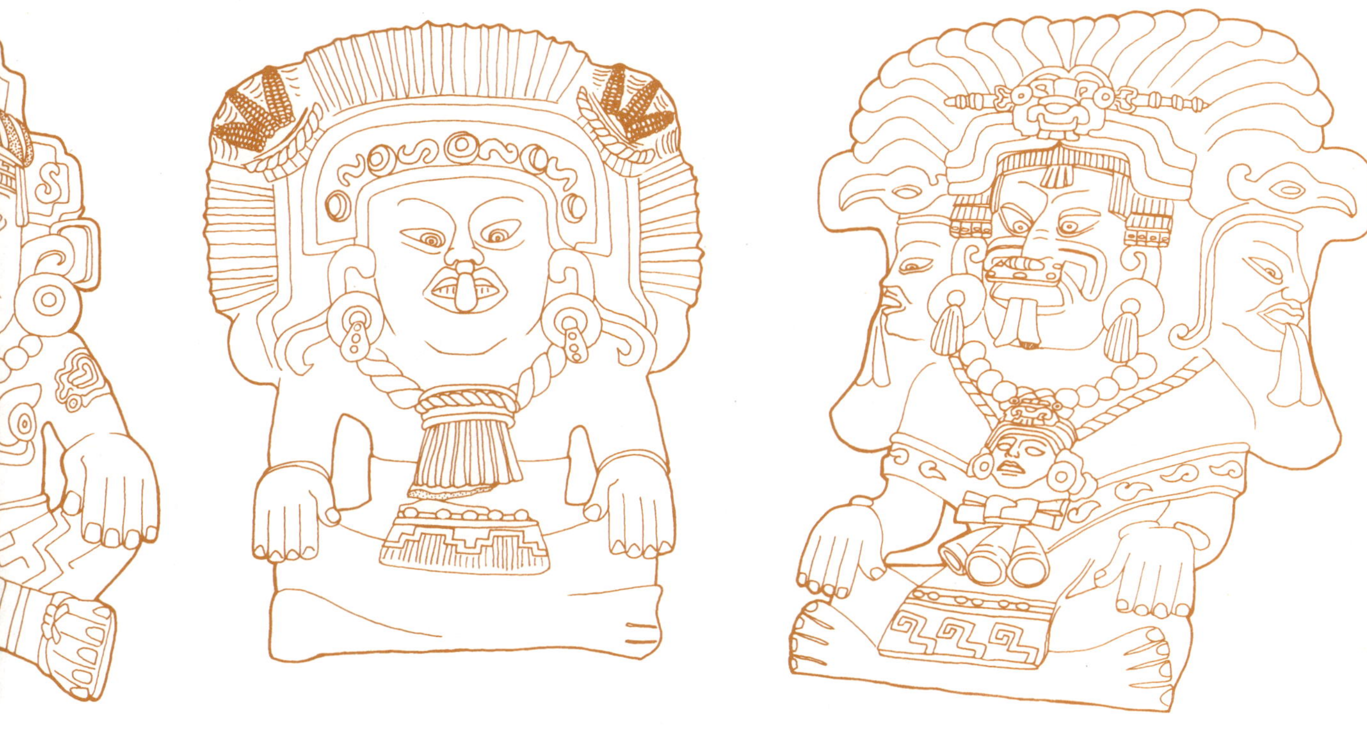

Guilt by Association

In a previous study, I examined dozens of Zapotec urns in the Rickards collection at the Royal Ontario Museum (ROM), and an interesting pattern emerged. Specific motifs that I could identify on originals in the ROM's collection—such as a face, a torso, or a unique decoration—appeared on fakes in museums all over the world. I came to the conclusion that most of the fakes had been made by combining these copied motifs in different ways (Sellen 2004). This type of creation can be called a pastiche, an artifact that has a credible appearance because its constituent parts are copied from ancient effigies, however the motifs are assembled in ways that violate the ancient Zapotec canons of composition. In a pastiche urn, the visual vocabulary is fine, but the "words" (motifs) are arranged in a different, and meaningless, grammar.

The Paulson urn in the Museo Nacional de Antropología can be considered a pastiche because its constituent parts are incongruous with ancient Zapotec iconography. Particularly, the incised glyphs on the arms and the chest of the object do not correspond to any known glyphs in the documented repertoire. In the middle of the headdress above the forehead, we can see a correctly executed and placed glyph C, but hanging down from the center of the glyph is an unusual lock of hair. Furthermore, the twisted roll that serves as the base for the headdress is a characteristic that corresponds to urns with female figures that have their hair braided and collected on top of their heads, but this figure is male because of his seated lotus position. The "vegetable" form held in the right hand is also atypical. Despite all these inconsistencies in the ancient Zapotec canon, as well as the surface treatment of the urn that belies its recent manufacture, it is the face that is the most revealing trait. With its particular expression and slanted eyes, a similar face can be found on other faux urns from collections around the world (Figure 3).

Figure 4
Faux urns in the Ethnographic Museum, Dahlem, catalog numbers 40641 and 35269

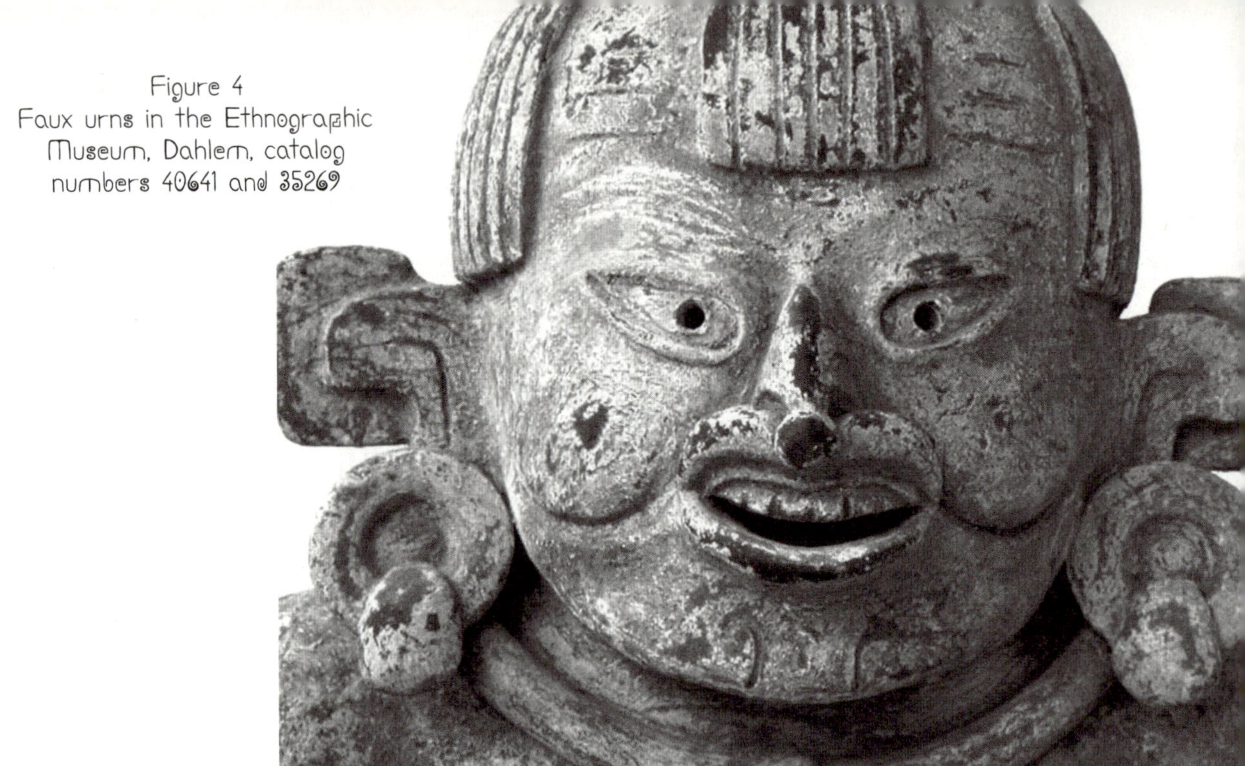

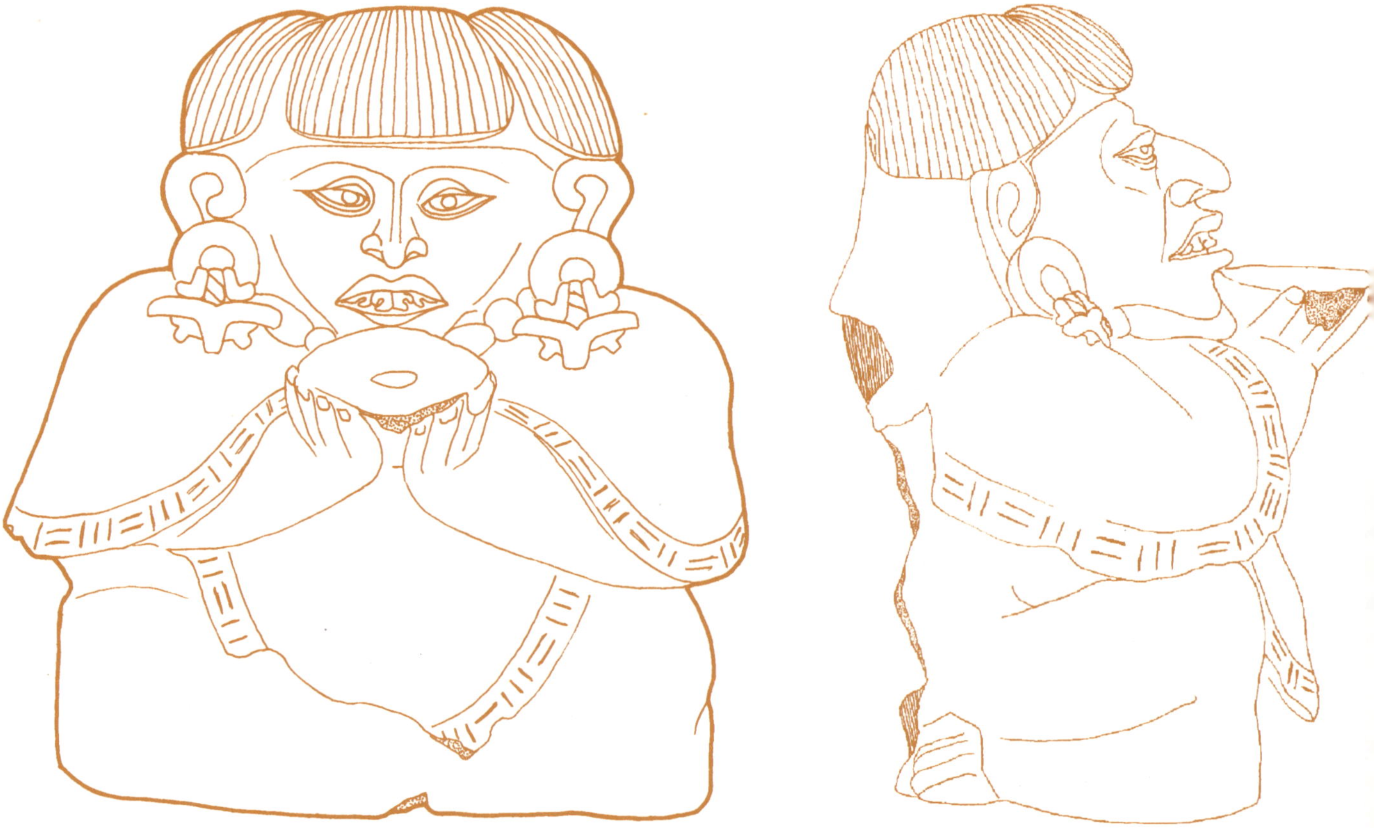

Figure 5. Effigy of a kneeling female, Royal Ontario Museum, cat. HM 1887

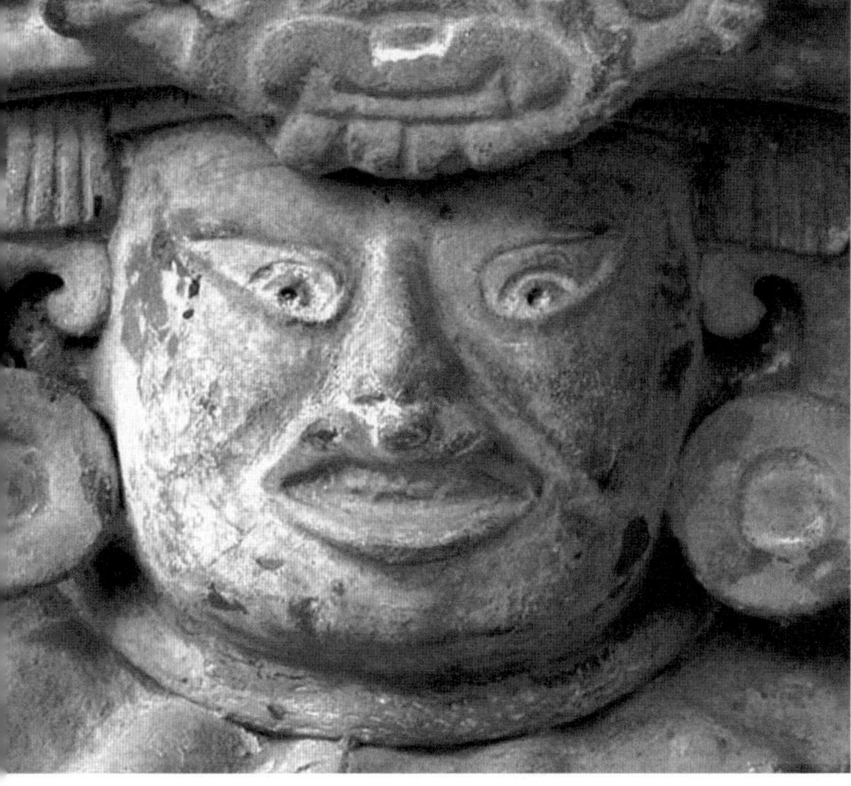

Although the general style and accoutrements of these urns vary, the distinct features of the face—Asiatic in character—is evident in all of them and suggests that a mold of a face was used to produce almost similar faces. For example, the faces on the two urns from the Berlin collection are almost identical, including a bead below the nose, which was omitted on the Paulson urn (Figure 4).

Since these four urns have been determined to be twentieth-century creations through TL tests, we have another element to consider: that the Paulson urn in Mexico is also part of the group, reaffirming Otto Kurz's maxim that "fakes hunt in packs" (Kurz 1967, iv).

Particular details on this group of urns allow us to make other observations. The peculiar hairstyle present on the artifact from the Ethnographic Museum in Berlin (Figure 3-a) has an echo in an original piece that is in the Royal Ontario Museum's collection: a seated female holding a small bowl to her mouth. Since this is a unique feature among known Zapotec urns, the hairstyle on the fake was probably copied from this original object (Figure 5).

A large effigy that is in the British Museum (Figure 3-e) originally belonged to Rickards, who took a picture of that effigy sitting on top of the cabinet that held his butterfly collection (Figure 6). Apparently, he often referred to this object affectionately as "la chinita," an urn that he sold or gifted to a man named Pike, a coworker at the British Consulate in Mexico City. Pike later donated the object to the British Museum in 1946.

Of course, these strands highly implicate Rickards in the forgery scheme, and in another study (Sellen 2004), I have provided ample evidence that he was using the originals in his own collection to produce the fakes. Motivated by a crippling financial situation he incurred with his silver mines, he created—with the help of local artisans—a staggering number of false urns during an eight-year period, between 1907 and 1915. These creations now comprise parts of museum collections around the world, including the Museo Nacional de Antropología.

Final comments

As a rule, experienced fakers avoid making exact copies of known works of art because such a practice would quickly reveal deception. Rather, the preferred modus operandi is to fabricate new pieces, emulating a particular style or period, by assembling elements from different genuine artifacts and creating news ones. This is precisely the nature of the Paulson urn.

Fakes are situated in time, reflecting contemporary trends and responding to demands from the market. The Paulson urn informs us about the intricacies of social agency and networks, as well as about the tastes and trends of a certain period. At the time these particular creations were being produced, many asserted that the origin of the American Indian was to be found in Asia, and the faces with strong Asian features may have played directly into this view.

Though the urn was "outed" as a fake in 1964, presumably by Ignacio Bernal, it continues to grace the exhibition hall as a genuine artifact, which speaks directly to its powerful aesthetic presence. Rather than withdraw the artifact from exhibition, perhaps it is time for the Museum to change the label into one that would reflect the enduring tradition fakes such as these represent in the annals of pre-Columbian art. This is a possible text:

> Fake Zapotec Urn
> At the beginning of the twentieth century, a company devoted to the falsification of objects was founded in the state of Oaxaca. Hundreds of newly manufactured artefacts were then scattered by collectors and travellers; occasionally some of these objects found their way into museum collections.
> Thanks to the implementation of objective techniques and a deeper knowledge of ancient iconography, it is now possible to distinguish falsifications from originals. Nevertheless, these objects are a testimony of an important epoch in Mesoamerican art.
>
> Valles Centrales de Oaxaca, 1907–1915.

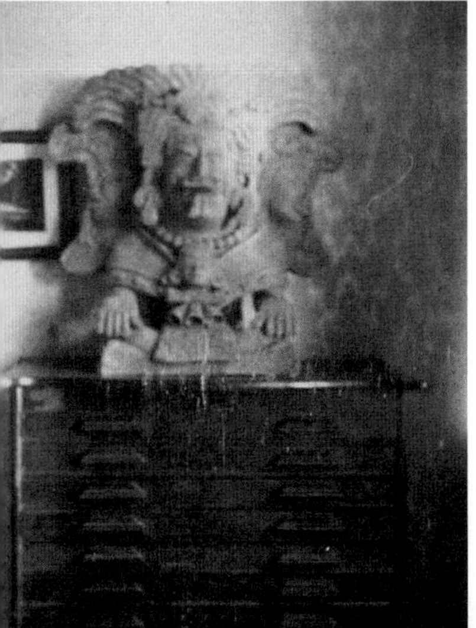

Figure 6
"La chinita." Faux Zapotec effigy in Constantine Rickards's collection, ca. 1907.

BIBLIOGRAPHY

Anton, Ferdinand. *Alt-Mexiko und seine Kunst.* Leipzig: VEB E.A., Seemann Buch-und Kunsterverlag. 1968

Batres, Leopoldo. *Antigüedades mejicanas falsificadas.* Mexico: Imprenta de Fidencio S. Soria, 1910.

Bernal, Ignacio. *Arqueología oaxaqueña.* (Reprinted with modifications from the English edition of *Handbook of Middle American Indians,* 1965). Mexico: La Colección Vidzu, 1992.

Boos, Frank. *The Ceramic Sculptures of Ancient Oaxaca.* New York: A. S. Barnes, 1966.

Brunius, Staffan. "A Greenstone Figure with Olmec Were-Jaguar Motif: Facts, Possibilities and Uncertainties." *Acta Americana* 10 (2) (2002): 47–65.

Carmona Macías, Martha. "Barros, Jades e Ouro a Arte da Oaxaca Ancestral." In *Tejedores de Voces, a Arte do México Antiguo,* 154–175. Portugal: Consejo Nacional para la Cultura y las Artes y Fundaçao das Descobertas/Centro Cultural de Belém, 1995.

Disselhoff, Hans-Dietrich y Sigvald Linné. *América Precolombina.* Barcelona: Editorial Praxis, S.A. and Editorial Seix Barral, S.A, 1960.

Eudel, Paul. *Trucs et Truqueurs.* Dijon: Imp. Darantiere, 1907.

Gendrop, Paul. *Arte Prehispánico en Mesoamérica.* Mexico: Editorial Trillas, 1970.

Goedicke, Christian, Sabine Henschel and Ursel Wagner. "Thermolumineszenzdatierung und Neutronenaktivierungsanalyse von urnengefassen aus Oaxaca." *Baessler-Archiv* 40 (1992): 65–86.

Kurz, Otto. *Fakes.* New York: Dover, 1967.

Les richness de l'Ancien Mexique. Les collections Zapotèque et Mixtèque du Musée de Mexico. Catalogue of the exhibition in *Galeries Lafayette.* Paris: Aeroméxico, Club Med, and Bancomext, April 8–30, 1994.

Linné, Sigvald. *Zapotecan Antiquities and the Paulson Collection in the Ethnographical Museum of Sweden.* Stockholm: Ethnographical Museum of Sweden 1938.

Sellen, Adam. "Is this the Face that Launched a Thousand Fakes?" *Rotunda* 36 (3) (2004): 32–39.

———. "Breve historia sobre la colección Rickards en el Museo Real de Ontario." *Estudios Mesoamericanos* 1 (2000): 14–23.

Toscano, Salvador. *Arte Precolombino de México y de la América Central.* Mexico: Instituto de Investigaciones Estéticas, UNAM, 1952.

Westheim, Paul. *Arte antiguo de México.* Mexico: Fondo de Cultura Económica, 1950.

———. *Obras Maestras del México Antiguo.* Mexico: Ediciones Era, 1977.

———. *Obras Maestras del México Antiguo.* Mexico: Siglo XXI Editores, 2000.

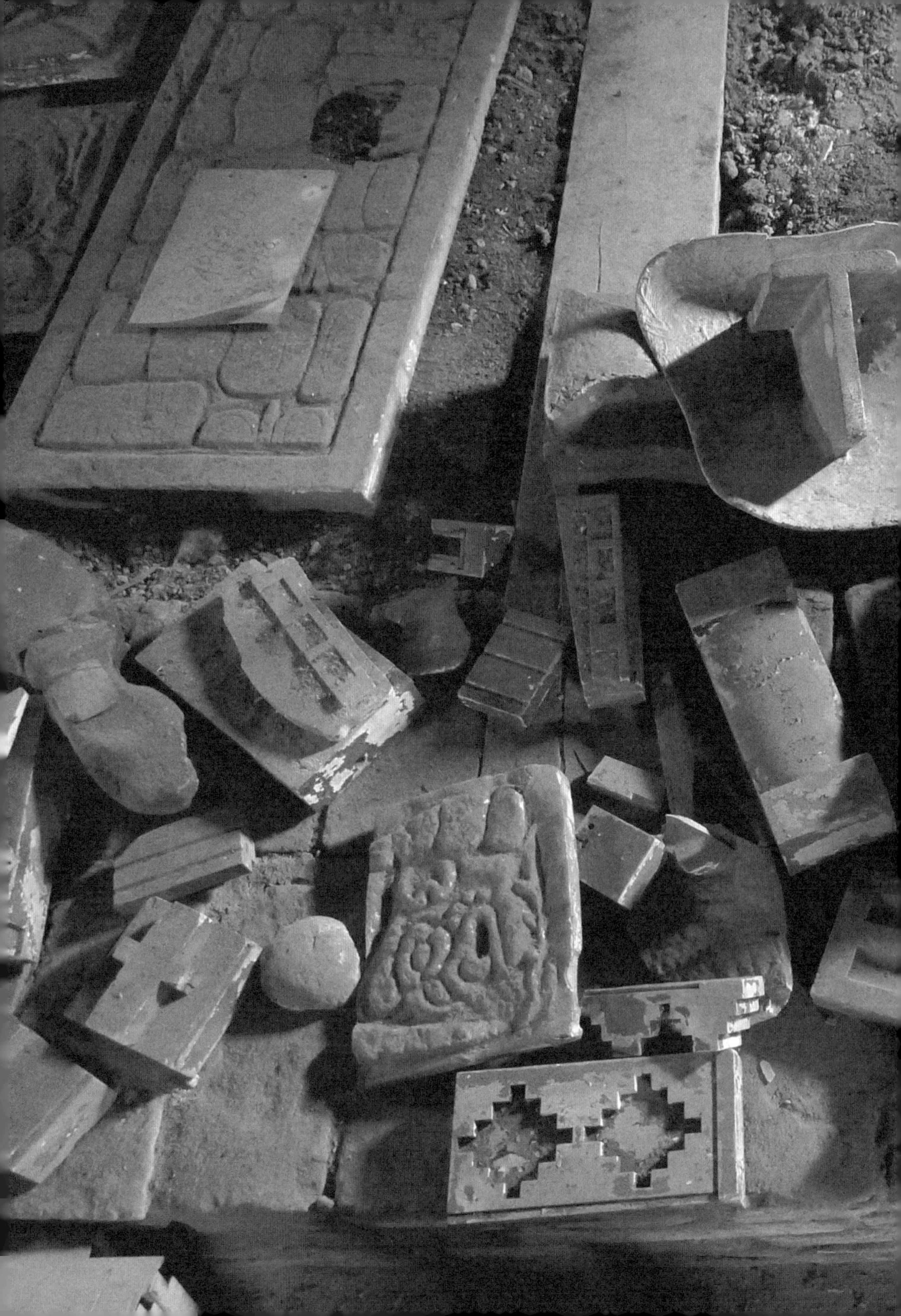

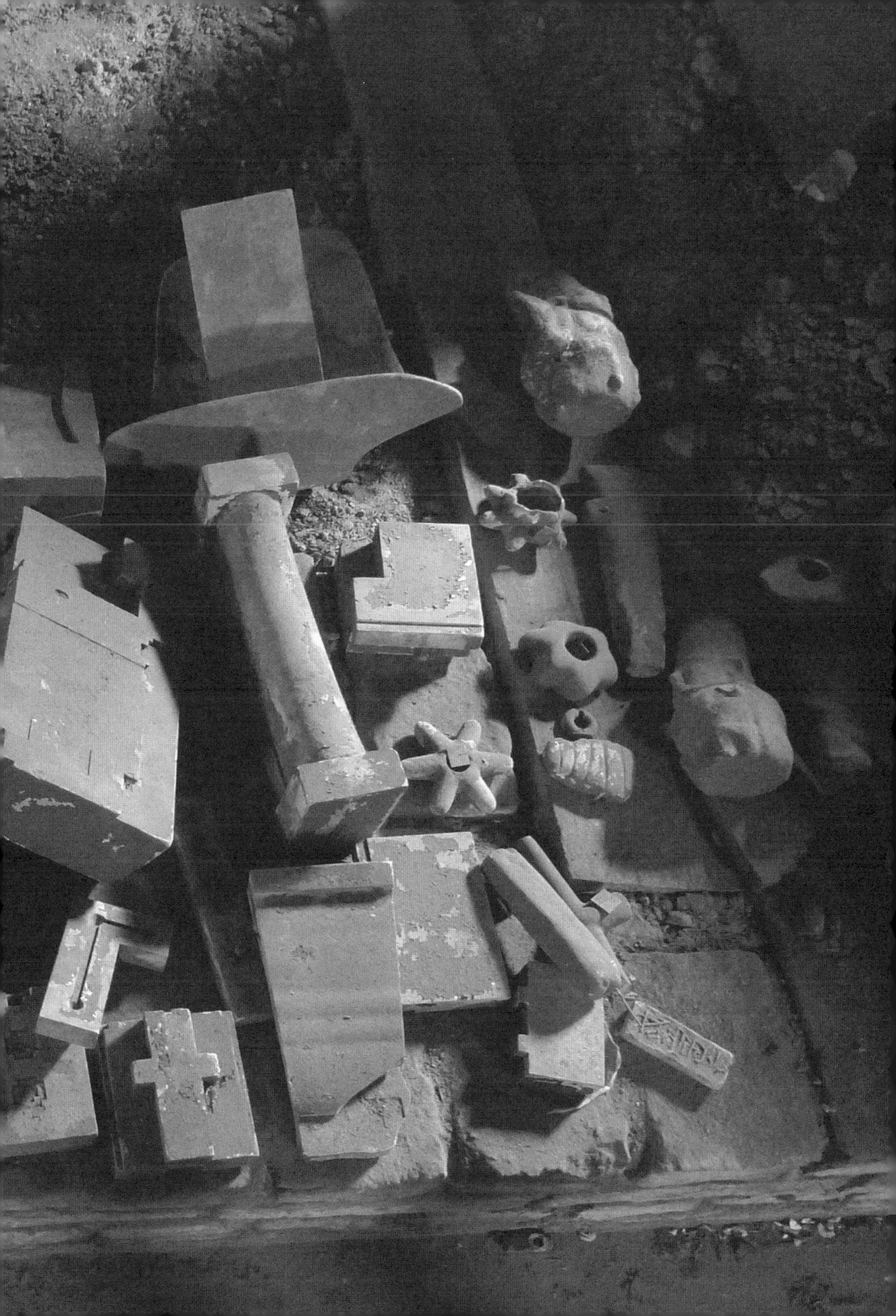

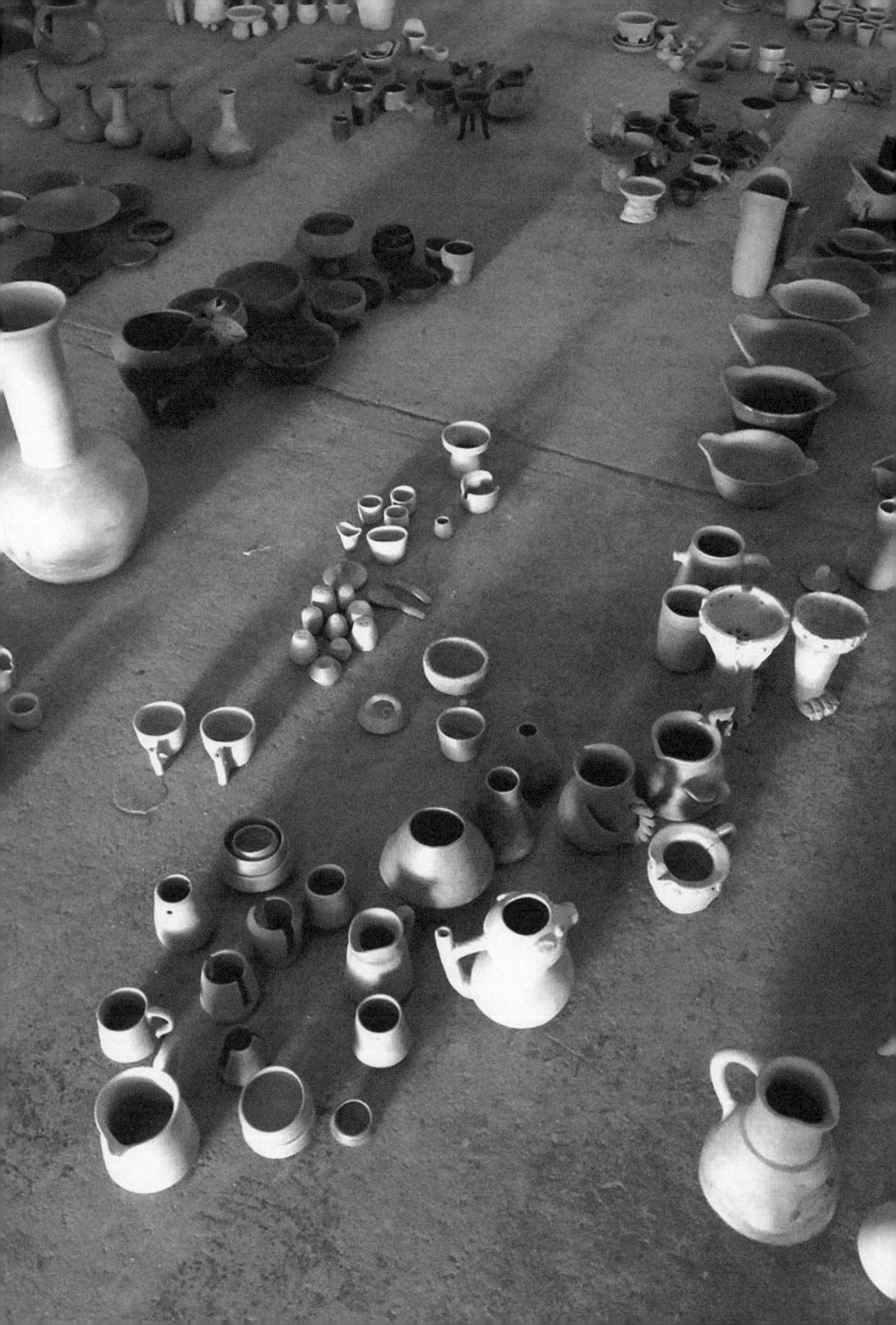

THE POLITICS OF CRAFTS

KYTHZIA BARRERA
INNOVANDO LA TRADICION
COLECTIVO 1050º

In collaboration with the potters of Santa María Atzompa, a village situated fifteen kilometers from Oaxaca in southern Mexico, Innovando la Tradición[1] has been conducting applied research into the reconstruction of local ceramist crafts. Of the population of six thousand, 99 percent are potters. This village is very well known for its traditional green glaze color in pottery.

The craft of pottery in Atzompa, as in most of the pottery villages in the state of Oaxaca, is very vulnerable and in danger of extinction. The pre-Hispanic traditions and talents are in crisis for a variety of reasons, primarily related to pressures of the global economy on marginalized communities. These problems manifest via difficulties in accessing markets, international regulation mandating lead-free pottery, local lack of social recognition, invasion of Asian plastic products, price competition, the increase in prices for fuel for firing the pottery, and changing lifestyles.

Together with Innovando la Tradición, art historian Mariana Rubio started working on a timeline of Atzompa's pottery, researching the morphology and genealogy of the village's ceramic objects. After identifying the archetypal shapes of Atzompa's pottery based on material evidence and interviewing members of the community, she continued her research in libraries, archives, and archeological sites.

After two months, she was able to draft a timeline. Nevertheless, the timeline still presented several gaps and incomplete sections, especially for the time after the Spanish conquest. These gaps were filled, though barely, by visiting the warehouse of the Museo Nacional de Antropología in Mexico City and by interviewing expert archaeologists in Oaxaca.

The archaeologist Leonardo Ruiz, working at the research laboratory for ceramics of the Instituto Nacional de Antropología e Historia (INAH), joined the team, and became a key figure in clarifying the mysteries, expanding the timeline for five hundred additional years. The resulting timeline is not complete, but it provides an overview of the history and morphology of Atzompa's pottery.

In order to give some context, following is an attempt to squeeze more than three thousand years of Atzompa's history into two paragraphs. It is important to mention that apart from our interest in the history of pottery in the region, at the core of our

1 Innovando la Tradición is a creative platform based in Oaxaca, where designers, artists, and artisans share knowledge and skills, contributing to building bridges among them. To do so, they develop research and experiment with ways of understanding these three disciplines, while using creativity as a common ground.

project is a reflection on how popular crafts are regarded, distributed, and studied in contemporary Mexico.

From 1,000 BCE until the nineteenth century, various transformations display a transition from Mesoamerican forms into Colonial shapes. Mixtec, Zapotec, Teotihuacan, and even Guatemalan features and influences are clearly identifible in the early years. It was not until the twentieth century, when Mexico was building national ideals, that handcrafted production was seen as an element of national identity. After the revolution, Mexican society turned to its past to seek true values through examining traditions, and crafts came to figure prominently in centenary independence celebrations, particularly once Dr. Atl's *Las Artes Populares en México* was published. This consisted of two exhibitions and a catalogue for the exhibition *Popular Mexican Art*, which took place in Mexico City and in Los Angeles, California. In 1934, the socialist government of Lázaro Cárdenas used it as a favorite media discourse: massive cultural diffusion was heavily promoted in the form of publications in other languages, meant to exploit curiosity among foreigners. For many years, it has been the State who speaks, promotes, manipulates, and uses cultural expression to communicate "lost" identity. We ask ourselves: Lost? Why lost? When one can easily find it here, in Atzompa, in houses and lives of the people?

In the 1950s, capitalistic Mexican culture appeared to be the big promise to "save" pottery. The Pan-American Highway brought many foreign tourists, and interest in indigenous communities increased. By 1957, pottery in Atzompa had transitioned into large-scale production, as it had been at the peak of Mixtec culture, in around 800 CE, when Atzompa was the main supplier of crafts to the primary city in the American continent, Monte Albán. In the 1970s, utilitarian production was set aside and decorative fabrication took its place; the market welcomed this through many American collectors of folk art. For the last two decades, traditional production and commerce has been threatened by prohibition, for the glaze contains lead. A government ban introduced in 1994 prohibited the use of leaded glazes without offering any retraining or suggesting other glazing techniques. This ban has made it almost impossible for the producers to create high-quality pottery that can find its way into the global market.

In all these different moments in history, culture has been promoted for the purpose of preservation inside a window, apart from the people, somewhere outside its original context, as a cabinet of curiosity that cannot be touched, but rather only observed from a distance, because it is exotic.

Once the first draft of our Atzompa timeline was ready, we met with the potters in the village to present our discoveries. The community of potters was amused and excited. Inovando la Tradición's idea was to expose Atzompa's potters to the timeline so that they could familiarize themselves with the different shapes and techniques that have emerged over time, creating empathy among them with their own context and enabling them to acquire a deeper knowledge around it. The timeline was taken as a starting point for recreating these historical pieces and thus for drawing a line linking contemporary production to the past. In order to draw this line, it was also necessary to take into account the information the objects provide, such as shape, material, and different kinds of clays.

Thereafter, Inovando la Tradición began to work with the potters on new pieces, recreating some of the objects in the timeline, and thus imagining how to fill up the historical gaps.

The sessions started on October 2013, when we brought together fifteen artisans, five designers, and three archeologists. We split into five groups, and each group worked in a different period. They started by copying and bringing to life 2 x 2 cm pictures into great 3-D masterpieces that expressed the punch of Mixtec and Zapotec culture very vividly. The discussions around the meaning of what was happening at that time are difficult to explain in words, because artisans were very sensitive and emotional about all the information displayed by the timeline and by the archeologists. The most shocking thing for them was to realize that the green color did not come from pre-Hispanic tradition, as they had proudly believed, and that in the old times, all of the production was for creating functional as opposed to decorative objects.

After a number of succesful working sessions, we organized an exhibition in the local museum, next to a historical site, recently "discovered" by INAH. We wanted to share our findings and exciting discussions with the rest of the villagers and our Oaxacan friends with an exhibition called "Miradas al Pasado" ("Glimpses Into the Past"). The use of the local museum in Atzompa had been exclusively given to the state institution, INAH. This was the first time that the inhabitants of Atzompa proposed that the space be used to display their own work. We approached the village authorities and the musuem director, and all agreed upon a space and date to launch the opening on a happy Saturday: December 14, 2013. One day before the opening, INAH authorities called the leaders of the artisans group, Rolando and Juan, to their office. They sat them in front of a "glossy" lawyer who asked them to sign papers stating that they were illegally reproducing replicas of pre-Hispanic pieces, and that they must give the rights to INAH to continue with the project research. Luckily, Rolando Regino and Juan Ruiz did not sign any papers, but the exhibition was canceled. More than fifty people attended the opening, including press, but the local musuem did not open its doors to the crowd outside the building. Two weeks after the bitter event, the artisans went back to the museum to pick up their work, to find that the museum was charging a 10-peso fee to view the pieces—a fee that went directly into INAH pockets. What a predictable coincidence! To whom does "our" material culture belong? What do we mean by "our culture"? Where shall we place a new emerging material culture created by a collective that for centuries has been denied access—or that has, in the best of the cases, been disrupted and remained invisible to the institutions that are suppose to support it?

After consultation with our lawyers in Mexico City, they explained us that the law related to replicas is very clear: it is indeed prohibited to make replicas without a permit from INAH, but this applies only when the replicas are intended for commercial purposes. There is no indication or specification that one cannot make reproductions for study or for exercising the pleasure of understanding oneself. It seems that a series of misunderstandings came along with a chain of assumptions on our side and a great deal of innocence on the side of the artisans.

We kept rowing: we continued the work with a stronger sense of group union. In February 2014, we again revised the timeline with the artisans during another four-day workshop. Finally, from March 10–27, with the generous support of the Finnish Minister of Foreigner Affairs, Finnish designers Pekka Harni and Yuka Takahashi were invited by Innovando la Tradición to guide a three-week workshop for product development with participatory design methodologies developed by Diego Mier y Terán and myself. The goal was to apply theories of object categories and evolution in design to the Atzompa timeline in order to develop products for specific functions and new contexts. This time we invited artisans from other villages in Oaxaca and designers from other cities in Mexico to integrate interdisciplinary teams. The design brief was to adapt an object from the timeline to a different context. In the first week, we worked to adapt ancient objects toward occupying new spaces, ranging from a bar in Copenhagen to a loft in New York to a house on a beach or a restaurant in Oaxaca city. In the second week, participants had to adapt another ancient object and function to a specefic meal, such as tamales or pozole, or to a restaurant or high-end dinner table in Mexico City. The third week, we selected pieces of a variety of styles that had been created in previous sessions, and participants were asked to pick one object and to invert the process, adapting tableware to the selected pieces.

A total result of more than one hundred masterpieces was the succeesful offspring of this exercise. Once again, the results will be exhibited (and this time we will try to avoid INAH authorities) in Oaxaca, Mexico City, and Helsinki in an exhibition titled "+3000 Atzompa and Ahead."

I cannot stop thinking that INAH authorities may show up again at the exhibition. They will certainly will go crazy when they look at what a group of master artisans and individuals—well organized, empowered by autonomy, and without the government's "help"—are able to do with their own heritage. I'll close my reflections with a celebrated story of an artisan who, when asked by the actual Oaxacan governor: "How can my government be of help to you?" she boldy replied: "Well, just stop fucking me up and that would be good enough for me!"

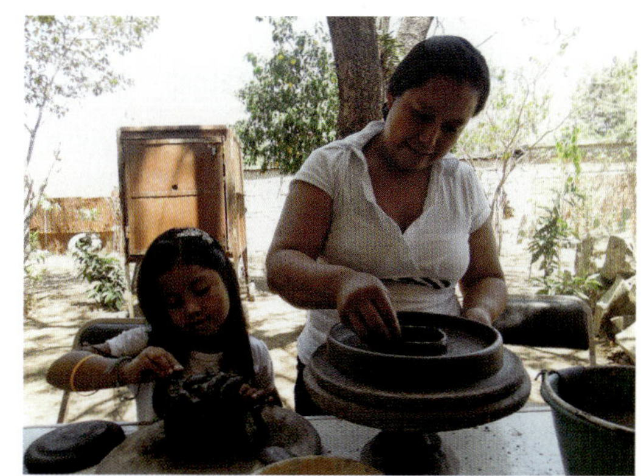

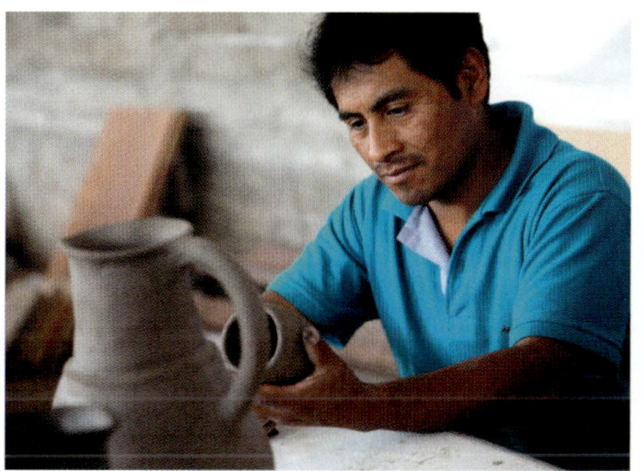

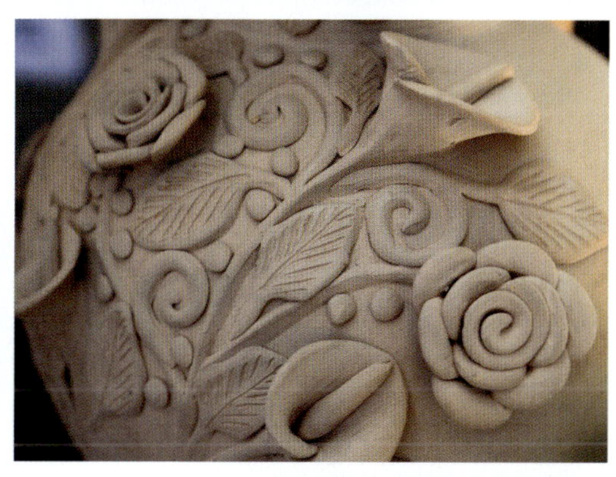

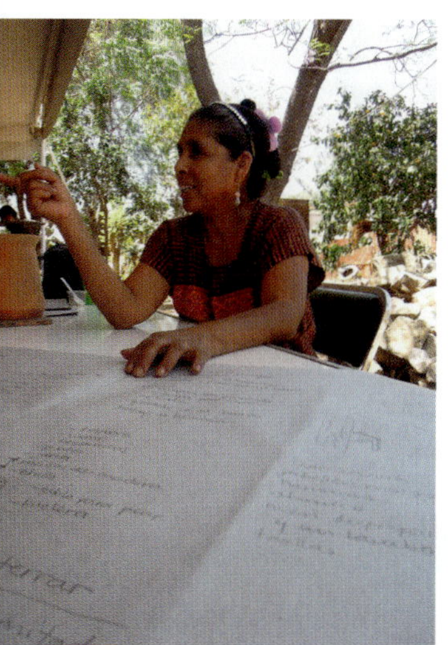

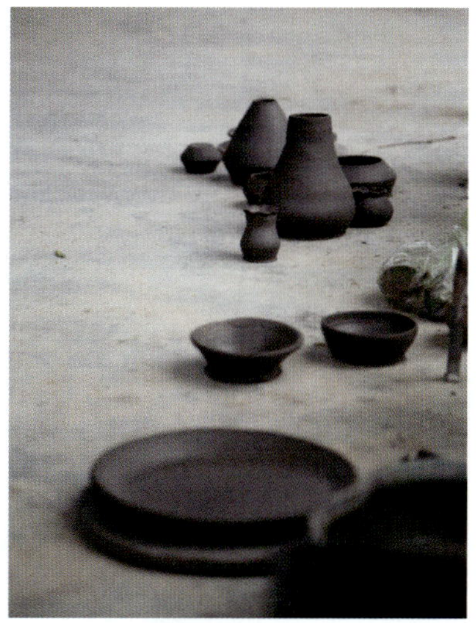

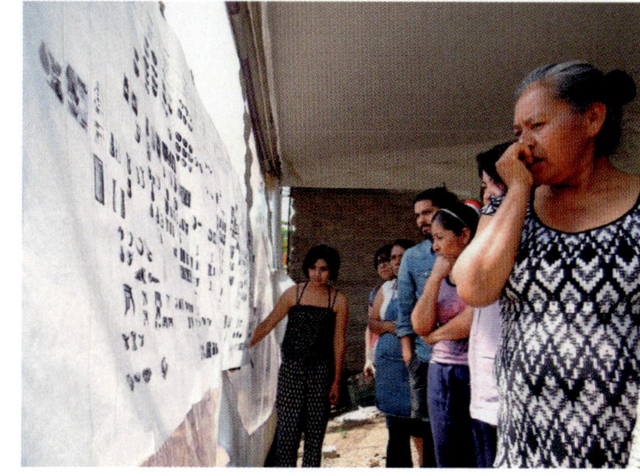

Timeline Azompa
Workshop
Images Diego Mier y Terán

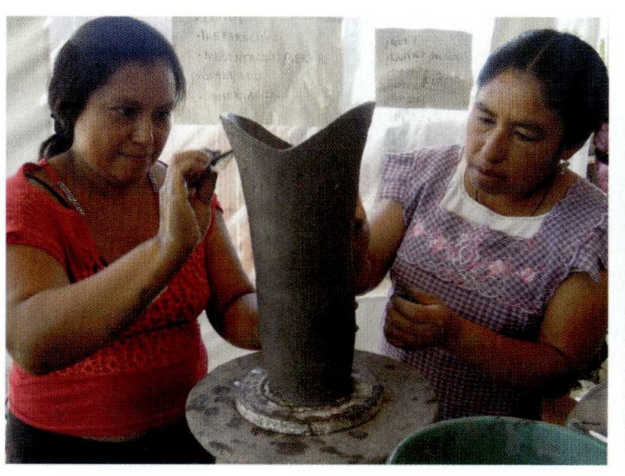

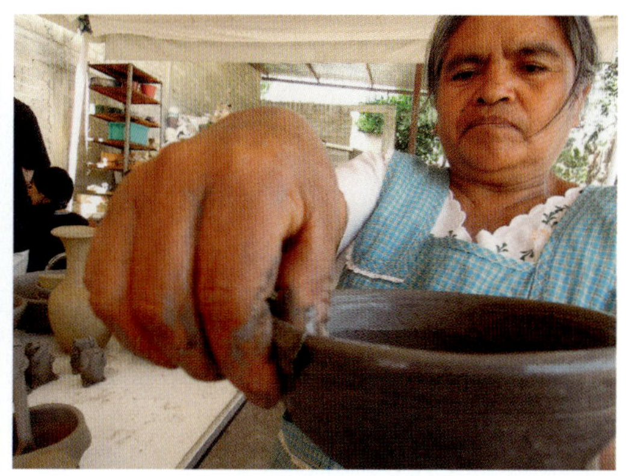

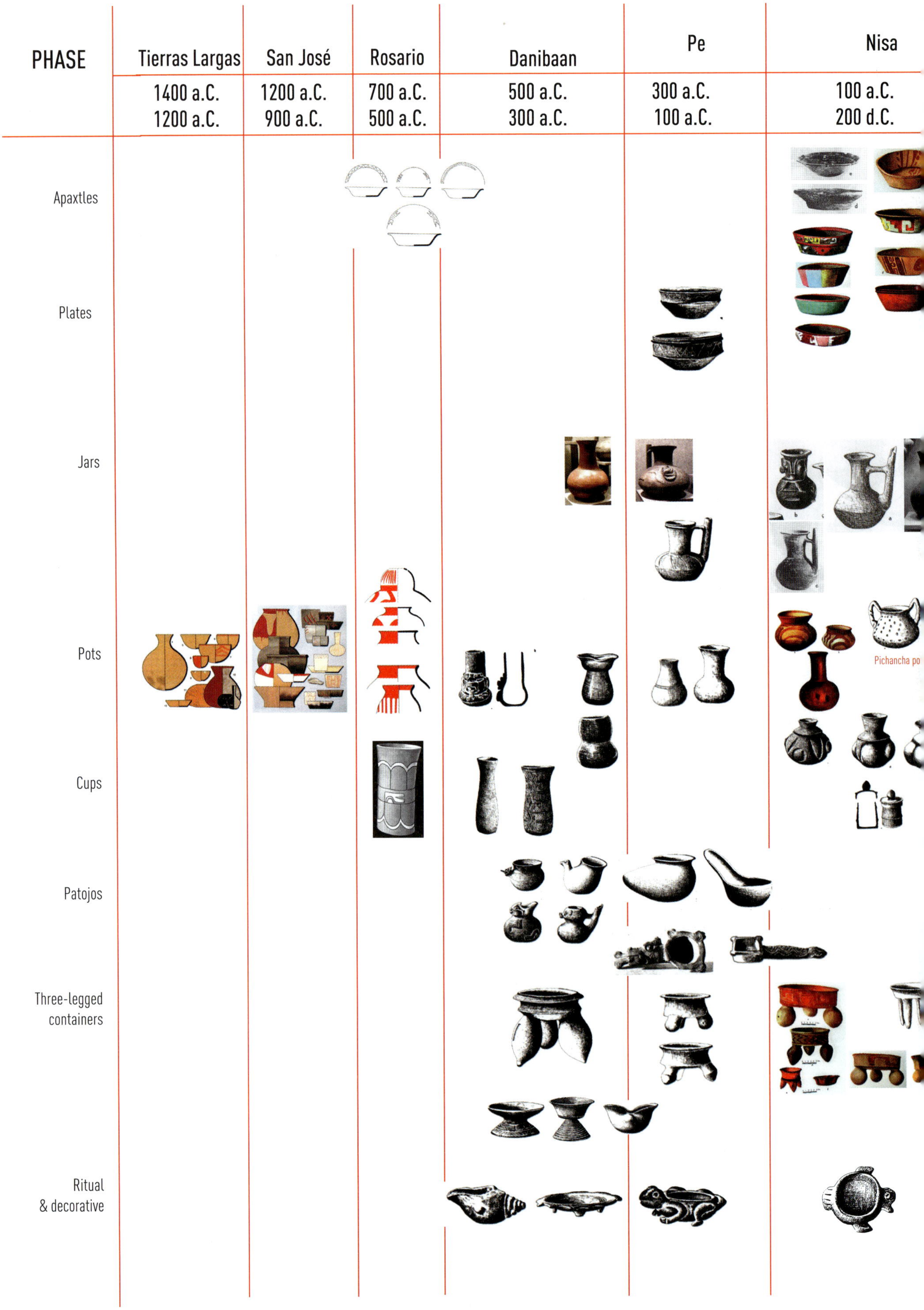

PHASE	Tierras Largas	San José	Rosario	Danibaan	Pe	Nisa
	1400 a.C. 1200 a.C.	1200 a.C. 900 a.C.	700 a.C. 500 a.C.	500 a.C. 300 a.C.	300 a.C. 100 a.C.	100 a.C. 200 d.C.
Apaxtles						
Plates						
Jars						
Pots						Pichancha po
Cups						
Patojos						
Three-legged containers						
Ritual & decorative						

Tani	Pitao	Peche	Xoo	Liobáa
200 d.C. 350 d.C.	350 d.C. 500 d.C.	500 d.C. 600 d.C.	600 d.C. 850 d.C.	850 d.C. 1150 d.C.

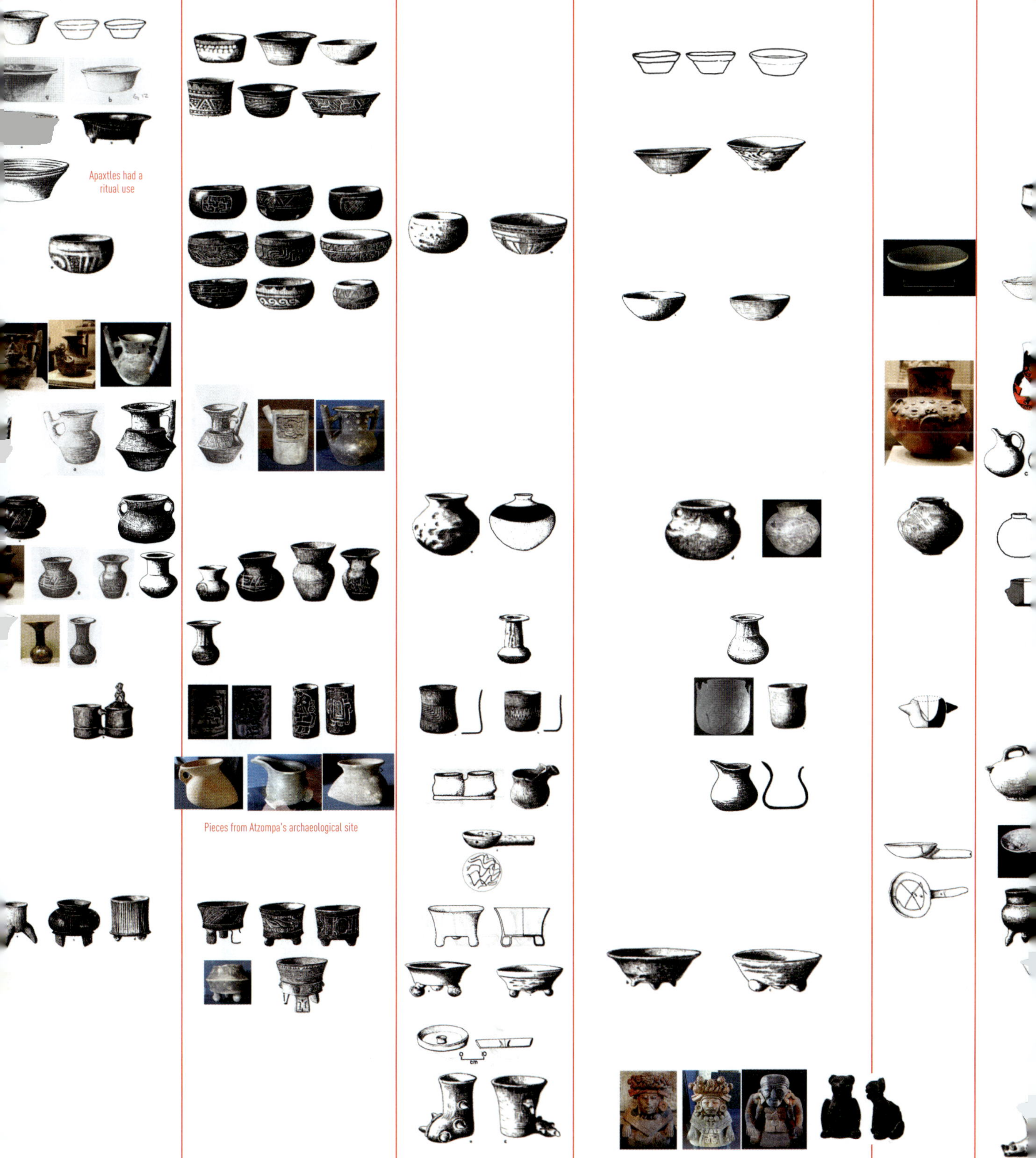

Apaxtles had a ritual use

Pieces from Atzompa's archaeological site

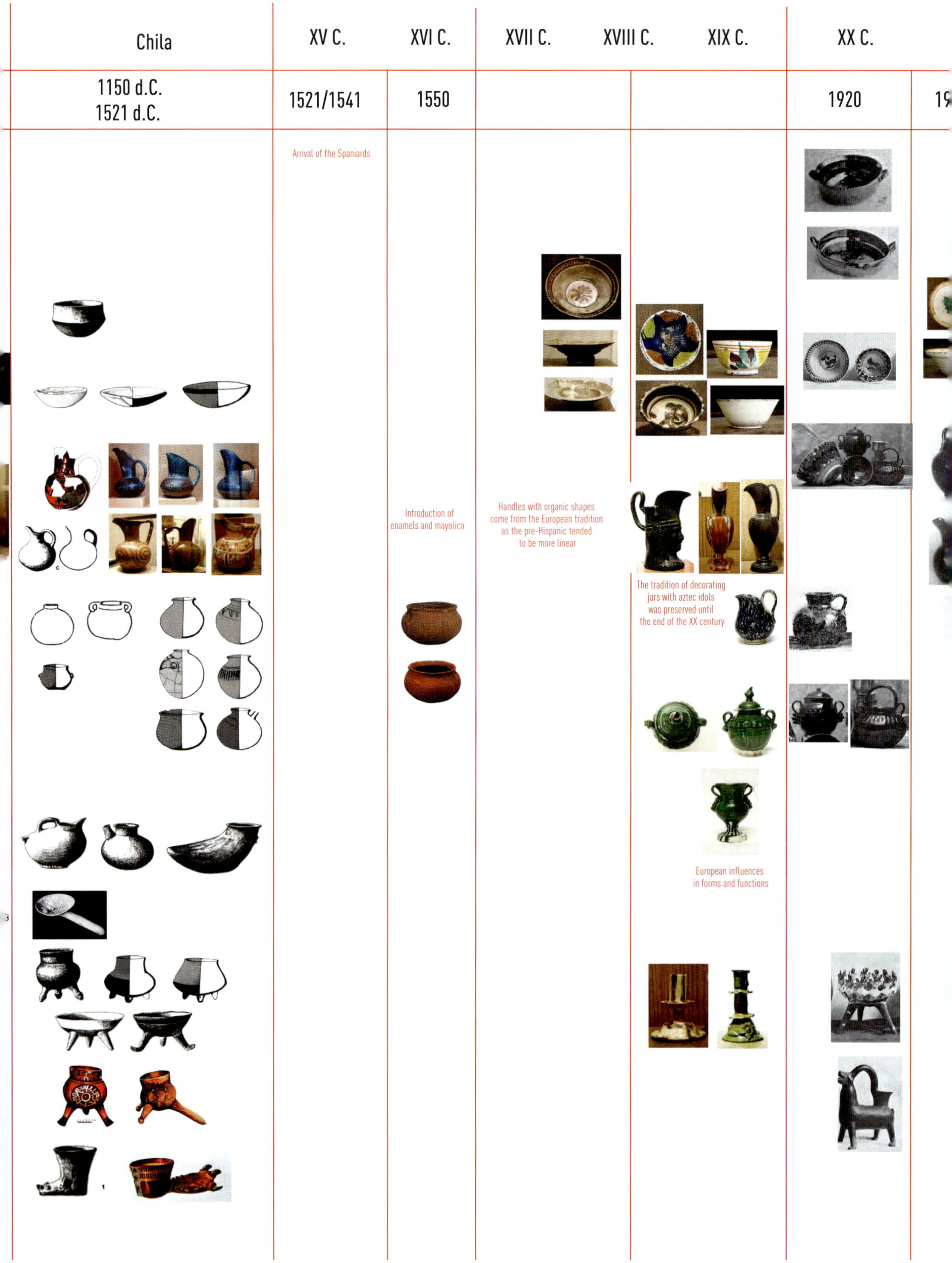

Chila	XV C.	XVI C.	XVII C.	XVIII C.	XIX C.	XX C.	
1150 d.C. 1521 d.C.	1521/1541	1550				1920	19

Arrival of the Spaniards

Introduction of enamels and mayolica

Handles with organic shapes come from the European tradition as the pre-Hispanic tended to be more linear

The tradition of decorating jars with aztec idols was preserved until the end of the XX century

European influences in forms and functions

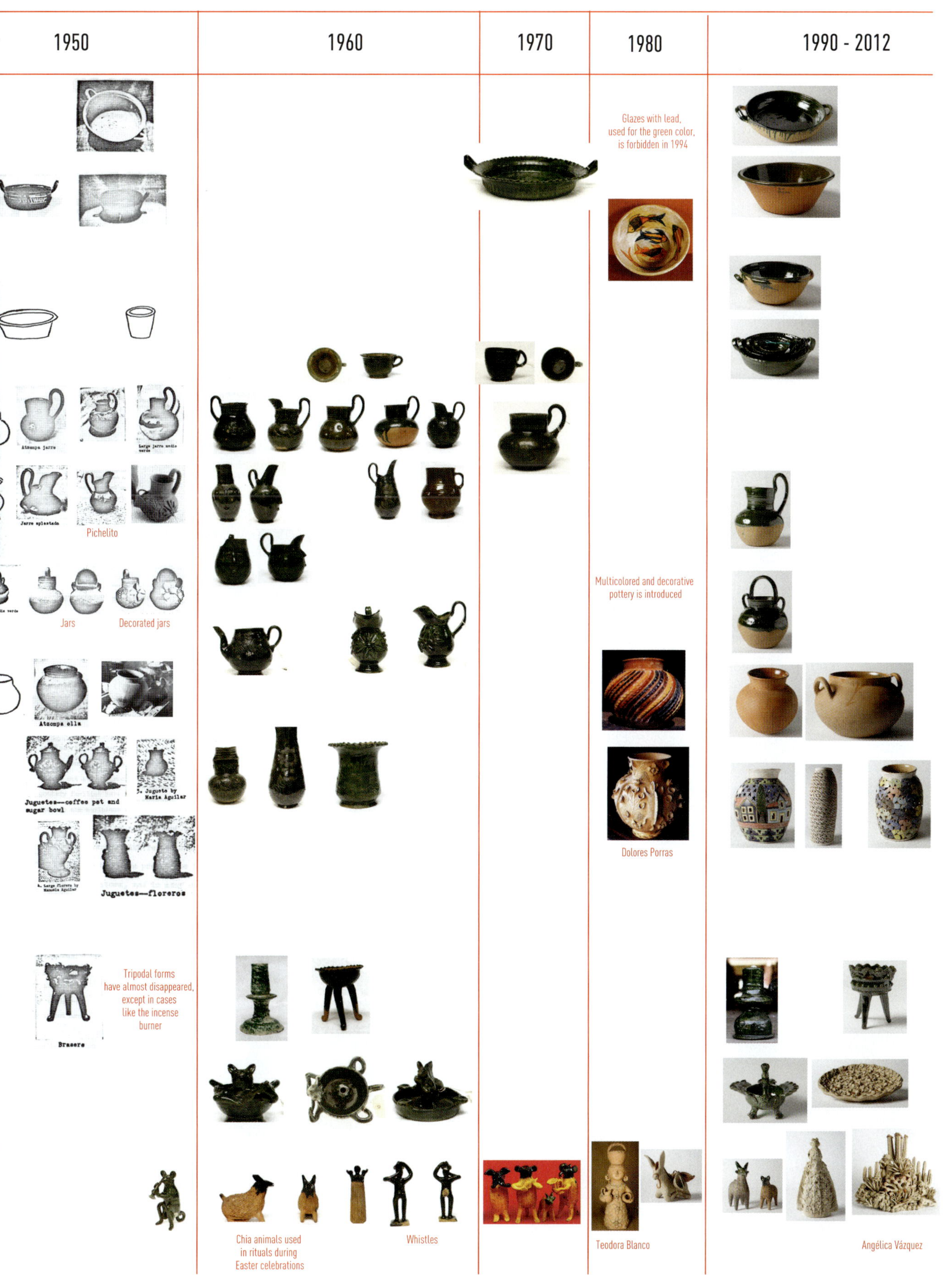

1950
1960
1970
1980
1990 - 2012
Glazes with lead, used for the green color, is forbidden in 1994
Pichelito
Multicolored and decorative pottery is introduced
Jars
Decorated jars
Atzompa olla
Juguetes—coffee pot and sugar bowl
Juguetes—floreros
Dolores Porras
Tripodal forms have almost disappeared, except in cases like the incense burner
Brasero
Chia animals used in rituals during Easter celebrations
Whistles
Teodora Blanco
Angélica Vázquez

Azompa 3000
Exhibition
Images Diego Mier y Terán

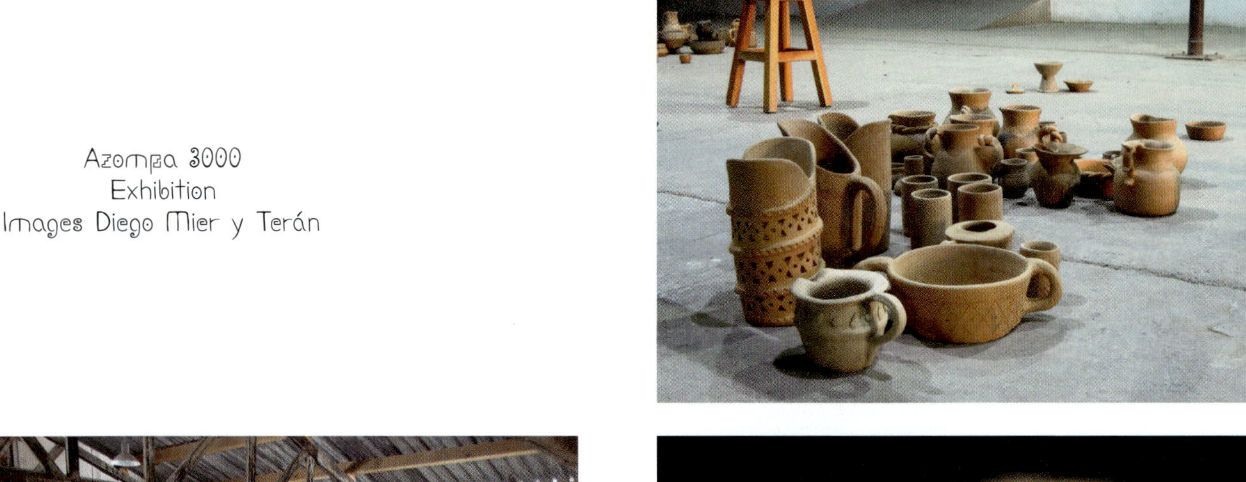

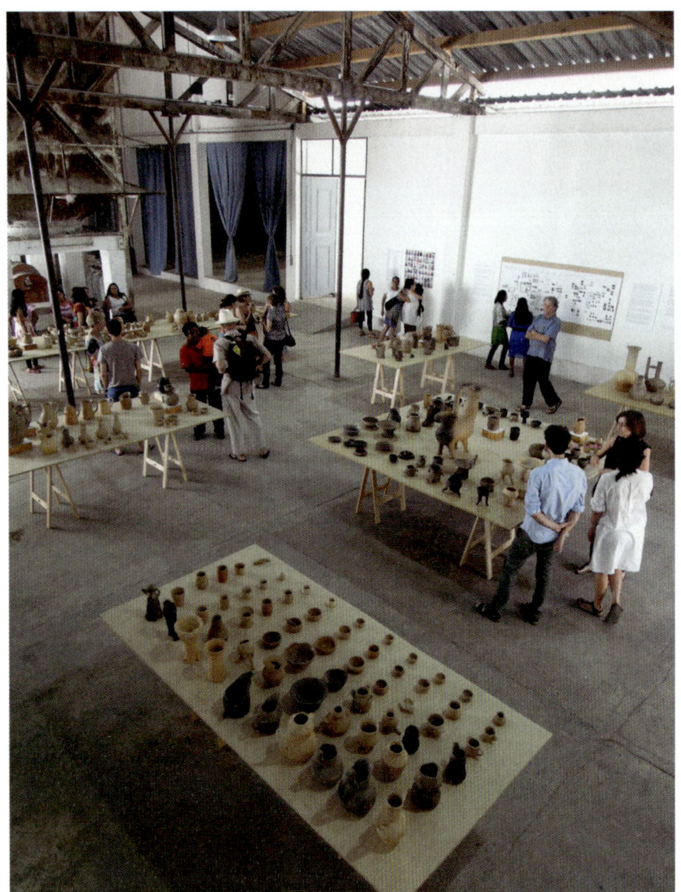

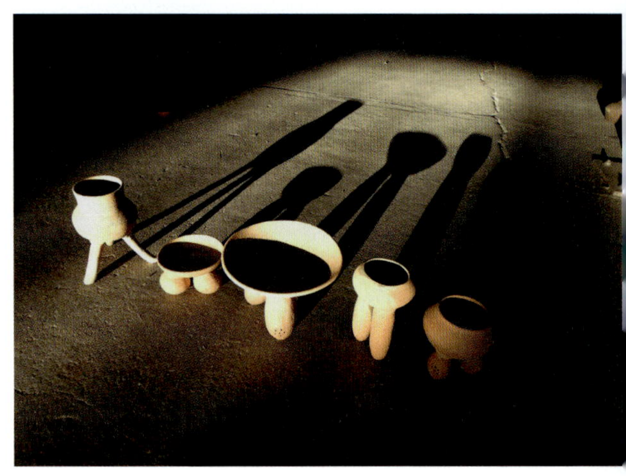

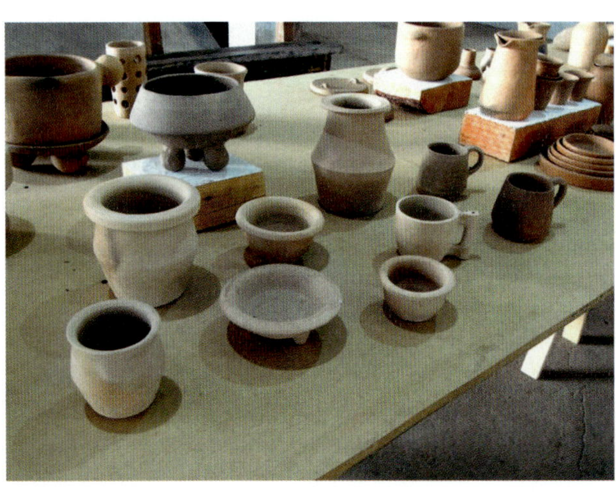

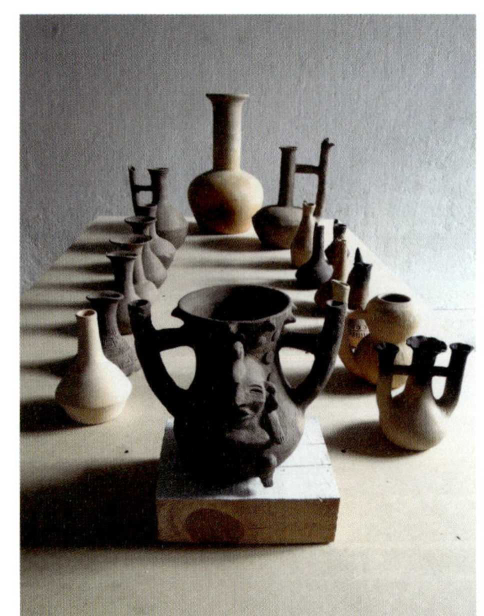

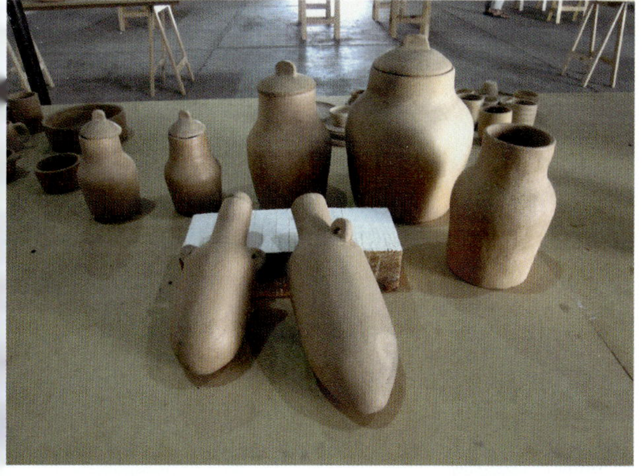
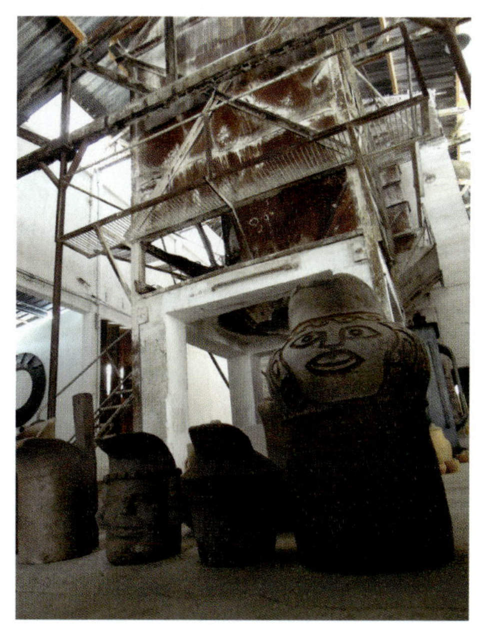
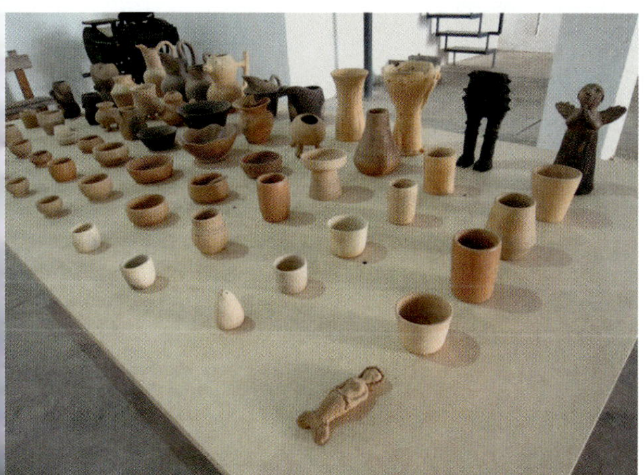
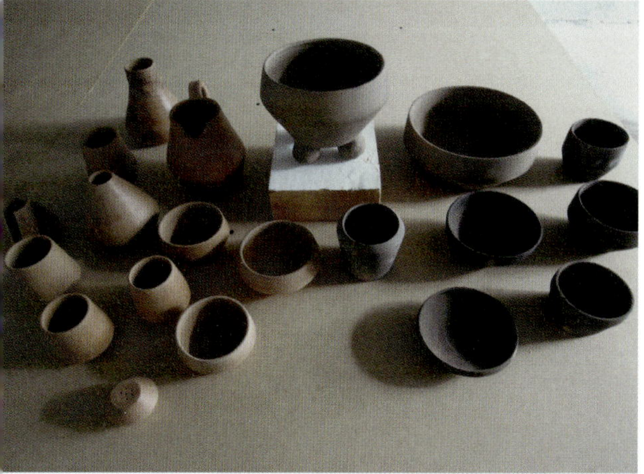
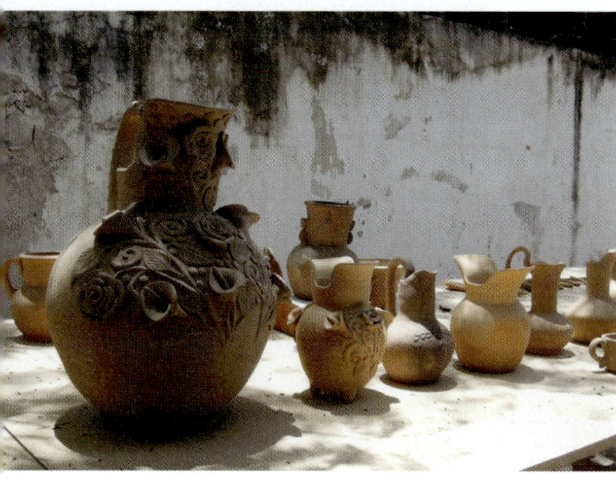
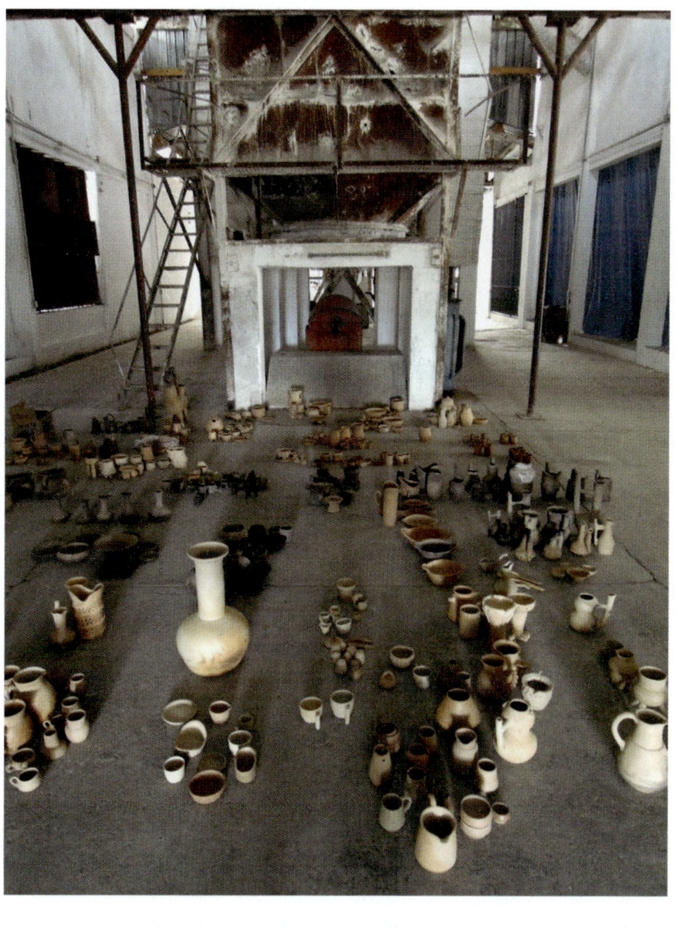

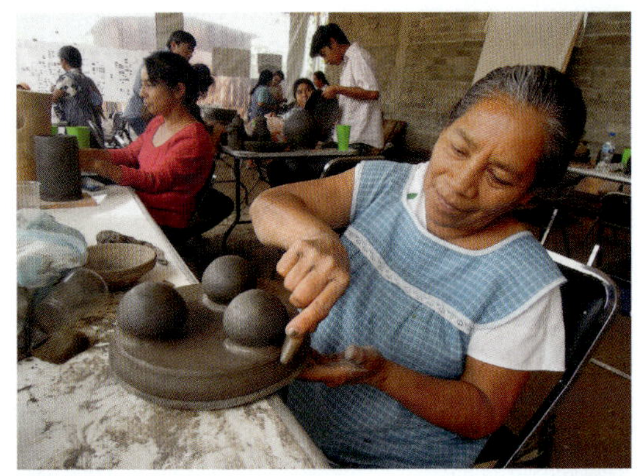

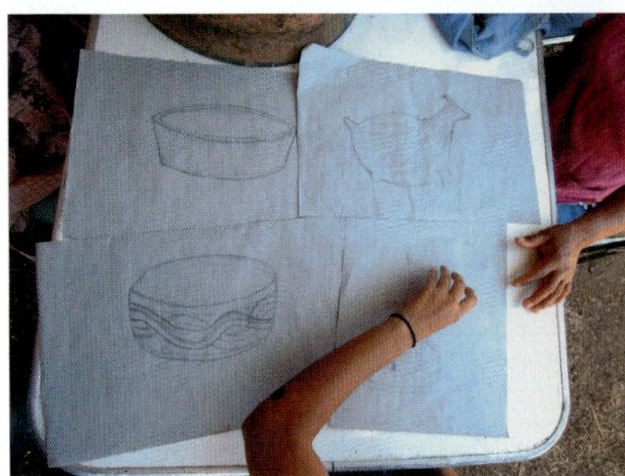

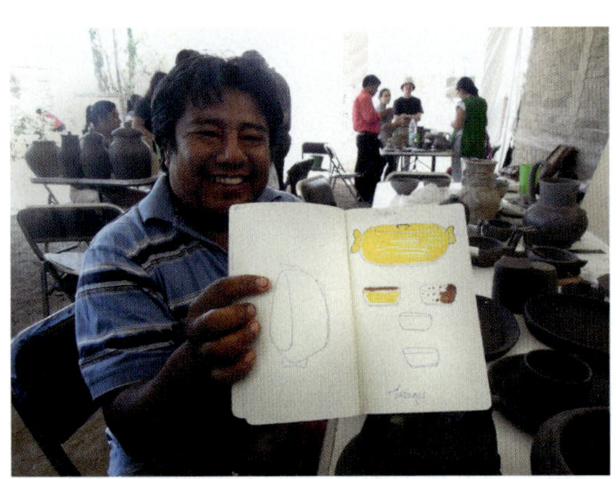

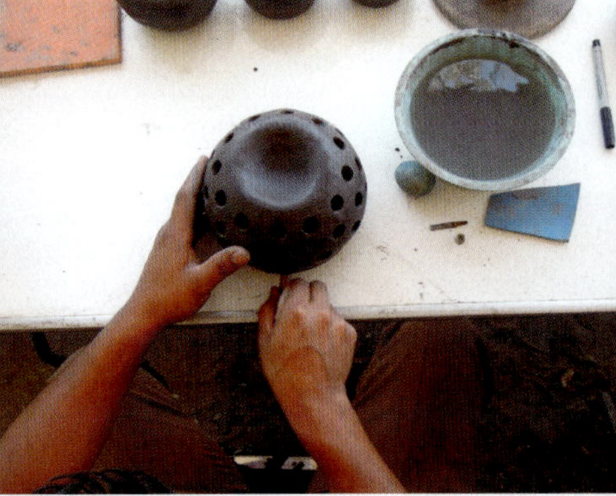

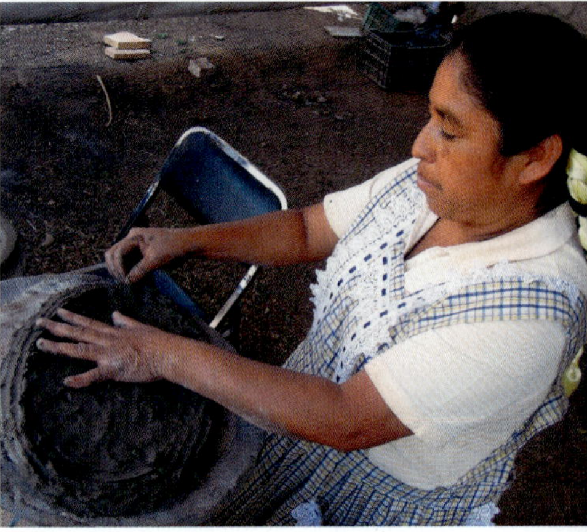

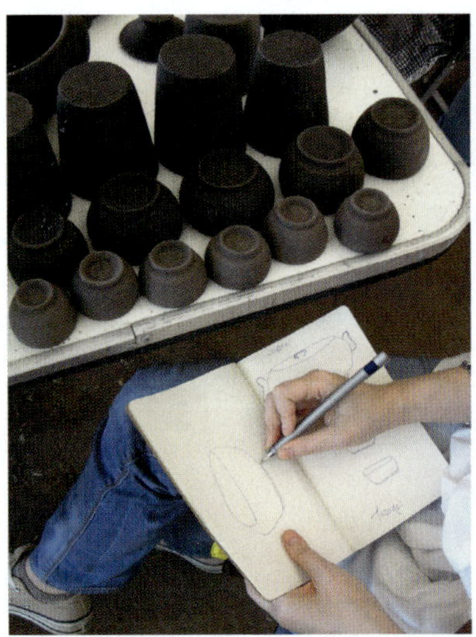

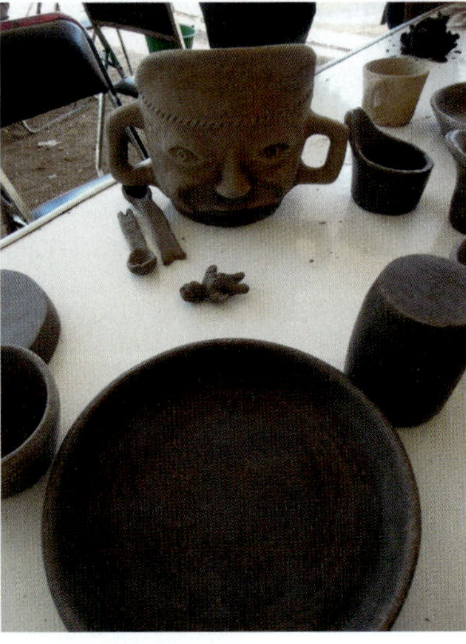

Timeline Azompa
Workshop
Images Diego Mier y Terán

BIOGRAPHIES

Kythzia Barrera is a designer and founding member of "Innovando la Tradición" and "1050°" collectives, organizations that try to support the development of pottery communities in the state of Oaxaca (Mexico).

Mariana Castillo Deball is a Mexican artist based in Berlin. She employs a variety of media including sculpture, installation, printing, and drawing. Besides her artistic practice, Castillo Deball is an editor and author. She has contributed to several publications and has published titles such as *A for Alibi* (in collaboration with Irene Kopelman, 2007) and *These ruins you see* (2008)

Dr. Maria Gaida is the curator of the Mesoamerican Collection at the Ethnologisches Museum, Staatliche Museen zu Berlin where, since 1999, she also works as Head of the Collection Department. Since 1996 she has been co-editor of the museum´s publication *Baessler-Archiv.*

Moosje M. Goosen is a writer based in Rotterdam. She has contributed to magazines such as *Metropolis M* and *Frieze,* and also writes fiction and essays in the framework of art exhibitions and events. She frequently collaborates with artists.

Pablo Katchadjian is an Argentinean writer. Some of his novels include: *La libertad total* (Bajo la luna ed., Buenos Aires, 2013), *Gracias* (Blatt&Ríos Ed., Buenos Aires, 2011), *Qué hacer* (Bajo la luna Ed., Buenos Aires, 2010) and *El aleph engordado* (Imprenta Argentina de Poesía Ed., Buenos Aires, 2009).

Historian and anthropologist Paula López Caballero is a researcher at the UNAM. She worked at CNRS in France and El Colegio de México. Her most recent research addresses from different historical and ethnographic observatories what she calls "national regimes of alteriry," meaning the way indigenous differentiation manifests, within the processes of state and nation formation.

Dr. Federico Navarrete Linares is an historian, anthropologist, and researcher at the Instituto de Investigaciones Históricas (UNAM) in Mexico City. He studies the indigenous conceptions about time and history and the transformations of the Amerindian societies after the Conquista to the present time. He has also written several historical novels about Amerindian cultures and their interactions with African European traditions.

Dr. Victoria Novelo Oppenheim is a Mexican anthropologist and professor emeritus at the CIESAS (Centro de Investigaciones y Estudios Superiores en Antropología Social) in Mexico City, institution at which she has been working for more than thirty years.

Sandra Rozental has worked as a museum curator and cultural journalist Mexico, and in 2012, received a PhD in anthropology from New York University. She is currently a professor and researcher at the Universidad Autónoma Metropolitana-Unidad Cuajimalpa in Mexico City. She has collaborated with artists and filmmakers to make her academic research reach other forums and audiences. The most recent of these collaborations, *The Absent Stone*, is her first feature-length documentary, co-directed with Jesse Lerner and winner of the Ann Arbor Film Festival Jury Award 2014.

Carlos Sandoval is a Mexican/German performer and composer based in Germany. He has written several articles and essays about music theory and aesthetics. www.carlos-sandoval.de

Dr. Adam T. Sellen is a researcher at the Peninsular Centre for Humanities and Social Sciences of the UNAM (Mérida/Yucatán). He specializes in ancient cultures from Oaxaca and around this subject he has worked on iconography, forgeries, and Zapotec epigraphy, focused on the artefacts commonly known as Zapotec urns.

Anna Szaflarski is an artist based in Berlin as well as the co-founder of artist book publishing collective AKV Berlin. Her graphic, sculptural as well as performance works search for the intersecting, yet quickly fleeting moment between form and language. In July she will be participating in the Stary Grunwald Sculptural Residency in Poznan, Poland.